The Buddhist Nirvāṇa and Its Western Interpreters

THE BUDDHIST NIRVĀṆA AND ITS WESTERN INTERPRETERS

Guy Richard Welbon

The University of Chicago Press

Chicago and London

Library of Congress Catalog Card Number 67–25535
The University of Chicago Press, Chicago 60637
The University of Chicago Press, Ltd., London W.C.1

Published 1968
Printed in the United States of America

FOR

My Family

PREFACE

I have a sinne of feare, that when I have spunne
My last thred, I shall perish on the shore. . . .
JOHN DONNE, "A Hymne to God the Father"

According to the Buddhists, a man's lot in this life is characterized by suffering (Sanskrit: *duḥkha;* Pali: *dukkha*). The texts make it clear that suffering is linked to ignorance. Indeed, in the Buddhist view, suffering and ignorance are invariably associated. The one is never found without the other. Most poignant and consequential among the aspects of ignorance, say the Buddhists, is man's failure to comprehend the basic truth about the phenomenal universe: no phenomenon is permanent—nothing abides. Ignorant of that truth, his proclivities (habitual thirst—*tṛṣṇā*, *taṇhā*—for objects and experiences) nurtured accordingly, a man lives out of harmony with himself, his fellows, his world. He suffers.

The Buddha is the compassionate physician, his pronouncements prescriptions. The Way of the Buddha is, in a manner of speaking, the way from disease to health. But of what does "health" in the Buddhist sense consist? To be sure, it is deliverance (*mokṣa*, *mokkha*) from suffering. It is described variously, most commonly as *nirvāṇa* (*nibbāna*).

Nirvāṇa is the absence—the destruction—of suffering (*duḥkhanirodha*). It involves the eradication of ignorance through the acquisition of wisdom (*saṃbodhi*)—knowledge, conceived classically in India not merely as intellection but as operational and effective knowledge. Yet, more specifically, more positively than the absence of debilities, what is nirvāṇa? The ultimate aspiration of all Buddhists, their *summum bonum*, what is its "essential" nature? What does attainment to it involve for the existence of the previously suffering individual? One of the oldest in the history of ideas, that question, in its various modes, has been debated furiously by Buddhists and non-Buddhists alike.

The inquiry that follows attempts an outline of the history of Western European (and North American) discussions on the meaning of the Buddhist nirvāṇa. Those interpretations of nirvāṇa that have been advanced by several distinguished authorities on Buddhist thought and practice will be examined in detail. The evaluations, never based exclusively on philological and historico-critical considerations, in every instance reflect the individual scholar's own personal commitment, his *sitz im leben*, and his understanding of the essence of Buddhism. The response to the question of nirvāṇa's meaning is at the same time an answer more or less complete to all questions about Buddhism.

Problems in intercultural hermeneutics can be approached most satisfactorily *sub specie particularis*. The present study concentrates on what Western Europeans have actually written and said about nirvāṇa. It may be taken as a footnote to the comprehensive understanding of European intellectual history in the nineteenth and twentieth centuries, but it is meant expressly to document a specific encounter. It is my hope that it will make some contribution to methodological debates concerning the study of non-Western *Geistesphänomena* and therefore be of interest to students in several disciplines. To what extent do cultural and social presuppositions determine the conduct and conclusions of the study of alien traditions? What role does the expanding body of ordered data play? These and many other kindred questions suggested by them tend always to the abstract. Examples from particular experiences are needed to illumine them, and the content of this book is offered as one such example.

There are many individuals to whom I am indebted for counsel, criticism, and solace during the course of my research and writing. To Mircea Eliade I owe much. The idea for this study is his. Without his unfailing interest and encouragement, his vast erudition, and his warm friendship I should have been totally lost at many points. J. A. B. van Buitenen, M. S. G. Hodgson, and James Redfield, giving freely of their time and learning, have guided me past several pitfalls. My thanks are due also to the Committee on Social Thought in the University of Chicago which accepted the original manuscript as a doctoral dissertation. The committee faculty and students—in fact, the committee "idea"—helped me in no small way to execute this project.

Provost McCrea Hazlett of The University of Rochester was instrumental in providing both the opportunity and the assistance for preparing the present manuscript. He and my other colleagues in the university have contributed greatly by establishing an intellectual environment in which fruitful revision was possible. Norma C. Mead, Olga Starnell, Lynne Poirier, Camella Wilson, Gary Hood, George Parks, and P. D. Herring graciously rendered help during several emergencies. And to my wife Julia, who cheerfully read the final drafts and proofs, corrected much of my precarious grammar and faulty spelling, and engineered compilation of the index despite the fact that work on this manuscript assaulted her courtship, afflicted our honeymoon, and plagued the early weeks of her first trip to India, I add those special thanks not easily expressed in words.

This manuscript incorporates and expands on the text of my article, "On Understanding the Buddhist Nirvāṇa," which originally appeared in *History of Religions* (Vol. V, no. 2 [Winter, 1966], 300–326). I thank the editors—Messrs. Mircea Eliade, Joseph M. Kitagawa, and Charles H. Long—and publishers (the University of Chicago Press) for permission to quote extensively from it here. Chapter III is essentially the same as my article, "Max Müller's Interpretation of the Buddhist Nirvāṇa," which was privileged to appear in *Numen* (Vol. XII, no. 3 [September, 1965] 276–300). I am delighted to thank *Numen*'s editor, C. J. Bleeker, and publishers, E. J. Brill, for permission to reprint it in this volume.

The heroic efforts and achievements of several generations of Western Buddhist scholars have made this book possible. That it is no better organized or written is my fault entirely. That no more interpretations of nirvāṇa have been included is a function of the time, space, and learning at my command. That no apodictically certain definition of nirvāṇa will be found on these pages is due to the nature of the idea itself.

A Note on Transliteration

In the following chapters passages dealing with technical terms will be quoted from a variety of works published over the past century and a half. Several transliteration conventions and typographical restrictions are evidenced in them. Often I have reproduced quoted material exactly as it appeared originally. Occasionally, however, it was considered advisable to regularize transliterations in accordance with contemporary scholarly practice. Hence, for example, nirvāṇa appears variously as "*nirvāṇa*," "nirvāna," "nirvâna," "nirvana," and even "nirwana." Some inconsistency will also be encountered in the use or absence of italics and diacritical marks elsewhere. Generally, consistency has been sacrificed to ease of understanding whenever the two conflict.

For the pronunciation and accent of Old and Middle Indo-Aryan, the reader is referred to any one of several grammars or primers on Indian history and culture.

GUY RICHARD WELBON

The University of Rochester

Contents

Introduction

Contacts between India and other centers of civilization extend back in a continuous, if often tenuous, line at least to the time of the efflorescence of cultural nuclei along the Indus and at Sumer—some five thousand years. Yet, Buddhism, one of India's most significant contributions to the arena of ideas and itself almost twenty-five hundred years old, was confronted first by Western Europeans only after it had undergone more than fifteen hundred years of systematization and fragmentation in the land of its origins and was very nearly extinct on the Indian subcontinent. In fact, only since the beginning of the nineteenth century has Buddhism been the subject of intensive studies in Europe. The veritable encounter with Buddhism as both idea and historical datum is even younger—only about a hundred years.

It is the purpose of this introduction to provide some foundations for the main body of investigations to follow by means of a cursory survey of the West's acquaintance with Buddhism before 1800. For convenience, this preliminary sketch is offered under four chronological rubrics: pre-Christian or classical antiquity; Christian antiquity and the Gnostic period; the Middle Ages and the period of commercial adventure; and, finally, missions and the commencement of critical evaluation in the seventeenth and eighteenth centuries.[1]

Contacts before the Christian Era

Father Henri de Lubac, distinguished scholar and historian of Buddhist studies, observes that "neither classical antiquity nor early Christianity has left any very important evidence concerning Buddhism." [2] Witnesses that do survive are not only few in number but, in most cases, are subject to a variety of conflicting interpretations. Thus it is that we are placed in the uncomfortable, perhaps even untenable, position of insisting, on the one hand, that there must have been meetings and exchanges between Buddhists and inhabitants of the Mediterranean area during the centuries immediately before and after the beginning of the Christian era and yet, on the other hand, being unable to single out one unambiguous reference to Buddhism in the whole of the extant literature from the period.

Such a dearth of solid information about Buddhism may be explained partly on the grounds that we do not have at our disposal all texts which might have included more or less specific references to Buddhism and Buddhists. Much of the

[1] A certain amount of overlapping of these divisions is inevitable, and, in any event, a very brief investigation is all that can be assigned to this "ur-geschichtliche" material. For the most comprehensive account of sources important for tracing early contacts between Buddhism and Western Europe, see Henri de Lubac, *La Rencontre du bouddhisme et de l'occident*, pp. 9–104. As will be obvious, my debt to this work is considerable. Containing hundreds of precise footnotes and invaluable references, the de Lubac volume suffers—as do so many French publications—for want of an index.

[2] *Ibid.*, p. 9. Unless otherwise indicated, the translations—occasionally impressionistic rather than literal—are my own.

material which we do possess from pre-Christian times onward has been preserved only in transcription or as "citations" in other texts. These latter purport to be accurate and complete but were produced by men innocent of present-day critical and historical research canons. Materials collected by the entourage of "scholars" who accompanied Alexander the Great to India, for example, have been preserved only fragmentarily—and then in such works as Flavianus Arrianus' *Indicus*, composed five hundred years after the "field work."[3]

I have mentioned that the so-called references to Buddhism which are found in extant texts are ambiguous themselves. That fact may well be a sign that one should not expect to recover accounts which could fill the lacunae in our knowledge of early Buddhist-European relations. The type of information we now have may be illustrated by means of a pair of examples.

Alexander the Great's Indian Raid, 327–325 B.C., ended abruptly on the west bank of the River Hyphasis (modern: Beas), where his infantry commanders refused to march any farther east. At that point of deepest Macedonian penetration, Alexander was still several hundred miles from the center of Magadhan hegemony and the growing circle of Buddhist influence. Second- and third-hand reports from the raid mention certain Indian wise men who were found in Northwest India, but there is no specific information about Buddhism. Gymnosophists, the so-called naked philosophers of India, are described in some accounts; but these ascetics were more probably Jainas or Brāhmaṇa saṃnyāsī-s than Buddhists.

Again, about 291 B.C., little more than a generation after Alexander's death (323 B.C.), there appeared the memoirs of Megasthenes, ambassador from Seleukos Nikator—heir to the easternmost portion of Alexander's empire—to the court of

[3] For Arrian's and other materials pertinent to Alexander's Indian campaign, no volume is more valuable than J. W. McCrindle, *Invasion of India by Alexander the Great as Described by Arrian, Q. Curtius, Diodoros, Plutarch and Justin* (London: Archibald Constable & Co., 1893).

Candragupta Moriya, usurper to the Magadhan domains and founder of the first all-India empire. In the fragments preserved from Megasthenes's work there are references to two types of Indian ascetics: "pramanikas" and "samanas." Nineteenth-century scholars—Robert Caesar Childers and Jules Barthélemy Saint-Hilaire among others—believed that the samanas (*śramaṇa*, *samaṇo*) were Buddhists. And, certainly, it seems probable that Megasthenes came across Buddhists during his extended stay in the Moriyan capital, Pāṭaliputta (modern: Patna). Still, Buddhist inscriptions and texts speak of both types of ascetics mentioned by Megasthenes as non-Buddhist in many instances. Moreover, it is apparent that the appellations were often used interchangeably as generic terms referring to all types of ascetics. Megasthenes, then, is a disappointing source for anyone interested in discovering the impact of Buddhism on Hellenistic Europeans.

> Nowhere among those fragments of his work which have been preserved for us can the Western reader find the slightest amount of precise information concerning Buddhist religion and thought.[4]

The Early Christian Period

Direct and informative testimony about Buddhism is almost nonexistent in the early centuries of our own era also. Clement of Alexandria observes in his *Stromata* (i.15) that

> philosophy, a thing of the highest utility, flourished in antiquity among the barbarians, shedding its light over the nations. And afterwards it came to Greece. First in its ranks were the prophets of the Egyptians; and the Chaldeans among the Assyrians; and the Druids among the Gauls; and the Samanaeans [cf. *śramaṇa* above] among the Bactrians; and the philosophers of the Celts;

[4] De Lubac, p. 11.

and the Magi of the Persians who foretold the Saviour's birth, and came into the land of Judaea guided by a star. The Indian gymnosophists are also in the number, and the other barbarian philosophers. And of these there are two classes some of them called Sarmanae (or Samanaei [*śramaṇa*]), and others Brahmins. And those of the Sarmanae who are called Hylobii neither inhabit cities, nor have roofs over them, but are clothed in the bark of trees, feed on nuts, and drink water in their hands. Like those called Encratites in the present day, they know not marriage nor begetting children.

Some, too, of the Indians obey the precepts of Buddha (*Boutta*); whom, on account of his extraordinary sanctity, they have raised to divine honours.[5]

Here, however, we have to do only with a casual—if tantalizing—reference in an apologetic tract. Beyond it we have only our imagination to proceed with.

Before reviewing the data on Buddhism provided by Marco Polo and others, I shall address a few words to the possibility of discerning an indirect witness to Buddhism in early sources. Out of the complex religious and ideological syncretism of the Hellenistic period, two great movements of ideas—one severely, the other loosely defined—emerged to challenge one another for dominance: Christianity and Gnosticism. Source materials indicate that Christian orthodoxy—or, rather, Christians struggling to formulate an orthodoxy—did not encounter Buddhism directly through apologies and polemics. Nonetheless, several questions still excite investigation and speculation. Does Christianity itself owe Buddhism anything in the matter of doctrine or emphasis? May not Christianity's very existence be a powerful witness to the encounter of Buddhism and the West? And what is the debt which Christianity has with regard to Gnosticism—a movement which, in its turn, may have developed under Buddhist influence?

Definite answers to these questions and others presupposed

[5] Clement of Alexandria, *Stromata*, i.15, in *Fathers of the Second Century*, Vol. II of *The Ante-Nicene Fathers*, ed. Rev. Alexander Roberts and James Donaldson (American ed. rev. A. Cleveland Coxe; Grand Rapids, Michigan: Wm. B. Eerdmans Publishing Co., 1951), p. 316b.

or suggested by them cannot be given at this time. And this state of affairs goes some way toward explaining the recurrence of quite fanciful "elucidations" of one or another Christian or Gnostic formulation through postulating a direct Buddhist antecedent. The trend is now to assert the independence of Christian and Gnostic traditions from any determining Buddhist associations. Consequently, such fantasies as the one which insists that Jesus of Nazareth was a member of the Essenian sect and that the latter was merely a displaced segment of the Buddhist order (*saṃgha*) seem unlikely to snare the attention of any serious student.[6]

While it is certain that Jesus was no more a Buddhist than He was an existentialist, it is true that much crystallization of the Church's dogma occurred in the second century and in direct conflict with the Gnostics. It is not so easy to answer questions concerning what the Church may have drawn from the Gnostics and in what precise ways it responded to that movement. That is to say, it is possible even now to ask if the Church may not have been influenced negatively by Buddhism via the instrument of Gnosticism.

However, the question of Buddhist "participation" in Gnosticism cannot be answered summarily. In the first place, this is due to the fact that students of Gnosticism do not agree as to the proper delimitation of the subject.

> "Gnosticism" has become one of the chameleonlike terms which are so dear to historical scholarship. The scholar can mold it to his liking. The vagueness and lack of precision in the present use of this concept has a double root. First, the complex nature of the movement in its manifold interlacement with the syncretistic world of the Near East asks for ambiguity in retrospect; to elucidate a syncretistic movement is one of the most difficult historical undertakings. The viewer's approach determines in advance the outcome of his research. Second, because every historical generalization is prone to break down at the borders of the period in question, margins can be narrowed or stretched *ad libitum*. It is a natural tendency to expand constantly the meaning of a term, precisely because one must—or can—always include

[6] De Lubac, p. 20 and footnote 60.

one more border case and then another. However, the wider the span is drawn, the more blurred will the actual content of the concept become. "Middle Ages" and "Renaissance" are two sad examples of ultimately meaningless generalizations.[7]

Adolf von Harnack viewed Gnosticism as an "acute Hellenization of Christianity"; but, after quoting Harnack, Hans Lietzmann countered that "we must recognize in addition an equally acute 're-orientalization.' . . . Among the gnostics, the god of oriental mysticism rose up in power and might to contend with the Father in Heaven to whom Jesus had taught His disciples to pray."[8] Robert M. Grant declares that Gnosticism is rooted in bankrupt Jewish apocalypticism.[9] Hans Jonas maintains that Gnosticism is a world religion emerging from the classical Hellenic milieu in conjunction with certain ideas from Syria and Iran to challenge every classical tenet and belief.[10] Some scholars speak of "gnosticisms" and cite the more or less systematic expositions of Simon Magus, Basilides, Valentinus, and Mani as separate schemes, independent of one another. Others speak comprehensively of an historical Gnosticism of which those men were representatives.

Direct discussion of the history and meanings of Gnosticism does not fall within the province of this study. Still, despite confusions arising at every statement made concerning the structure of this phenomenon, we can point out certain features of Gnosticism (or the several gnosticisms) on which scholars are in general agreement: the pronounced dualism

[7] Samuel Leauchli, *The Language of Faith: An Introduction to the Semantic Dilemma of the Early Church* (New York: The Abingdon Press, 1962), p. 16.

[8] Hans Lietzmann, *The Beginnings of the Christian Church*, trans. Bertram Lee Woolf (3d ed. rev.; London: Lutterworth Press, 1953), p. 295.

[9] Robert M. Grant, *Gnosticism and Early Christianity* (New York: Columbia University Press, 1959) as cited in Leauchli, p. 17, footnote 3.

[10] Hans Jonas, *The Gnostic Religion*—the most comprehensive and imaginative one-volume treatment of the subject in English; includes extensive bibliography.

of the Gnostic systems (a dualism in cosmology, psychology, and so on exemplified most clearly by Manichaeanism and Mandaeanism); docetism; radical displacement of ethics and morality from preeminent status for the man seeking salvation (and a consequent tendency to develop the full range of possibilities of antinomianism); asceticism; and the consistent and extreme use of negative terminology when referring to the nature of the religious and ontological ultimates. These features, and there are others, of course, have suggested an Eastern origin of certain strains of Gnosticism. It is commonly conceded that the Mediterranean hosted Indians and Buddhists during Gnosticism's rise to prominence (though data about the Buddhist community which is supposed to have existed in Alexandria are singularly elusive to modern historical scholarship). And may not the roots of Gnosticism be in India and Iran?

Lamentably, no historian of Gnosticism has been at the same time either an Indologist or a student of Buddhist thought. Indeed, there has hardly been any serious dialogue between experts in those several areas of inquiry. During the nineteenth century many scholars insisted that Gnosticism, diversely conceived, owed much to India and Buddhism. It was stated on various occasions that *gnosis* was merely a translation of the Sanskrit *prajñā* (Pali: *paññā*); that Gnosticism was "prajñā-ism"; in short, that Gnosticism was an Indian salvation scheme. Basilides, the most consistently brilliant of the Gnostic systematizers, was especially pointed out as a crypto-Buddhist. In 1902, the *Journal of the Royal Asiatic Society* published an article entitled "Buddhist Gnosticism, the System of Basilides" in which the author, J. Kennedy, attempted to show that Basilides' system was nothing other than a clever fusion of materials drawn from Buddhist merchants in Alexandria and representatives of the Church.[11] Apropos of the questions of Buddhist influence on

[11] J. Kennedy, "Buddhist Gnosticism, the System of Basilides," *Journal of the Royal Asiatic Society* (1902), pp. 377–415. Kennedy's article draws on Thomas William Rhys Davids for information about

Gnosticism and that latter article in particular, Father de Lubac remarks wisely:

Proofs are lacking. That Basilides doubtless pressed "negative theology" further than anyone else; that he had supposed an identity in principle between absolute existence and the absolute "nothing"; that he believed in metempsychosis—attaching to it both moral and soteriological significance; and, finally, that he had conceived of the final restoration of the universe as a return to "The Great Ignorance"; all this is not at all sufficient to establish that he had tried to construct a sort of fusion between Buddhism and Christianity or that, being a Christian, he had interpreted his own religion by means of a Buddhist metaphysics. Although there is an undeniable analogy between the way he spoke about the First Principle—as neither comprehensible nor incomprehensible—and the ways in which the Buddhist authors spoke, that does not prove that there was the slightest influence of Buddhism on him.[12]

Arguments for Buddhist influence on the Gnostics are somewhat stronger in the case of Manichaeanism. Mani, born about A.D. 216 in Babylonia, traveled extensively in the "farther East," and it is reasonably certain that he went at least as far as the Northwest sector of the Indian subcontinent. His own religious formulations constituted an explicit syncretism in which the Buddha was accorded high recognition. But of specifically Buddhist doctrine—of the idea of nirvāṇa, for example—there is no indication. Rather, the Manichaean mélange is dominated by the specific dualism of corrupted Zoroastrianism and a severe asceticism. References to identifiably Buddhist principles are limited to elements pertaining to discipline.[13]

From the epoch of Alexander the Great on through the entire Hellenistic period and the first millennium of the Church's existence, sources from fifteen centuries tell a

---

Buddhism. See especially p. 409 and footnote for Kennedy's conclusions regarding nirvāṇa and its "equivalent" in Basilides' scheme. The *Journal* is cited hereafter as JRAS.

[12] De Lubac, p. 23.

[13] See Jonas, pp. 206–237, 297–299.

monotonously similar tale: other than isolated references—often dubious, always brief—there is no indication of a direct confrontation between Buddhism and the European–Mediterranean West. During the first fifteen hundred years of its history, Buddhism, "perhaps the most powerful movement of ideas in the history of Asia," [14] neither drew specific attack from the civilized West nor contributed positively to the formation of European thought systems. There was no "encounter," strictly so called.

Attractive in its seeming vulnerability, that tentative conclusion invites refutation. Nevertheless, it has yet to be challenged effectively. Further investigations may uncover new and positive evidence, of course; but only the most naïve diffusionist could undertake such research convinced that there *must* be historical connections. Fortunately, most scholars have learned that to be heedless of the manifest, creative continuities within individual traditions is to forsake critical study in order to serve popular fancy or private fantasy.

The Middle Ages

The first direct, authentic, and somewhat documented knowledge that she [Christian Western Europe] acquired of the Buddhist world was to come toward the end of the thirteenth century from the great ambassadors and missionaries and the illustrious Venetian traveler Marco Polo.[15]

It is in the writings of the Franciscan Friar William of Rubrock [Willem van Ruusbroec], "the best informed and wisest of Marco Polo's predecessors," that this first secure in-

[14] Th. Stcherbatsky, *Buddhist Logic*, I, xi.
[15] De Lubac, p. 32.

formation about an encounter between Buddhism and the West is found. In the spring of 1253, the friar began a journey east to the court of one of the great Tartar khans as an emissary of Louis IX of France. The information he transmitted was the first of any consequence which Europeans received about Buddhism. For that reason, the title "Discoverer of Buddhism" is deservedly his.

Throughout the several centuries preceding Friar William's journey, Christian Europe's knowledge of Asia was gleaned almost exclusively from reports of merchants and traders who, to impress buyers, did everything possible to stress the fantastic and exotic origins of the cloth, jewels, and spices that they sold. Those advertising and salesmanship techniques did nothing to increase Europe's knowledge (as opposed to speculations and fantasies) about the Near and Far East, but the exaggerated reports had no deleterious political effects during the period (and this is not the place to estimate the cumulative economic side effects).

By the time of the Crusades, however, Europe's lack of dependable information about the "Orient" was considered to be a serious, indeed a critical, liability. The Church faced an ambitious, belligerent, organized enemy in the armies of Islam. Rumors in the twelfth century suggested that a great horde of fighting peoples deep in Asia were moving westward. Those fighters were the Mongol–Tartar tribesmen. The measure and balance of factors inspiring those predatory migrations are still deliberated. Presumably, the shifting fortunes of weather, geographical readjustments of the Chinese populations, and the policies of the Chinese administrative hierarchies played roles of importance. In any case, led by a series of brilliant military commanders-cum-administrators, the Mongol–Tartars posed a serious threat to a Europe whose Charles Martel lived no longer except in the songs of bards.

European interest was captured by further rumors reporting that there were Christians among the Mongols. Leaders spiritual and secular were excited and apprehensive. If Europe were faced with another enemy, all would be lost. But if it were true that part of the Mongol hordes were Christians—or, at least, not hostile to the Church—they might ally themselves with Europeans against a common Muslim enemy. In the most favorable circumstance, the Mongols could be played off against the Islamic forces, leaving Roman Catholic Europe to watch the gladiatorial combat without becoming involved. So it was that the Papal court sent several ambassadors to the Tartar strongholds on expressly political missions in the early thirteenth century. In the main, these missions were composed of Dominican friars who, totally unprepared and uninformed about the Tartars, failed miserably when they confronted the shrewd and sophisticated court of the khans. Moreover, the Dominicans had a notoriously short tolerance for any type of "idolatrous paganism." The various religious practices which they encountered excited not curiosity but anger.

With but few exceptions, the reports from the missions to the East were conflicting, sketchy, even incoherent. That fact inspired France's Louis IX to send the reliable and prestigious Friar William to obtain solid intelligence. The friar—then thirty-eight years old and in no mood to wander about in the midst of barbarians—objected as vehemently as was politic and grudgingly set out for the court of the Turkish khan. His assignment was to confirm the existence of Christians there and to convert as many as possible to the Roman Church. The friar did find Christians and in considerable numbers. But they were Nestorians. To make matters worse, Friar William noticed almost as many Muslims.

The final insult was the presence of "idolaters." The situation irritated the friar, but not so much as it had his Dominican precursors. Friar William was inspired to hold public debates on religious topics rather than pout over the depravity of the natives. Mongka (Mongu) Khan, distressed to find the delicate equilibrium of religious sects threatened by this interloper, managed to rid the court of the Franciscan in six months. The results of Friar William's mission were six baptized converts and a magnificent book of memoirs, *Itinerarium*, justly described as one of the most original and interesting masterpieces in the whole of medieval Latin literature.

Through the *Itinerarium*

> Friar William was able to make known for the first time to ignorant Westerners the Buddhist cults, and Buddhist rites as practiced especially by the resident Tibetan lamas. . . . But he made no attempt to penetrate the spiritual depths and doctrinal substance of the various cults. On the other hand he gives a vivid picture both of the religious rivalries around the imperial throne and of the enlightened policy followed to maintain peace and tolerance amid so much dogmatic ferment and so many latent conflicts. The descriptions of the public discussion held between the friar and representatives of Oriental religions records the first direct Catholic contact with Asian clergy in an age of fierce universal religious controversies, and it has no equal for vivacity and exactitude in all the medieval literature that stemmed from it. It was through this report that the Western world learned for the first time dependably some of the fundamental principles of Buddhist doctrine, which Tibetan Lamaism had diffused in Mongolia from the time of Chinghiz Khan.[16]

From 1271 to 1295, the young Venetian Marco Polo, accompanied by his father and uncle, journeyed through Mongol Asia. On Marco's return to Italy, and while he was in a Genoa prison, he dictated a "description" of his experiences. In the masterful *Marco Polo's Asia*, Leonardo Olschki observes that the depiction of Marco as primarily a merchant—with the

[16] Leonardo Olschki, *Marco Polo's Asia*, trans. John A. Scott, pp. 69–70. For a recent and lively translation of the *Itinerarium* of Brother William of Rubrock (it has been suggested that his name derives from Rubruc near Cassel rather than from Ruisbroek in Brabant), see *The Journey of William of Rubruck*, trans. a nun of Stanbrook Abbey, *Mission to Asia: Narratives and Letters of the Franciscan Missionaries in Mongolia and China in the Thirteenth and Fourteenth Centuries*, ed. Christopher Dawson (New York: Harper & Row, 1966 [originally published as *The Mongol Mission* (London and New York: Sheed and Ward Ltd., 1955)]), pp. 89–220, especially pp. 187–94. Dawson's introductory essay concisely summarizes the historical background and the nature of these "missions," pp. vii–xxxv.

"commercial mentality" and "poetic prestige" which are ascribed and accorded to him as such—"makes of Marco a type and not an individual, a professional and sociological cliché rather than a historical personage. . . ." [17]

Marco seems to have been a very practical, curious, honest man—jarring as this may be to lingering romantic sensitivities. "Marco was neither a merchant nor a missionary, strictly speaking, and least of all an adventurer, as many still like to call him." [18] Olschki comes away from *Il Milione* with the impression that Marco was an unusually flexible and versatile fellow.

> Marco was something of both man of the world and man with a mission, according to circumstances, and adapted himself empirically to becoming expert in various activities, without any specific vocation, without professional instruction, and without any specific task, amid the thousand and one vicissitudes of a long and varied career.[19]

We seek a reliable witness, and, as Olschki observes, Marco's very lack of imagination testifies to the validity and authenticity of the episodes and descriptions in *Il Milione*.

> Marco's psychological make-up is, indeed, a guarantee of the authenticity of his reminiscences, even when they cannot be made to agree with the reality of historical and natural facts. A man so devoid of imagination and literary ability could never have produced and kept up without betraying himself a fiction so varied and on so vast a scale.[20]

In *Il Milione*, as in Friar William's *Itinerarium*, the religious devotees seen in Asia are described as being either Christians, Muslims, or "idolaters." Now, with regard to the last named,

> though Marco knows that they belong to different sects, practice various rites, and are grouped in independent religious organiza-

[17] Olschki, p. 97.
[18] *Ibid.*, p. 118.
[19] *Ibid.*
[20] *Ibid.*, p. 120.

tions, he nevertheless attributes all these diverse manifestations of Asiatic idolatry to a common founder, identified in the person of the Buddha.[21]

He refers to the Buddha by the Mongol name Sagamoni Borcan. Sagamoni is apparently the Mongol corruption of the Indo-Aryan compound, Śākyamuni. Borcan would be "an Altaic word which among the Turkish and Mongol tribes of upper Asia was used to describe not only a divinity, but also . . . its image, or, as Marco has it, its idol." [22]

Buddhism in *Il Milione*, then, is a phenomenon far removed from the various forms of Indian Buddhism, and the Buddha is hardly recognizable. This is consistently the case in the work despite the fact that Marco visited Ceylon in 1293 and refers to the existence of Buddhism on the island. For him, the Mongolian variety remained the standard of reference. And Sagamoni Borcan—not the Buddha of history, but an idealized fragment of a transcendent, shamanistic miracle worker—was the central cult figure. By means of Mongol tribesmen's interpretations of the idiosyncratic Buddhism of the Tibetan lama-missionaries, the Buddha had been "transformed into a concrete materialization of a supernatural power that was vaguely apprehended and never specified, and finally became a supreme divinity worshiped in the images which represented it." [23]

Both the peculiar forms of this Buddhism—not all of which were Buddhist at all—and Marco's own lack of concern for or insight into speculative matters conspired to prevent the appearance of a probative account of Buddhism in *Il Milione*.

Although Marco attempted to see further into the mystery of this idolatry, so often described or mentioned by him, he was never able to penetrate those speculative depths that were the ultimate concern of the meditations and doctrines of Sakyamuni's followers and that determined the transcendental humanity of the Buddha. These were not understood even in the court and govern-

[21] *Ibid.*, p. 253.
[22] *Ibid.*, p. 254.
[23] *Ibid.*, p. 256.

ment circles where Marco had observed the manifestations of the cult. Hence, the Buddhism that he knew and portrayed in his book is essentially different from the Buddhism of the Chinese; and different also, in certain respects, from Lamaistic teaching. . . .[24]

There are hints that Marco understood the bare outlines of the belief in transmigration (*saṃsāra*, "going around, wandering"); but he knew nothing—or at least reveals no knowledge—of a doctrine that declares the absolute release from the round of rebirths and the wandering from existence to existence.

Nowhere in Marco Polo's account do we find mention of the fundamental concept of *nirvāṇa* as a willed and definitive liberation from this cycle of rebirths, a cycle determined by moral qualities and conduct in secular life, but especially by the systematic sacrifices of the monastic life.[25]

Through Marco's *Il Milione*, several centuries of Western Europeans learned almost all that was to be known in the West about Buddhism. The patently misleading nature of many of Marco's descriptions and the fact that, in the main, he observed at close hand only the most peculiar ramifications of the earlier, Indian Buddhist practice mean, of course, that his was hardly a definitive account. Still, *Il Milione*, in a most interesting fashion, both exhibits and contributes to a Western European attitude of mind which has played a notable role in the course of Buddhist studies.

Henri Baudet has commented arrestingly on an aspect of the European consciousness which, though for the most part unnoticed in the pedestrian course of our twentieth-century lives, continues to affect the way in which we view the "East." It is "our mythical image of the 'noble savage': the myth of the natural and fundamental goodness of primitive man."[26]

[24] *Ibid.*, p. 257.
[25] *Ibid.*, p. 292.
[26] Henri Baudet, *Paradise on Earth: Some Thoughts on European Images of Non-European Man*, p. 10.

Disconcertingly enough, this myth has intertwined with the "factual" political awareness of the extra-Western since the classical Hellenic age. Until the time of the Crusades, Jean de Plan Carpini, Friar William of Rubrock, and Marco Polo, however, the existence of this golden man and his golden, cultureless—hence, burdenless—society was referred to "an unimaginably remote past at an immeasurable distance of time." [27]

During the Crusades and more especially with the distribution of accounts from missionary-ambassadors and merchants, there was a radical alteration of Europeans' geographical awareness. Thereafter the imaginative could conceive of their noble savage not as long ago but, rather, as far away.

> The image thus became a geographical reality. It was removed from a distant past to a distant present. Where at first it had been characterized by the distance in time, it now became increasingly invested with a contemporary character. The distance became a matter of geography.[28]

Even in the face of degenerate, bizarre forms of Buddhism, Marco was able to declare soberly of the Buddha: "For a certainty, if he had been baptized a Christian he would have been a great saint before God." [29] Projected on the barely perceived person of the historical Buddha was an image of Western Europe's noble savage. Spatially and temporally distant, the Buddha was an ideal subject for this mythologizing. Proper appreciation of the nature of this projection—this cloak of sanctified primitiveness—and the impulses which inspired it will help illumine later intellectual and emotional struggles with the supposed substance of the Buddha's teachings and the many blind refusals to concede even the possibility that he could have preached the way to annihilation.

[27] *Ibid.*, p. 11.
[28] *Ibid.*, p. 15.
[29] As quoted in Olschki, p. 256.

Threshold of the Scientific Period

During the sixteenth, seventeenth, and much of the eighteenth centuries, Europe's additional knowledge about Buddhism came from a variety of travelers, mostly missionaries. A good deal of reliable information was obtained from these sources, but it was superficially descriptive for the most part. In India, China and Japan, missionaries encountered culturoreligious institutions and traditions which they were generally unable or unwilling to fathom at the level of ideas. The solid information conveyed by them bears rather on the behavior of Buddhists, on the appearance of their rites, and on the contributions made by Buddhists to the Eastern civilizations. Resemblances between aspects of Buddhist and Roman Catholic ritual trappings and procedures were scrupulously noted, but the designation of Buddhists as vulgar idolaters combined with the persistence of the Christian apologists' polemic spirit to exclude them from any profound doctrinal understanding.[30]

Although reports from the period usually characterize Buddhists simply as idolaters, occasionally the analysis is more "delicate" and two levels of Buddhist thought and practice are distinguished: idolatrous and atheistic. According to most accounts in which Buddhists are differentiated in that fashion, the idolaters are said to follow a "lower" law, and the atheists a "higher." [31]

[30] Materials are being discovered and edited which may lead to a modification of this judgment. See, for example, *I Missionari italiani nel Tibet e nel Nepal*, ed. Luciano Petech (*Il Nuovo Ramusio*, II; Rome: La Libreria dello Stato, 1952–56).

[31] Voltaire observed caustically:

"These sects are tolerated in China for the use of the common people as a sort of coarse food for their nourishment, while the magistrates and literati nourish themselves on a purer substance. It would seem

In 1700, in his *Apology of the Dominican Missionaries of China*, Noël Alexander wrote:

The secret doctrine of the ministers of the god Fo [a Chinese equivalent for Buddha] is unalloyed atheism. The void which they consider to be the principle of all things is, they say, completely perfect and tranquil, without beginning or end, unmoving, without knowledge, and without desire. That is why those who wish to be happy ought to devote all their efforts to becoming like this principle, overcoming and suppressing all their passions to the extent that they become oblivious to everything and that—lost in the highest contemplation, without reflection, without any use of their reason—they will enjoy that divine repose which is the only happiness for man. When they have arrived in this state, they can teach the doctrine and common discipline of life and practice it outwardly, applying it inwardly to themselves only in order to enjoy that secret tranquillity which characterizes a celestial existence. Here is the mystery of this sect which at bottom does not distinguish at all between good and evil; which makes a virtue neither of thinking nor of working to be virtuous; which acknowledges no rewards nor punishments after death; which believes in neither providence nor the immortality of the soul; which reduces everything to a confused void with a simple nothing as its beginning and end; and which considers that perfection consists in perfect indifference, apathy, and an undisturbed quietude.[32]

The content and tone of Alexander's statement reverberated through the eighteenth century: Buddhist quietism, analogies between Buddhists and Stoics. In most cases the judgments were stern. (H. T. Colebrooke, in the early decades of the nineteenth century, used some of the same comparisons but without the condemnatory overtones. Some, however, would

---

that the masses do not deserve a reasonable religion." *Oeuvres complètes de Voltaire*, Vol. XX: *Essai sur les moeurs et l'esprit des nations* (2d ed.; Paris: Baudouin Frères, 1827), p. 343. See also de Lubac, pp. 103–4.

[32] De Lubac, pp. 86–87. Speaking in the same register, Pierre Bayle said it all more succinctly: "They [*i.e.*, Buddhist adepts, whom, somewhat confusingly, Bayle groups together with Brāhmaṇas] have some very bizarre notions about nothingness and a moral philosophy which greatly resembles the visions of our quietists." "Brachmanes," *Dictionnaire historique et critique de Pierre Bayle* (Nouvelle éd.; Paris: Desoer, 1820), IV, 94b.

choose to see in this latter merely Colebrooke's own sovereign disinterest in Indian metaphysical systems. See below, Chapter I.) Apathy, ataraxy, void, nothingness, annihilation—as these and other slogan characterizations of Buddhist doctrine became current in the late seventeenth and early eighteenth centuries, polemical activity increased without inspiring a commensurate intensification of inquiry. De Lubac offers this summary of the prevailing Enlightenment attitude toward Buddhism:

> Buddhism always appears simply as a "monstrous religion," as an "abominable sect" founded by a "very wicked man." It is a "plague," a "gangrene." Chinese philosophers and statesmen have had reason to combat it not only as a "ridiculous doctrine" but as a "moral monster and the destruction of civil society." [33]

Disdain and an overwhelming sense of superiority and indignation came to dominate one level of almost all the writings on Buddhism during this period. One level, but not all; for the latent power of that urge to mythologize about the Buddha contended with and moderated the scorn. The eighteenth—the philosophical, universalist, ahistorical—century. Excitement about China. Voltaire's *Mohammed*. At first glance this was a century very likely to fix tolerant attention on Buddhism.

> With the eighteenth century in mind, one might state that the less a period thought in *historical* terms, the more it stressed contemporary expectations of perfect happiness and identified these expectations with the contemporary world. That might explain why the eighteenth century, with its protesting attitude toward the whole of history—an attitude also displayed to some extent by our own century—felt so strongly attracted to the other world known or thought to exist outside Europe. And it might also explain the universalism that went with it.[34]

Unfortunately for the myth and the myth makers, a certain amount of "factual" evidence was accessible to the Western European intelligentsia during the period. Perhaps idolatry

[33] De Lubac, pp. 89–90.
[34] Baudet, pp. 74–75.

could be reconciled in the quest for the simple society; but atheism and nihilism could hardly be accommodated. Paramount was the "virtue of simplicity,"[35] and even Deists blanched in the face of Buddhism's reputed atheism and annihilationism.

Of the solid information passed to Europe in the seventeenth and eighteenth centuries, the contributions of Engelbert Kaempfer and La Loubère deserve special notice. Kaempfer, "physician to the Dutch embassy to the [Japanese] Emperor's Court," published his *The History of Japan together with a Description of the Kingdom of Siam* in several folios from 1690 to 1692. He seems to have been the first European to be impressed by the complex diversity of Buddhism in its various manifestations throughout Asia while at the same time being mindful of its basic unity.

> The origine of this religion, which quickly spread thro' most Asiatick countries to the very extremities of the East, (not unlike the Indian fig-tree which propagates itself, and spreads far round by sending down new roots from the extremities of its branches,) must be look'd for among the Brahmines. I have strong reasons to believe, both from the affinity of the name, and the very nature of this religion, that its author and founder is the very same person, whom the Brahmines call Budha, and believe to be an essential part of Wisthnu, or their Deity, who made its ninth appearance in the world under this name, and in the shape of this man. The Chinese and Japanese call him Buds and Siaka.[36]

La Loubère, ambassador from Louis XIV to the king of Siam in 1687 and 1688, published his discerning *On the Kingdom of Siam* in Paris in 1691. To him we owe not only one of the first references to the Buddhist nirvāṇa by name in European literature (I cannot find an earlier one) but an amazingly modern evaluation of the term. " '*Nireupan* [nirvāṇa],' " he commented,

[35] *Ibid.*, p. 35 *et passim.*

[36] Engelbert Kaempfer, *The History of Japan together with a Description of the Kingdom of Siam, 1690–1692*, trans. J. G. Scheuchzer (3 vols.; Glasgow: James MacLehose and Sons, 1906), II, 56.

is not a place, but a way of being. . . . Nireupan, they say—that is, this soul has disappeared. It will not return again to any world. And it is this word which the Portuguese have translated as follows: *it is annihilated* and also as: *it has become God;* even though, according to the Siamese, it is neither true annihilation nor the acquisition of any divine nature.[37]

For more than one hundred years there were to be no more penetrating observations than these. Sir William Jones, whose efforts in India opened Sanskrit studies to the West,[38] never attained to them. Early in the 1790's, he dismissed the Buddha as some sort of bastard manifestation of the Egyptian sun god. It remained for the nineteenth century to pick up Buddhist studies from the point at which they had been left in fact since the work of Kaempfer and La Loubère and, by virtue of an increasing competence in the languages that Jones had helped make known, to inaugurate the scientific period of these investigations.

[37] De Lubac, p. 99.

[38] The best short account of Jones' life and contributions will be found in A. J. Arberry, "The Founder: William Jones," *Oriental Essays: Portraits of Seven Scholars* (London: George Allen & Unwin, Ltd., 1960), pp. 48–86. See also Franklin Edgerton, "Sir William Jones: 1746–1794," *Journal of the American Oriental Society*, 66 (1946), 230–39; and Suniti Kumar Chatterji, "Sir William Jones: 1746–1794," *Sir William Jones Bicentenary of his Birth Commemoration Volume 1746–1946*, (Calcutta: Royal Asiatic Society of Bengal, 1948), pp. 81–96. Both of the latter are now conveniently reprinted in *Portraits of Linguists: A Biographical Source Book for the History of Western Linguistics*, ed. Thomas A. Sebeok, I, 1–36. And several articles of interest on Jones will be found in the *Bulletin of The School of Oriental and African Studies*, XI, Part 4 (1946); especially Alfred Master, "The Influence of Sir William Jones upon Sanskrit Studies," pp. 798–806.

[CHAPTER I]

Earliest Scientific Buddhist Studies

Although, as we have seen, Europe did not "discover" Buddhism in the nineteenth century, the early 1800's did witness the beginnings of a scientific study as distinct from fabulous reports, desultory descriptions, and unfounded conjectures. The ideas and discussions of pre-nineteenth-century "commentators" on Buddhism—whatever their interest may be for antiquarians of our own time—patently had not been widely circulated, nor had they aroused sustained interest on the part of scholars or laymen. Only the most ingenious enthusiast would attempt to make a case for the ordered development of a body of knowledge concerning Buddhism before the end of the eighteenth century.

Henry Thomas Colebrooke, Brian Houghton Hodgson, Alexander Csoma of Körös, and Eugène Burnouf—these are the men who founded the tradition of Buddhist studies that continues today in both hemispheres. It is to their achievements that this and the following chapter are dedicated.

In order to begin the study of Buddhism—not merely in certain late, often bastard, states, but in its authentic tenor, in its origins, in the development of its branches, and in the great periods of its history—it was first necessary to learn the principal languages in which its enormous literature was redacted or translated.[1]

Chief among those languages were Sanskrit and Pali (*pāḷi*). Regular instruction in Sanskrit began on the Western European continent in 1814 when Antoine-Léonard de Chézy was appointed as the first occupant of the chair "pour la langue et la littérature des Sanskrites . . . au Collège royal de France." [2] Formalization of Sanskrit instruction was the necessary first stage in founding the historical and critical study of Buddhism. (Subsequently, hesitantly, and always as an aspect or stepchild of Sanskrit curricula, Pali studies were developed.) Only after the effective discovery of Sanskrit could nirvāṇa be introduced to serious consideration in the West.

Henry Thomas Colebrooke

Between 1820 and 1830, the two languages essential for the historical study of Buddhism began to be known in Europe. But this was still the accomplishment of only a very few scholars. And of Buddhism itself these same scholars knew scarcely anything if they were not, in fact, ignorant of it altogether.[3]

Henry Thomas Colebrooke's contributions to Sanskrit studies entitle him to a place among the foremost giants of that discipline. Fortunately, complete studies of his life and work are

[1] De Lubac, *La Rencontre du bouddhisme*, p. 107.

[2] Sylvain Lévi, "Les Origines d'une chair: l'Entrée du sanscrit au Collège de France," *Mémorial Sylvain Lévi* (Paris: Paul Hartmann, 1937), p. 161.

[3] De Lubac, p. 115.

readily available, hence obviating the need to present a satisfactorily complete biographical sketch here. Born June 15, 1765, the son of Sir George Colebrooke, chairman of the court of directors of the East India Company, Colebrooke first went to India (Bengal) in 1782 as a minor civil service employee. In 1814, he returned to England, having become professor of Sanskrit and Hindu law at the College of Fort William and judge in the new court of appeal of Calcutta (1801), president of the court of Calcutta (1805), and member of the council of Greater India (1807). During the years between his homecoming and his death in London on March 10, 1837, he wrote numerous papers on the languages, law, philosophy, and literatures of India.[4]

Of Colebrooke's scholarship, Raymond Schwab writes:

> His virtues of accuracy, patience, penetration, and balance show up exceptionally well in one work which has been the object of almost undiminished admiration for more than a century: the *Essays on the Philosophy of the Hindoos*, a subject he had learned thoroughly in the first years of his colonial appointment although he allowed his study to mature for thirty years before publishing the results. It exercised a decisive influence in European cultural circles. Moreover, in his respect for all varieties of mankind, Colebrooke followed Anquetil. As scholar and judge, his unfailing dedication to the truth caused him to deal with beliefs differing from his own in terms of verifiable facts and as equally valuable elements in a single whole. This integrity is to be held to the credit of the English school—of which Colebrooke is one of the foremost representatives—as a compensation for the political ambitions of certain men of action and the blindness of their rigid and narrow beliefs.[5]

That is high praise indeed, and it is far from being mere homage in retrospect. Colebrooke's essays deeply impressed his learned contemporaries. In fact, several years before they were translated into French, they had become the basis for

[4] For biographical data, see especially T. E. Colebrooke [H. T. Colebrooke's son], *A Life of H. T. Colebrooke*, Vol. I of H. T. Colebrooke, *Miscellaneous Essays*, ed. E. B. Cowell (3 vols.).

[5] Raymond Schwab, *La Renaissance orientale*, p. 45.

university lectures on Indian philosophy at the Collège de France.[6]

On February 3, 1827, Colebrooke read the fifth part of his *On the Philosophy of the Hindus* to a public meeting of the Royal Asiatic Society, London. "In the present essay," he began, "it is my intention to treat of the heretical systems of Jina and Buddha; . . . and to notice certain other Indian sects, which, like them exhibit some analogy to the Sankhyas, or followers of Kapila or of Patanjali." [7]

With characteristic straightforwardness, the phlegmatic Colebrooke admitted that he had not consulted any primary source texts for his sketch.[8] He was perfectly satisfied, however, he added casually, that the materials obtained from "polemical" sources were essentially correct. At that time and for many decades thereafter, it was not possible to refute his claims. And it is a particular tribute to his scholarly accomplishment that he said so few things about Buddhism which are exceptionable in light of present-day research.

Declaring that both Jainas and Bauddhas (Buddhists) were "originally Hindus," [9] Colebrooke proceeded to outline

[6] "At the Collège de France in 1829, Victor Cousin devoted the fifth and sixth lectures of his course in the history of philosophy to Hindu doctrines. From the beginning, he freely avowed: 'I declare that for me, who cannot read the originals, Oriental philosophy reduces to Indian philosophy. Further, I declare that Indian philosophy for me is almost entirely contained in Colebrooke's Memoirs, published from 1824 to 1827 in the early volumes of the *Transactions of the Asiatic Society of London*.' " (*Ibid.*, p. 104.)

[7] H. T. Colebrooke, "On Indian Sectaries," *Miscellaneous Essays*, II, 402.

[8] *Ibid.*, pp. 403–4. His sources: "[The] 4th, 5th, and 6th adhikaraṇas of the 2d chapter of the 2d lecture of *Uttara-mīmāṃsā* devoted to Buddhists (4 and 5) and Jains (6); *Pūrva-mīmāṃsā*, scattered references—especially 3d chapter, 1st book; and the *Sāṃkhya* (Kapila), one chapter on Bauddhas." (*Ibid.*)

[9] *Ibid.* On the controversy concerning the discoverer of Buddhism's birthplace, see de Lubac, p. 112; and also consult Ernest Renan, "Premiers travaux sur le bouddhisme," *Nouvelles études d'histoire religieuse* (Paris: Lévy Frères, 1884), pp. 43–44. I cannot understand how it is that Colebrooke has been overlooked as the scholar who unquestionably established that Buddhism was born in India. And, too,

the metaphysics and philosophical assertions of each system. Then he addressed the problem of nirvāṇa.

In published accounts of the religious opinions of Bauddhas and Jainas, derived principally from oral information, doubts have been expressed as to the sense attached by them to the terms which they use to signify the happy state at which the perfect saints arrive. It has been questioned whether annihilation, or what other condition short of such absolute extinction, is meant to be described.[10]

For more than a century and a quarter the question has remained for Western Europeans substantially as Colebrooke framed it. Because he was the first of them to essay a direct answer—supported by *some* reliable textual evidence at least—the various aspects of his answer deserve examination in some detail.

Colebrooke begins his study of nirvāṇa by considering common features among the Indian sects regarding the goal of human life. "Both these sects [Jaina and Buddhist], like most others of Indian origin, propose, for the grand object to which men should aspire, the attainment of a final happy state, from which there is no return." [11]

Mukti or *mokṣa*, Colebrooke explains, signifies the attainment of this goal. And he mentions such terms as *amṛta*, *apavarga*, *śreyaḥ*, *niḥśreyasa*, *kaivalyam*, and *niḥśaraṇa* which are descriptive—if not definitive—of this attainment. "But," he continues,

the term which the *Bauddhas*, as well as the *Jainas*, more particularly affect, and which however is also used by the rest, is *nirvāṇa*, profound calm. In its ordinary acceptation, as an adjective, it signifies extinct, as a fire which has gone out; set, as a luminary which has gone down; defunct, as a saint who has passed away: its etymology is from *vā*, to blow as wind, with the preposition *nir* used in a negative sense: it means calm and unruffled.[12]

Engelbert Kaempfer, more than a century and a quarter earlier than Colebrooke, had conjectured about the Indian roots of Buddhism.

[10] H. T. Colebrooke, *Miscellaneous Essays*, II, 424.

[11] *Ibid.*

[12] *Ibid.*, p. 425. Compare the analysis of Sir M. Monier-Williams, *A Sanskrit-English Dictionary*, p. 557bc.

Colebrooke carefully underscores one signification from among the etymological analyses and customary usages:

> The notion which is attached to the word in the acceptation now under consideration, is that of perfect apathy. It is a condition of unmixed tranquil happiness or ecstasy (*ānanda*). . . . A happy state of imperturbable apathy is the ultimate bliss to which the Indian aspires: in this the *Jaina*, as well as the *Bauddha*, concurs with the orthodox *Vedāntin.*[13]

Colebrooke grants that it is a trifle confusing to try to picture a state of perfect apathy—which resembles nothing so much as deep, dreamless sleep, he says, following the favored image in the Upaniṣads—as a happy or blissful state in itself. But, continuing the analogy of profound slumber, he suggests that the pleasure and refreshment experienced by a person awakening from such sleep is "referred back to the period of actual repose." To describe nirvāṇa as unmixed happiness or ecstasy is, then, by Colebrooke's own statement to speak of it in relative terms. That is to say, apathy is bliss only to the person who contemplates it beforehand or afterward. Relatively conceived, it is blissful only when compared with present experience. Articulate witnesses to apathy as a present experience are excluded by definition.

For the *Vedānta*, according to Colebrooke, deep sleep is the closest analogy to the condition of union with the Supreme. Such an idea of union after emancipation is anathema to the Buddhists and Jainas. He goes on to say:

> But neither do they consider the endless repose allotted to their perfected saints as attended with a discontinuance of individuality. It is not annihilation, but unceasing apathy, which they understand to be the extinction (*nirvāṇa*) of their saints; and which they esteem to be supreme felicity, worthy to be sought by practice or mortification, as well as by acquisition of knowledge.[14]

Colebrooke's evaluation has been praised often for its balance and moderation. Yet, one should not forget that he had no direct acquaintance with any Buddhist texts. As a con-

[13] H. T. Colebrooke, *Miscellaneous Essays*, II, p. 425.
[14] *Ibid.*

sequence, there seem to be some inconsistencie tion of Buddhism. Consider, for example, what *cittavijñāna*, the second of the five *skandha*-s (aggregates which, according to the Buddhist an bine to form phenomenal existences under the i *karman*):

> It is intelligence (*citta*), which is the same with self *man*) and knowledge (*vijñāna*). It is consciousness of sensation, or continuous course and flow of cognition and sentiment. There is not any other agent, nor being which acts and enjoys; nor is there an eternal soul: but merely succession of thought, attended with individual consciousness abiding within the body.[15]

Apparently there is a hiatus between such a statement, on the one hand, and Colebrooke's insistence, on the other, that nirvāṇa is not annihilation. Buddhists, he writes, recognize no *jīva* or *ātman* as distinct from *citta*. Many scholars were dissatisfied with his explanation that nirvāṇa is merely apathy, not annihilation. How, they asked—attempting to follow the logic of the Buddhist system to its conclusion—could the absence of suffering (*apatheia*) be anything less than total annihilation? [16]

Colebrooke's *Mīmāṃsaka* and *Sāṃkhya* sources brand the Buddhists *nāstika*-s, "atheists, or rather, disowners of another world." [17] Hence, we would expect him to be less charitable toward the Buddhist concept of nirvāṇa. And we wonder why, at the very least, he did not acknowledge this problem: to what surviving entity does that apathy which is nirvāṇa appertain? Would it be *citta?* Scarcely, for *citta* is not unceasing. It is not an eternal *ātman*.

[15] *Ibid.*, pp. 418–19.

[16] Cowell's long footnote (p. 426) summarizes the interpretations of nirvāṇa given by European scholars during the half-century that followed original publication of Colebrooke's essay. Completely convinced by the theses of Robert Caesar Childers (for which see below, Chapter IV), he assures his readers that nirvāṇa is annihilation, for "all existence is absolutely an evil to the Buddhist, and consequently its absolute extinction is the only summum bonum."

[17] *Ibid.*, p. 418.

While Colebrooke tries to distinguish the Buddhist nirvāṇa from the *Vedānta*'s conception of release and final bliss, he does not make the same effort with regard to the *Sāṃkhya*-s' notions. Consequently, his description of Buddhist nirvāṇa sounds discomfortingly like the *kaivalyam* of the *Sāṃkhyayogadarśana*. And it also strongly resembles doctrines which are distinctive to the Jainas.

Two points should be mentioned in order to help us understand the apparent inconsistencies in Colebrooke's essay. First, I am convinced that he was not altogether secure as to what beliefs differentiated Buddhists from Jainas. And that criticism would seem to hold true despite the fact that he knew that the idea of an eternal *jīva* was utterly foreign to the Buddhists. The polemics which were Colebrooke's sole literary sources must be blamed for much of this confusion. Even today it is not always clear to what sect a given native critique is directed. At the same time, it is apparent that the polemicists themselves were by no means always sure of the distinctions which characterize various sects.[18]

Second, I want to point out that Colebrooke describes nirvāṇa as a "state of mind" rather than orienting it ontologically—that is, as a mode of being. Certainly he did not define nirvāṇa as "apathy" because of the pejorative connotations which that word might have for his audience.[19] Rather, it was the most satisfactory definition of nirvāṇa as a *psychological* phenomenon. In eschewing talk of nirvāṇa on a metaphysical plane and at the same time denying that it is annihilation,

[18] This point is important because it underscores the undeniable fact that hard lines of distinction between the various *darśana*-s and also the so-called sects are not for every period so clear and plentiful as we wish they were. Consequently, the reliance on analogies with Christian denominationalism that has been manifest in the work of many scholars has often inhibited a proper understanding of the Indian phenomena.

[19] Both before and after Colebrooke, serious students and laymen found that the so-called Buddhist apathy was the most damning feature. Especially in the latter half of the nineteenth century, Europeans often seemed to be far more outraged by Buddhist quietism than by Buddhist nihilism.

Colebrooke did more than pamper his own predispositions. He spoke more prudently, more sensitively, more as a Buddhist than perhaps he himself realized.[20]

Brian Houghton Hodgson

As important as Colebrooke's study of Buddhism has been, the distinction of founding a "true" study of Buddhism belongs to his countryman Brian Houghton Hodgson. It was he who presented the first collections of Buddhist texts to the Western European scholarly community.

Born in Cheshire County on February 1, 1800, Hodgson entered the East India Company's Haileybury College in 1816 to prepare for a career in India. In December, 1817, he left Haileybury as first man in his term class, with prizes in Bengali and classics. At the College of Fort William the following year he continued his studies and began to read for honors in Sanskrit. Overpowered by the Calcutta climate, however, he fell desperately ill. His physician advised him to leave the India service and return to England. To stay in sultry Calcutta would mean death.

The only other alternative to returning to England and an overcrowded home was to obtain "a hill-appointment"—that is, an appointment in the drier, less demanding climate (for an Englishman) of the Himalayan foothills. Only two such

[20] See Shoson Miyamoto, *Studies on Nirvāṇa: I. Is Nirvāṇa Nichts or Peace?* reprinted from *Toyo Shiso Ronshu* (Tokyo, 1960), p. 8, footnote 7. In Miyamoto's "list of 7 groups, into which various modern scholars of Buddhism could be classified, according to the concepts of *Nirvāṇa* held by them," Colebrooke is the only one to appear under two rubrics: "*Nirvāṇa* is yogic, hypnotic ecstasy plus religious beatitude" and "the standpoint of practical ethics . . . *Nirvāṇa* as 'peace' as opposed to nihilism."

posts were open to a junior civil servant in the entire Bengal presidency: assistant commissionership in Kumaun (a region adjoining the western boundary of Nepal and about eleven thousand square miles in area) and the assistant residentship in Nepal. Still less than twenty years old, Hodgson was awarded the former post.

In Kumaun, Hodgson's health improved rapidly, and he quickly adapted himself to the new rigors of mountain life—even to the point of becoming a skilled climber. In 1820, after barely two years in Kumaun, he accepted the assistant residentship in Nepal. He returned to Calcutta late in 1822 as deputy secretary of the Persian department in the Foreign Office.

After barely five years in India, Hodgson's great chance in life came to him. The Deputy-Secretaryship was in itself one of the chief prizes of the junior service. It might lead to the very highest positions—to Governor-General's Agencies, to Council, or to the government of a province. . . . [But] the Calcutta autumn of 1823, like that of 1819, tried him severely, and by the end of the year the old alternative was once more forced upon him, an appointment in the hills or a grave on the plains.[21]

Early in 1824, Hodgson returned to Katmandu (Nepal) as postmaster.

For more than a year he recruited his health in that subordinate post. In 1825 the assistant-residentship again fell vacant, and Hodgson was reappointed to it. But the hope of a career in the great arenas of Indian diplomacy and administration, opened up by the deputy-secretaryship in the Foreign Office had closed to him forever. He knew that if he were to live in India his life must be spent in Nepal.[22]

Speculations as to what might have been the course of European Buddhist studies had young Hodgson not been "exiled" to Nepal have no place in this study. But the preceding sketch sheds some light on the circumstances which contrib-

[21] Sir William Wilson Hunter, *Life of Brian Houghton Hodgson*, p. 64.

[22] *Ibid.*, p. 65.

uted to Hodgson's becoming "the founder of the true study of Buddhism through texts and monuments."[23]

Hodgson had a passion for collecting. By rare good fortune he found himself set down in a part of Asia isolated from European scholarship and as a field for the collector absolutely untouched. Within a few months of his definite return to Nepal in 1824 a stream of manuscripts, specimens, and antiquarian curios of many sorts began to flow into the Asiatic Society in Calcutta from the young Assistant Resident at Kathmandu.[24]

Sir William Hunter, Hodgson's biographer, lists three contributions to Buddhist studies made by Hodgson: first, the collection of "a larger body of original documents on Buddhism than had up to that time been ever gathered together either in Asia or in Europe";[25] second, serious study of many of these manuscripts, which resulted in the writing and publication of several valuable essays; and third, the donation of numerous manuscripts to the scholarly organizations best qualified to examine them in detail.[26]

The second contribution most concerns us in the present context, although Hodgson's personal scholarship was the least important part of his legacy. Admittedly, his essays are no longer requisite to an adequate understanding of Buddhism. In fact, they are cumbersome, often misleading, and incomplete. Nevertheless, "the results arrived at by Hodgson from his personal study of the materials which he had collected . . . amounted to a new revelation to the Western world of scholarship."[27]

Before I examine Hodgson's Buddhist studies as they relate to our theme, it will be worthwhile to ascertain as far as possible the reasons behind his efforts. Hunter, whose major concern is to show Hodgson to best advantage as a brilliant and

[23] Eugène Burnouf (trans. and comm.) *Le Lotus de la bonne loi*, dedication.

[24] Hunter, pp. 261–62.

[25] *Ibid.*, p. 264, quoting Burnouf.

[26] *Ibid.*, p. 266, where a comprehensive list of Hodgson's donations will be found.

[27] *Ibid.*

tireless public servant, asserts that Hodgson collected texts and studied Buddhist thought and practice always with the aim of benefiting company and crown. "Hodgson," he insists, "commenced the collection of the materials for them [the essays] when Assistant Resident, as part of a systematic scheme for bringing Nepal within the knowledge of the British Government." [28]

Though insufficient as an explanation in itself, Hunter's point is well taken, for Hodgson seems to have embraced any task which he felt would improve his efficiency as an administrator. In this regard, he is of a kind with his precursor H. T. Colebrooke, who had learned Sanskrit originally for the immediate purpose of gaining access to the various compendia of Hindu laws.[29] In a letter to his youngest sister, October 22, 1833, Hodgson writes:

> The antiquities, too, of the land afford me much entertainment. I pore over the pictorial, sculptural, and architectural monuments of Buddhism by the light of the ancient books of the sect; and *the learned Thebans of your isle* [my italics] appear to gather up my gleanings with eagerness. But the past chiefly interests me as it can be made to illustrate the present—the origin, genius, character, and attainments of the people.[30]

That Hodgson incorporated his Buddhist studies into a comprehensive framework designed to aid the residency in Nepal does not detract from his achievement. It *is* illuminating, however, for it helps elucidate his "style," providing at least partial answers to such questions as: Why did he concentrate on

[28] *Ibid.*, p. 104.

[29] Taught Sanskrit in the traditional Indian mode—methods at that time still vital throughout India—Colebrooke acquired a mastery of the language that may well never again be attained by a non-Indian. "It must be added that he took on the whole more pride in his skill with a shot-gun than in his Sanskrit" (Philip Woodruff [Philip Mason], *The Men Who Ruled India*, Vol. I: *The Founders* [London: St Annes, 1953], p. 213). Of all the Sanskrit literature he encountered, Colebrooke was most interested in works on the "exact" sciences, mathematics and astrology-astronomy.

[30] Hunter, p. 78.

certain facets of Buddhism to the exclusion of others? And why did he present those data in the way he did?

Hunter's portrait almost completely ignores another contour which is interesting to anyone wishing to place Hodgson's contributions to Buddhist studies: Hodgson's personal ambitions and his sense of exile. The second appointment to Nepal was a severe defeat (though the Calcutta climate's victory is hardly exceptional). Many of his efforts thereafter seem to be traceable to a concern for reputation which mere performance of official duties would not earn. Much of Hodgson's enthusiasm for investigations in Nepal is explicable as a function of his quest for recognition—if not within the company, then in scholarly circles elsewhere. At some level, certainly, he was mindful of an obligation to those scholars; but one cannot ignore the fact that this was a man struggling to salvage a career.

While one ought to be careful not to attribute too much premeditation and calculation to Hodgson's efforts, an inquiry into the chronology of his presentations and donations is revealing. The first series of gifts, manuscripts, and so on was to Calcutta, where their impact on company overseers would be high. On his return to Nepal, Hodgson contrived his essays, and only following published criticisms did he send manuscript collections to Western Europe. It is with this in mind, I suggest, that the opening—and apparently praiseworthy—statement in his "Sketch of Buddhism" be read:

> Soon after my arrival in Nepal (1821), I began to devise means of procuring some accurate information relative to Buddhism; for, though the regular investigation of such a subject was foreign to my pursuits, my respect for science in general led me cheerfully to avail myself of the opportunity afforded, by my residence in a Bauddha country, for collecting and transmitting to Calcutta the materials for such investigation.[31]

[31] Brian Houghton Hodgson, "Sketch of Buddhism, Derived from the Bauddha Scriptures of Nepal," *Essays on the Languages, Literature, and Religion of Nepal and Tibet*, p. 35. All eleven of Hodgson's papers on Buddhism are available in this volume together with comprehensive notes concerning the previous publication of each. Hodgson

Hodgson desired to do no more than "sketch" Buddhism, to provide an outline of fundamental philosophic and religious beliefs. Because of his practical bent, his conception of the duties of a resident, and his concern to control authentic information about Buddhism, he aimed at a sort of handbook explanation of major Buddhist ideas. When Abel Remusat, the French sinologist, asked why Hodgson had not explained the significance of the *tathāgata* and the theory of divine incarnations in Buddhism, Hodgson was plainly annoyed. "I confess I am somewhat surprised," he observes in a rejoinder,

> . . . since whatever degree of useful information relative to Buddhism my essays in the Calcutta and London Transactions may furnish, they profess *not* to give *any*, (save *ex vi necessitatis*) concerning the "veritable nonsense" of the system. And in what light, I pray you, is sober sense to regard "une infinitie" of phantoms, challenging belief in their historical existence as the founders and propagators of a given code of laws? [32]

A few paragraphs further on, Hodgson re-outlines his reasons for writing about Buddhism. They may be read from several starting points.

> The purpose of my two essays on Buddhism [33] was to seize and render intelligible the *leading* and *least* absurd of the opinions and practices of these religionists, in order to facilitate to my countrymen the study of an entirely new and difficult subject in those original Sanskrit authorities which I had discovered and placed within their reach, but no living interpreters of which, I knew were accessible to them in Bengal or in Europe.
>
> I had no purpose, nor have I, to meddle with the interminable sheer absurdities of the Bauddha philosophy or religion; and, had I not been called upon for *proofs* of the numerous novel statements my two essays contained, I should not probably have recurred at

became the nineteenth century's most renowned authority on Himalayan flora and fauna. See Hunter, pp. 302–9, and bibliography, pp. 368–75. Plants and animals seem to have been far more interesting to Hodgson than were Buddhists!

[32] Hodgson, "European Speculations on Buddhism," *Essays*, p. 96.

[33] Namely his "Sketch" and his "Notices of the Languages, Literature, and Religion of Nepal and Tibet," *Essays*, pp. 1–35.

all to the topic. But sensible of the prevalent literary scepticism of our day and race, I have answered that call, and furnished to the Royal Asiatic Society, a copious selection from these original works which I had some years previously discovered the existence of in Nepal.[34]

It is not easy to discover how Hodgson interpreted nirvāṇa. Two factors account for the difficulty. First is the set of motives behind his study of Buddhism. He did not allow Buddhism to challenge him personally. What many recent twentieth-century writers are fond of calling a confrontation or an encounter did not occur to Hodgson as a possibility apropos of Buddhism. His motives dictated the questions which he asked and the degree of detail permitted to any answer. Nirvāṇa?—an "absurdity" which he almost neglects to mention by name.

Second must be mentioned the characteristics of Nepalese Buddhism. Tantric elements penetrate to the core of Buddhism in Nepal, transforming it into a quite distinct genre.[35] Now, much of Hodgson's material came to him in answer to questions which he posed formally to a Buddhist *paṇḍita.* Hodgson occasionally confesses that he finds many inconsistencies between these oral answers and those given in the texts. But he was neither equipped for critical text study (his knowledge of Sanskrit was minimal) nor inclined to delineate contradictions and obscurities. As one consequence, there is no dialectic in his writings—the view of Buddhism which he holds in the earliest essay remains unchanged throughout his career.

Hodgson discusses nirvāṇa in *one* paragraph. And he does not mention it by name.

In regard to the destiny of the soul, I can find no essential difference of opinion between the Bauddha and the Brahmanical sages. By all, metempsychosis and absorption are accepted. But absorbed into what? into Brahma, say the Brahmans, into

[34] Hodgson, "European Speculations," pp. 98–99.

[35] On this point, see David Snellgrove, *Buddhist Himalaya* (Oxford: Bruno Cassirer, 1957), especially pp. 91–120.

Sunyata, or Swabhava, or Prajna, or Adi Buddha, say the various sects of the Buddhists. And I should add that by their doubtful Sunyata, I do not, in general, understand, annihilation, nothingness, but rather that extreme and almost infinite attenuation which they ascribe to their material powers or forces in the state of Nirvṛtti, or of abstraction from all particular palpable forms, such as compose the sensible world of Pravṛtti.[36]

In order to understand that statement, it will be necessary to glance at Hodgson's exposition of Nepalese Buddhist sects. He identifies four of them: Svābhāvika, Aiśvarika, Yātnika, and Kārmika. Each subjoined a number of subsects which, according to Hodgson, consist in

divers reconciling theories of the later Bauddha teachers, who living in quieter times than those of the first Doctors, and instructed by the taunts of their adversaries, and by adversity, have attempted to explain away what was most objectionable as well as contradictory in the original system.[37]

It is interesting, I think, that Hodgson scarcely ever tries to discover the *Ur*-Buddhism underlying these divisions.

The Svābhāvika, according to Hodgson, was the oldest of the four sects. Its members denied any substantiality but matter. And matter, they are said to have insisted, exists in two modes: *pravṛtti* and *nirvṛtti*, "action and rest, concretion and abstraction." The original and proper state of matter is *nirvṛtti*, a condition of actionless potentiality from which the phenomena of *pravṛtti* proceed under the impetus of ignorance (*avidyā*). Inanimate objects exist only in *pravṛtti* and, at all events, only temporarily.

But animate forms, among which man is not distinguished sufficiently, are deemed capable of becoming by their own efforts associated to the eternal state of Nirvṛtti; their bliss in which consists of repose or release from an otherwise endlessly recurring migration through the visible forms of Pravṛtti.[38]

36 Hodgson, "Notices," p. 26.

37 *Ibid.*, p. 23.

38 *Ibid.*, p. 24. Compare Eugène Burnouf, *Introduction à l'histoire du buddhisme indien*, pp. 393–94, 460–61.

Of the two modes of matter or nature, then, *nirvṛtti* is the proper one. It seems that nirvāṇa describes in some way man's reattainment to this condition. One notices also, as does Hodgson, that, according to this exposition, nature, "the universal material principle . . . [is] very nearly akin to the *Pradhāna* of the Kapila Sāṃkhya." [39]

The soteriological aspect of the Svābhāvika scheme is transparent in Hodgson's essay. *Pravṛtti* is the mode of activity and tangible phenomena. It is also the mode of existence that is characterized by pain, suffering, and transmigration. According to Hodgson, the attainment (that is, the reattainment) of *nirvṛtti* depends on understanding what it is. This realization requires discipline—a discipline which will abstract the Buddhist from the state of actual forms to the state of potential or attenuated forms. Realization of the character of *nirvṛtti* is tantamount to release, and he who attains this knowledge is a Buddha even while "lingering in pravṛtti."

Hodgson observes that not all Svābhāvikas accept the idea that there will be an existence of any sort once the *pravṛtti* is transcended.

> Some of the Swabhavikas have expressed much doubt, while others of them have insisted that it is eternal repose, and not eternal annihilation (Sunyata); though adds this more dogmatical school, were it even Sunyata, it would still be good; man being otherwise doomed to an eternal migration through all the forms of nature; the more desirable of which are little to be wished; and the less so, at any price to be shunned.[40]

At this point, Hodgson finds the light growing dimmer.

> The Swabhavika doctrine of Sunyata is the darkest corner of their metaphysical labyrinth. It cannot mean strictly nothingness, since there are eighteen degrees of Sunyata, whereof the first is Akasa: and Akasa is so far from being deemed nothingness that it is again and again said to be the only real substance.[41]

[39] Hodgson, "Remarks on M. Remusat's Review of Buddhism," *Essays*, p. 104.

[40] Hodgson, "Notices," p. 24.

[41] Hodgson, "Sketch," p. 59. Compare Hodgson, "Quotations from Original Sanskrit Authorities in Proof and Illustration of the Preceding Article," *Essays*, p. 83, footnote.

His patience failing, Hodgson finally confesses that

> language sinks under the expression of the Bauddha abstractions; but by their Sunyata I understand sometimes the *place* and sometimes the *form*, in which the infinitely attenuated elements of all things exist in their state of separation from the palpable system of nature.[42]

According to Hodgson, the Prājñika school unifies and deifies the *nirvṛtti.* The Kārmika and Yātnika schools, he declares, "owe their origin to attempts to qualify the extravagant quietism of the primitive Swabhavikas, and even of the Aiswarikas. . . ." [43] All Buddhists, Hodgson claims, are "idealists," for they attribute merely provisional reality to the forms in *pravṛtti.*

The so-called idealism which Hodgson attributes to the Buddhists, however, is not basically philosophical.

> The ideal theory or denial of the reality of the versatile world, has, in some of its numerous phases, a philosophical foundation; but its prevalence and popularity among the Buddhists are ascribable principally to that enthusiastic contempt of action for which these quietists are so remarkable. Their passionate love of abstraction is another prop of this theory.[44]

Hodgson often notes an inconsistency in Buddhist thought, but he remains unperturbed. He is often amazed but never appalled. He does not consider nirvāṇa to be the most important idea in Buddhism. In fact, he does not analyze the word, leaving his readers to puzzle over the statement: "*Nirvṛtti* means abstraction, and *pravṛtti*, concretion—from *nirvāṇa* is formed *nirvṛtti*, but *pravṛtti* has no *pravāṇa*." [45]

The practical consequences of Buddhist thought most interest Hodgson. Later writers have often condemned the ideas and practical ramifications which Hodgson merely reported—albeit perhaps with tongue in cheek.

[42] Hodgson, "Sketch," p. 59, and compare p. 61.

[43] Hodgson, "Quotations," p. 89. See also Hodgson, "Notices," pp. 25–26.

[44] Hodgson, "Quotations," p. 89.

[45] Hodgson, "Sketch," p. 58, note 17.

Genuine Buddhism never seems to contemplate any measures of acceptance with the deity; but, overleaping the barrier between finite and infinite mind, urges its followers to aspire by their own efforts to that divine perfectability of which it teaches man is capable. . . .[46]

According to Hodgson,

The old Bauddha philosophers seem to have insisted that there is no sufficient evidence of immaterial entity. But, what is truly remarkable, *some* of them, at least, have united with that dogma a belief in *moral and intellectual* operations; nor is there one tenet so diagnostic of Buddhism as that which insists *that man is capable of extending his moral and intellectual faculties to infinity.* True it is, as Mr. Colebrooke has remarked, that the Hindu philosophy recognizes it, and that is all: whereas, the Bauddhas have pursued it into its most extravagant consequences, and made it the cornerstone of their faith and practice.[47]

Alexander Csoma of Körös

Not a drop of romance can be distilled from the biography of the lonely, bitter Brian Hodgson, "the hermit of the Himalayas." It is quite otherwise in the case of his contemporary in those foothills and mountains, Alexander Csoma of Körös [Kōrösi Csoma Sándor]. Csoma's Tibetan investigations and discoveries equal, where they do not surpass, Hodgson's. And he lived a life of adventure unparalleled in the modern history of Asian exploration.

Csoma was the personification, on the one hand, of the courage and personal sacrifice so characteristic of explorers and missionaries in the centuries before the beginnings of the scientific study of Buddhism; and, on the other hand, he rep-

[46] *Ibid.*, pp. 60–61, note 29.
[47] *Ibid.*, p. 58, note 18.

resents the spirit of scholarly inquiry to which these studies continue to aspire. Indeed, the insistence of Csoma's major biographer, Theodore Duka, that "his name will never be omitted from any work bearing upon Tibetan literature or Buddhistic learning,"[48] is redundant.

Csoma was born in Transylvania, April 4, 1784. He was descended from the Śzeklers—military nobles who had protected Hungary's easternmost frontiers against the Turks for centuries. From 1799 to 1807 Csoma studied at the College of Nagy Enyed. During those school days, he and two comrades solemnly vowed to conduct a scientific expedition in search of the origins of the Hungarian people. Csoma devoted his life to the vow. His comrades forgot.

After a few years as a tutor, Csoma left Hungary to study at Göttingen as the first recipient of a traveling fellowship for Nagy Enyed graduates which had been established by private contributions in England. (Evidently this is one of the principal sources of that sense of indebtedness which he so often displayed toward the British and which prompted him to write all his subsequent studies in English.) In Germany, he studied history and Arabic, laying additional foundations for the fulfillment of his vow. Returning to Hungary, he announced—on February 7, 1819—his intention to travel to the East.

On New Year's Day, 1820, Csoma set out on foot in quest of the original home of his countrymen. He intended to go directly to Constantinople, where, or so he believed, he would be able to consult Arabic manuscripts which would give him information about the inhabitants of Central Asia. But Constantinople was being ravaged by a plague, and Csoma traveled by ship to Alexandria instead.

For more than two years Csoma walked and wandered ever farther east. The major Muslim–Arabic libraries were closed to him as the menace of the plague overspread the entire

[48] Theodore Duka, *Life and Works of Alexander Csoma de Koros*, p. v.

Middle East. Each time he attempted to proceed north, something blocked his path. And the money with which he started the journey—only twenty pounds sterling!—had been exhausted quickly despite his amazing frugality. In mid-April, 1822, he reached Kashmir.

From Kashmir the Himalayas prevented egress north to Csoma's goal: Mongolia. Moving on to the capital of Ladakh, he discovered that he still could not go north and from Ladakh could travel no farther east. Disheartened, he doubled back. On July 16, 1822, he met the English explorer William Moorcroft.

> I acquainted him with all my circumstances and designs, and by his permission remained with him. I accompanied him on his return to Leh, where we arrived on the 26th of August. In September, after Mr. Trebeck's [Moorcroft's expedition partner] arrival from Piti, Mr. Moorcroft gave me to peruse the large volume of the Alphabetum Tibetanum, wherein I found much respecting Tibet and the Tibetan literature. . . .[49]

Moorcroft convinced Csoma that the reputed libraries in Lhasa contained the materials about Hungarian origins which Csoma so persistently sought. (We have no idea on what Moorcroft could have relied as an authority for this preposterous claim. The generous assumption would be that Lhasa was so famous as a center of learning and at the same time so difficult of access that it was commonly presumed to be a sort of academic El Dorado.) Csoma, accepting Moorcroft's tale, dedicated himself to learning Tibetan. Through the autumn and winter, 1822–23, he studied the grammar and dictionary of Giorgi and took instruction from a Tibetan *paṇḍita* (the language of instruction was Persian). However, the materials were inadequate. Financed by Moorcroft, he moved to a Buddhist monastery in Tibet (Yangla, Zanskar) for sixteen months.

Csoma returned from the monastery with a plan for financing his researches in Tibet and Mongolia. To the British authorities he proposed the following: he would prepare a

[49] *Ibid.*, p. 28.

Tibetan grammar, a large Tibetan–English dictionary, and a thorough study of Tibetan literature and history in return for an allowance of a mere fifty rupees a month!

> Both the Sanskrit and the Tibetan literature open a wide field before me, for future speculation on the history of mankind. I possess the same ardour as I felt at the beginning, when I planned and determined to come East. Should these first rough drafts of my labours, arguments, and sentiments have the Government's approbation, I shall be happy if I can serve them with my ulterior literary researches.[50]

As soon as that proposal was accepted, Csoma devoted every energy to fulfilling his new pledge. He twice returned to Tibet for extended stays in monasteries. In April, 1831, he arrived in Calcutta to assist the editing and publication of the materials which he had collected. Late in November, 1835, these tasks completed,[51] he traveled into East Bengal to learn Bengali and Sanskrit. Two years later, he returned to Calcutta to become librarian for the Asiatic Society.

The project which Csoma had set for himself so many years before was not forgotten despite the extended Tibetan and Indian hiatus. In February, 1842, he announced his intention to tour Central Asia, and in March he was again on the road to Lhasa. His hopes were high after so many delays and frustrations. "What would Hodgson, Turnour, and some of the philosophers of Europe not give to be in my place when I get to Lassa!" But in Darjeeling Csoma's hardy constitution which had sustained years of privations succumbed to the fever he had so long avoided. He died there at the age of fifty-eight on April 11, 1842.

Because Alexander Csoma's life was unusually exciting, I am tempted to detail it more completely. Rather than do that —an effort Csoma would certainly have disapproved of—I shall mention a few points which may assist the formulation of a just estimate of his contributions to Buddhist studies.

[50] *Ibid.*, p. 65, citation from Csoma's letter.
[51] In 1834. See bibliography of Csoma's works, *ibid.*, pp. 169–70.

"As regards intellectual powers, Csoma was not considered in any way a genius, but rather looked upon as an example of industry and perseverance." [52] That, according to Duka, was the learned opinion voiced by Csoma's teachers at Nagy Enyed. If there is more substance to it than is typically found in a biographer's pious hindsight, one wonders whether those same teachers ever realized the ludicrous extravagance of its understatement.

At about the same time that Csoma began his Asian pilgrimage, Franz Bopp was presenting his epoch-making comparative grammar which established the foundations for a true linguistic science. Csoma's own comparative language studies were grounded on verbal resemblances, a method which Bopp's achievement transcended and discredited.[53] But Csoma did not read Bopp and was never to know that he sought a linguistic and historical mirage.

Csoma, inadequately prepared to solve linguistic puzzles, was convinced that the first wave of Hun migrants from Central Asia had peopled Hungary. He expected to find the first home of those original Huns in Mongolia. Apropos of this, Sir William Hunter observed that Csoma needs no apologist for the nature of his historical fantasies or the inadequacies of his philological techniques. "It is Csoma's glory," Hunter wrote, "that starting from one set of old errors, he

[52] *Ibid.*, p. 6.

[53] Bopp's own method and conclusions were by no means unassailable. For biographical data and estimates of Franz Bopp's (1791–1867) contributions, see the following: Holger Pederson, *The Discovery of Language: Linguistic Science in the 19th Century*, trans. John Webster Spargo (reprint; Bloomington: Indiana University Press, 1962), pp. 254–58; John T. Waterman, *Perspectives in Linguistics: An Account of the Background of Modern Linguistics* (Chicago: University of Chicago Press, 1963), especially pp. 30–31; Russell Martineau, "Obituary of Franz Bopp," *Transactions of the Philological Society*, 12 (1867), 305–12; August Leskien, "Bopp," *Allgemeine deutsche Biographie*, III (1876), 140–49; and Pieter A. Verburg, "The Background to the Linguistic Conceptions of Franz Bopp," *Lingua*, II (1950), 438–68. The latter three articles are now reprinted in Sebeok, I, 200–250.

arrived at quite a different set of new truths; that in pursuing a dream he accomplished a reality."[54]

That statement cannot be gainsaid. However, one must acknowledge that Csoma's methodological poverty does dim his analytical and commentatorial achievements. His impeccable honesty and caution assure the permanent worth of his contributions as an explorer-scholar. "Csoma's principal trait of character was his regrettable diffidence," Duka writes, "—almost, we might say, an overstrained *vaunting* of ignorance—and his own too modest estimate of himself."[55] Csoma's only European visitor during his third stay in the Himalayas found the Hungarian's personality frustrating. "I am almost afraid to risk making known, from mere recollection, the attainments he has already arrived at, and the discoveries he has made," the guest wrote after returning from Csoma's mountain retreat,

> because he is so scrupulously tenacious of correctness in everything related to and said of him. . . . In his conversation and expressions he is frequently disconsolate, and betrays it in involuntary sentiment, as if he thought himself forlorn and neglected. . . . Yet he told me with melancholy emphasis, that on his delivering up the Grammar and Dictionary of the Tibetan language, and other illustrations of the literature of that country, he would be the happiest man on earth, and could die with pleasure on redeeming his pledge.[56]

As visionary as his own life quest was, Csoma was not blind to practical matters. He was deeply interested in the reception that Europe would give to the new materials on Buddhism. In his first letter to Brian Hodgson, December 30, 1829, he acknowledges Hodgson's perplexities about Buddhist philosophy and provides some clues for understanding his own attitude. He writes:

[54] Sir William Wilson Hunter, "Csoma de Koros: A Pilgrim Scholar," *The Life and Teachings of Buddha* (Calcutta: Susil Gupta, 1957), p. 6. Article first published in *The Pioneer*, Allahabad, 1885.

[55] Duka, p. 22.

[56] *Ibid.*, pp. 84–85, citing Gerard's letter of January 21, 1829.

Since the Buddhistic works consist not merely of wild metaphysical speculations, but contain several volumes of practical topics also, we should get acquainted with the whole and judge accordingly. When Europeans shall have been acquainted with the practical part of the Buddhistic doctrine, with the language of Tibet, and the several useful popular works it contains, then I think they will excuse them in some degree for the dogmatical part of their religion.[57]

Cold and unsympathetic toward Buddhism, Hodgson did not grasp its essence. Csoma came closer, for he was more taken with ethics and practice. He allowed himself to be affected by Buddhism, and he seems to have been more interested in the personal benefits which Europeans might derive from Buddhism than was his colleague. He wanted "to excite the curiosity of the learned to search after the ancient state of the Buddhists, and to respect a religion which is founded on the same moral principles with our own, namely, on the love of all men." [58]

Manifestly enchanted by the moral precepts of Buddhism, Csoma does not exhibit a similar interest in matters more philosophically technical; and it is difficult to gauge his comprehension. Nirvāṇa does not come in for a direct analysis in those among Csoma's writings which have been accessible to me for study. Apparently he translated nirvāṇa rather consistently as "deliverance from pain." [59] Eugène Burnouf declares in his *Introduction à l'histoire du buddhisme indien* that Csoma translated the Tibetan equivalent of nirvāṇa as "the being-delivered from suffering, death, emancipation." [60]

[57] *Ibid.*, p. 108. For further information on the life and work of Csoma, see E. Denison Ross, "Körösi Csoma Sandor," *Körösi Csoma Archivum* (Budapest: Körösi Csoma-Társaság, 1932), II, 333–45; and Louis J. Nagy, "Tibetan Books and Manuscripts of Alexander Csoma de Körös in the Library of the Hungarian Academy of Sciences," *Analecta Orientalia Memoriae: Alexandri Csoma de Körös Dicata* (Budapest: The Academy, 1942), pp. 29–56.

[58] Duka, p. 60, citation from the letter.

[59] See *The Life and Teachings of Buddha*, p. 60.

[60] Burnouf, *Introduction*, p. 17 and footnote where Csoma, *Tibetan-English Dictionary* (Calcutta: Asiatic Society of Bengal, 1834), pp. 134 and 194 are cited.

It is in Csoma's succinct account of Tibetan Buddhist schools, "Notices on the Different Systems of Buddhism," [61] that one finds the only other traces of his evaluation of the term.

Following an introductory discussion of the *trikāya* doctrine—in which he defines the *dharmakāya* as "the primary essence of all things . . . existing . . . without beginning, duration, and end" [62]—Csoma identifies four Tibetan Buddhist schools or sects. They are the "dogmatical" Vaibhāṣika and Sutrātika (Sautrāntika) and the "philosophical" Yogācāra and Mādhyamika "which are studied by the learned few."

Csoma next declares that Buddhists may also be classified under three headings according to their individual capacities. It is strongly indicative of his practical concern that he concentrates on the *triyāna* for the balance of the article.

> [§ 1] Men of a common capacity must believe that there is a God, that there is a future life, and that all will obtain, according to their deeds in this life, a reward hereafter.
>
> [§ 2] Men of a middle degree of intellectual or moral capacity, in addition to the above doctrines, must understand that every compound thing is perishable; that there is no reality in things; that every imperfection causes suffering, and that deliverance from suffering, and eventually from final existence, is *final beatitude*.
>
> [§ 3] Men of the highest capacities will know that between the body and the supreme soul nothing exists by itself, nor can we prove whether the supreme soul will continue forever, or absolutely cease; because everything exists by a causal concatenation.[63]

Those compendious statements are so tantalizing! Obviously subsection 2 cannot be read out of context or one would be forced to say that Csoma interpreted the "final beatitude" of the Buddhists as a "deliverance from final existence"—annihilation assuredly. Comparing the above with the views "Regarding Salvation" affords some clarification.

> Those of the first degree, seeing the miseries of those who, by virtue of the metempsychosis, suffer in the bad places of transmi-

[61] Duka, p. 195.

[62] *Ibid.*

[63] *Ibid.*, pp. 196–97.

gration as beasts, etc., desire to be born again among men, or among angels (asuras), or among gods.

Those of the second class are not content with the lot of the former, and wish to be entirely delivered from all bodily existence.

The highest class, regarding existence, under whatever form, as suffering, crave for final emancipation, and by arriving at the supreme perfection, are enabled to assist others out of their miseries.[64]

Lamentably, Csoma does not use the term nirvāṇa at all, for we have no record of his conclusions regarding the Sanskrit texts. And from his summaries it is difficult to know at what point he is dealing with the Tibetan equivalent: *mya-ṅan-las 'das-pa.* However, reconsidering subsection 2, above, in light of the second statement concerning salvation, it now appears that the "middlers" seek a terminus or annihilation only of bodily existence, according to Csoma's interpretation. A new problem develops: what distinguishes the third group from the second? Evidently it is either the intention to help others or the lesser degree of "substantial" existence sought by those men of highest capacities.

The latter possibility hinges on the interpretation given to Csoma's words "existence, under whatever form." Because he does not attempt as sophisticated an analysis as Hodgson's, Csoma is vague about the details of Buddhist ontology. It would be most reasonable to insist that, whatever Csoma means, he certainly does not mean utter annihilation. Rather, it would be the type of existence properly belonging to the *Buddhadharmakāya.* In that case, the compassionate attitude, such as that which particularly characterizes the Bodhisattva, is the differentiating feature of the third class.

Thus, the three scholars consulted in the course of this chapter rejected the notion that nirvāṇa is annihilation. It is true, of course, that these first Buddhist scholars could not be expected to have digested all the voluminous material they had discovered. It is equally true that they faced up to the term nirvāṇa and were not overwhelmed by it. Their "mild" inter-

[64] *Ibid.*, p. 197.

pretations, though perhaps partly a function of a lack of depth understanding of the intricate systems which they were the first to explore, display an intelligence and moderation of judgment which often eluded later investigators. Surely it would be utter nonsense to suggest that these men distorted their presentations because they found any notion of complete annihilation personally repellent.

[*CHAPTER* II]

Eugène Burnouf and His Disciples

The publication of Hodgson's first essays produced an extraordinary sensation in Europe. They came at a time when scholars had grown tired of polite speculations about Buddhism, and wanted to know what it really was.[1]

Such an enthusiastic estimate of the significance of Brian Hodgson's essays is understandable enough—coming, as it does, from his biographer's pen. But Sir William Hunter has overstated the case. It is true that some scholars were receptive to solid information about Buddhism or any other historical and cultural aspect of greater Asia. And it is undeniable that Hodgson's early writings roused measurable interest. One must add quickly, however, that the response to those essays was rather reserved on the whole. Certainly there was no overwhelming rush to join Hodgson in this field of inquiry.

In fact, the scope and intensity of the reaction help explain

[1] Hunter, *Life of Brian Houghton Hodgson*, p. 276.

Hodgson's declining interest in Buddhist studies. There had been a small, reasonably attentive audience for his essays in the late 1820's and early 1830's, but the manuscripts which he gave to the learned societies of Europe and India lay untouched. He had opened a door to that mysterious mansion which was Buddhism; yet hardly anyone seemed interested in crossing the threshold. Several years after he himself had ceased to contribute articles on Buddhism, Hodgson commented on the fate of the Buddhist materials which he had obtained:

> Nearly all were eventually procured, chiefly, and in the first place solely, for Calcutta. They were deposited first with the Librarian of the College of Fort William, then with the Asiatic Society, but were for years utterly neglected, and still are so I fancy; so also the copies sent to London and Oxford. Those sent to France met with a far different reception. . . .[2]

In France, it was Eugène Burnouf who realized the significance of Hodgson's donations. "Mr. Hodgson certainly did not send two collections of this extent to Paris so that they could sleep peacefully on the shelves of a library."[3] Uniquely qualified to disturb the slumber of these texts, Burnouf devoted most of the rest of his life to translating and elucidating them. When he died in 1852, fifteen years after the Bud-

[2] Hodgson, "Sketch," p. 35, footnote. As the first edition of this essay appeared in 1828—and doubtless was written a year or more earlier—this cannot be an original note. In the Serampore collection of his essays (1841—I am still looking for a copy) he would not have been able to refer his readers to Burnouf's *Introduction*, which latter was published in 1844. The following paragraph from the "Editorial Notice" to *Essays* is the only statement offering any clarification:

"Mr. Hodgson's 'improved and extended views [reference here to a quote from J. Summers in *Phoenix*, Vol. I (July, 1870)],' so far as Buddhism is concerned, were found embodied in numerous marginal notes in his own copy of 'Illustrations . . . (1841).' In the same way many manuscript additions were made by him in his own copy of the 'Selections.' All these corrections and additions have been introduced into the text of the present reprint, though they represent, as is only just to Mr. Hodgson to state, various phases of his views, ranging over a period of nearly thirty years." (P. v.)

[3] Burnouf, *Introduction*, p. 5. See following note.

dhist materials had arrived in France, his project was not yet complete. Nevertheless, his *Introduction à l'histoire du Buddhisme indien* [4] and his annotated translation of the Saddharmapuṇḍarīkam (*Le Lotus de la bonne loi*) [5] constitute the first substantial monuments of the critical study of Buddhism in Europe. Indeed, they remained touchstones for serious scholarship and controversy throughout the nineteenth century. Even today they retain considerable value both in content and in the conscientious method to which they testify.[6]

Eugène Burnouf

Eugène Burnouf was born April 8, 1801,[7] the only son of the famous French classicist Jean-Louis Burnouf.[8] A brilliant

[4] Burnouf's *Introduction* was originally published in Paris. I refer throughout to the 1876 reprint, which differs only in pagination and the inclusion of a preface by Jules Barthélemy Saint-Hilaire, "Notice sur les travaux de M. Eugène Burnouf." Indicative of Burnouf's uncompromising method is the transliteration scheme he adopted. Generally, the French have been curiously out of step in such "trivial" matters—an observation with which Islamicists in particular will concur. In his review of the *Introduction (Journal des Savants* [1845], 233–44, 257–69, 337–49), Biot makes a point of "correcting" Burnouf's spelling: "The author writes *Buddhism* with a simple *u*, having conventionally adopted the Italian pronunciation of this letter in the words he transcribes from Sanskrit into French. *In order not to embarrass the majority of our readers by disturbing their habits* [my italics], we resume our usual pronunciation in the following extracts. Thus we write *bouddhisme*, *Bouddha*, *Pourâna*. . . ." (p. 233, footnote.)

[5] *Le Lotus de la bonne loi*, trans. Eugène Burnouf, published posthumously. My references are to the 1925 reprint.

[6] Space limitations prohibit citing here a representative sample of the tributes that have been paid to Burnouf. See, for example, Sylvain Lévi's "Préface," *Le Lotus*, pp. i–iv; and Schwab, *La Renaissance orientale*, pp. 309–16 *et passim*. For a review of Burnouf's life and scholarship, consult also Ernst Windisch, *Geschichte der Sanskrit-*

student at the Lycée Louis-le-grand, he entered l'Ecole des Chartes in 1822. Unsure of what career to pursue after receiving the licence-es-lettres and licence en droit in 1824, he returned to the study of Sanskrit under the tutelage of his father and Léonard de Chézy.[9] His genius in language studies was announced only two years later when he published, in collaboration with Christian Lassen, the *Essai sur le pâli.*[10] Shortly thereafter, he was elected to membership in the Société asiatique. Professor in Comparative and General Grammar at l'Ecole Normale from November, 1829, to February, 1833, Burnouf then succeeded de Chézy in the Sanskrit chair at the Collège de France. In that same year he published his *Commentaire sur le Yaçna*, introducing and firmly grounding Avestan studies in Europe.[11]

Even this abbreviated biographical account will substantiate the claim that Burnouf was the only scholar in Europe competent to analyze the manuscript collections sent from Nepal. Before he was thirty-five, Burnouf had been instrumental in solving two major questions in the study of Indo-Iranian linguistics. And at the Collège de France he was to exert a greater influence on the course of Sanskrit and Bud-

---

Philologie und indische Altertumskunde, pp. 123–40. Here and elsewhere in the course of the present book, my indebtedness to that classic study in the history of indology will be obvious.

[7] Sources are divided concerning the exact date. I follow Barthélemy Saint-Hilaire, "Notice," *Introduction*, p. VIII; Jules Mohl, *Journal asiatique*, 4e série, XX (1852), 22; Naudet "Notice historique sur MM. Burnouf, père et fils," *Mémoires de l'Institut Impérial de France*, t. 50e (1861—read on August 18, 1854), p. 305; and *Dictionnaire de biographie française*, ed. M. Prevost et Roman d'Amat (Paris, 1956), VII, 703a. Windisch, *Geschichte* (p. 123) and the major French, German, Italian, Spanish, and American encyclopedias, however, insist that Burnouf was born on August 12, 1801; e.g., *Encyclopaedia Britannica* (U.S.: 1929–61), IV, 438b.

[8] On Jean Louis Burnouf's life, see Naudet, pp. 287–305, and Eugène Burnouf's letter to Julien Travers (November 18, 1844), *Choix de lettres d'Eugène Burnouf* (Paris, 1891), pp. 357–61.

[9] See Naudet, pp. 306–8.

[10] Eugène Burnouf et Christian Lassen, *Essai sur le pâli ou langue sacrée de la presque'île au delà du Gange* (Paris, 1826).

[11] Paris, 1833.

dhist studies in Europe than would any other man in the nineteenth century.

Obviously it will not be possible here to enumerate all the contributions which Burnouf made to Buddhist and classical Indic studies, far less to examine them in detail.[12] Before I turn to what he said about the Buddhist nirvāṇa, however, some comments are in order concerning his plan of study, the object of his inquiry, and the style of his presentation.

In the first place, notice must be taken of the plan and chronology of Burnouf's study of Buddhism. In 1837, he was Europe's acknowledged master of Sanskrit and Pali. Several decades were to pass before another scholar appeared with similar credentials. The point is that Burnouf had the refined skills necessary for the study of early Buddhism as documented in Northern as well as in Southern sources. And he knew very well that a history of Buddhist thought and institutions in India—not to mention a cogent presentation and analysis of Buddhist *naya* or *Dharma* ("doctrine")—could be written only after close, comparative study of both Sanskrit and Pali materials.

About 1840, Burnouf translated the Saddharmapuṇḍarīkam into French. He had chosen the text as the most representative of those manuscripts at his disposal in Paris. A number of notes would be essential, however, if the text were to be intelligible to the uninitiated reader. As Burnouf prepared those annotations for his translation, he became more convinced of the enormous scope and complexity of the interpretive problems.

Now, Burnouf harbored no wild hopes about the popular appeal of Buddhism in France—or anywhere else in Europe or the Americas for that matter. The wisest course, then, seemed to be to publish a general work on the history of Buddhism in India before attempting to present the translation of a single text. That decision seems to have been made in

[12] See the list of works in Barthélemy Saint-Hilaire, "Notice," *Introduction*, pp. XXIII–XXVII; and Naudet, pp. 329–37 (in part borrowed from Barthélemy Saint-Hilaire or vice versa).

1842 (about the time he had intended to submit the Saddharmapuṇḍarīkam to the printers). Notes and other materials were readily at hand, and the *Introduction* appeared two years later.[13] "This first volume," he explained in the *avertissement*,

> conducts the reader to the point at which Buddhism enters history. Hence, I have not taken pains to present the chronological framework for the facts describing the birth and development of this religion. According to the plan of my work, the exposition of this system has its place after the analysis of the sacred collection of the Sinhalese.[14]

Unhappily, Burnouf did not live to complete that analysis of the Pali texts. The insight explicit in his plan of study impressed surprisingly few of his successors, for many discussions about Buddhism over the past hundred years have been hampered because the participants often spoke as if either the so-called Northern (= Mahāyāna) or the Southern (= Hīnayāna or Theravāda or Pali) tradition alone existed. Had Burnouf lived another decade, doubtless we should have been spared much of the sterile nonsense characteristic of a disconcertingly large number of subsequent "studies."

That Burnouf did not accomplish his program should alert the wary student to an important consequence: what he published on the question of nirvāṇa must be regarded as a tentative estimation. How much more rapidly investigations on that subject could have advanced had such a scholar as Jules Barthélemy Saint-Hilaire—who knew a fair amount of Sanskrit—devoted his talent and energies to the continuation and completion of Burnouf's project! On the contrary, however, he became absorbed totally in the "implications" of a term which had not yet been fully examined in context. Burnouf inquired. Barthélemy Saint-Hilaire reacted.

The objectives of Burnouf's investigations were historical rather than philosophical. His primary interest in the com-

[13] See Burnouf's two letters to Theodore Benfey (April 9, 1841 and April 30, 1842), *Choix de lettres*, pp. 326–29, 346.

[14] Burnouf, *Introduction*, p. xxxvii.

parison of the Northern and Southern Buddhist manuscript traditions was, as he states, to help establish a secure chronology of Buddhism. In particular, he sought to discover the dates of the Buddha's birth and death. The Sanskrit texts provided little help. There was no such thing as a historical sense among the Indians, he admitted with a sigh.[15] A discrepancy of several hundred years divided the Sanskrit and Pali traditions on this matter. And, familiar with Turnour's work on the *Mahāvaṃsa* and *Dīpavaṃsa*—the two famous Sinhalese chronicles—Burnouf hoped that the Southern texts would provide whatever answers were to be had relative to Buddhist chronology.[16]

A third consideration important for those attempting to assess Burnouf's scholarly accomplishments is his constant, balanced, and dispassionate attitude. His writings are remarkably free from those personal asides and exclamation points which punctuate so many of the works on Buddhism since his day. Laudable though his calm presentation is, it *does* hinder efforts to discover his private attitude regarding Buddhist thought. In short, it is extremely difficult to get inside Burnouf; and, in a scholar of his stature, that inscrutability deprives the historian of a valuable perspective.[17]

[15] *Ibid.*

[16] An almost complete translation of the *Mahāvaṃsa* was found among Burnouf's papers after his death. See Barthélemy Saint-Hilaire, "Notice," *ibid.*, p. xxv.

[17] In a footnote concerning a particularly involved passage in the Laṅkāvatārasūtra, Burnouf allows himself the luxury of an exasperated comment: "Here is true philosophic nonsense: many words for few ideas." (*Introduction*, p. 461). It is a mild enough observation considering the passage in question. An indication of Burnouf's over-all attitude towards Indic studies will be found in his "Discours d'ouverture: De la langue et de la littérature sanscrite" (read at the Collège de France, February, 1833), *Révue des Deux Mondes*, t. 1er, 2e série (1833), pp. 264–78. The conclusion is of interest: "We should not close our eyes to the most brilliant light that may ever have come from the Orient, and we shall attempt to comprehend the grand spectacle offered to our gaze. It is India, with its philosophy and myths, its literature and laws, that we study in its language. It is more than India, gentlemen, it is a page from the origins of the world, of the primitive history of the human spirit, that we shall try to decipher

E. J. Thomas was not being entirely fair when he dismissed Burnouf's interpretation of the Buddhist nirvāṇa in two abrupt sentences: "Colebrooke's view was first discussed by Burnouf, but as he had to depend chiefly on Tibetan translations the question was not much advanced. He assumed that extinction meant extinction of the individual." [18] One remembers that Colebrooke, whose interpretation is much praised by Thomas, did not read *any* Buddhist materials. Not a little of Thomas' distaste for non-Pali Buddhism is apparent here. And Edward Conze's quip is apposite: "E. J. Thomas' *The History of Buddhist Thought* is good on Theravāda, but he obviously had never taken much interest in the Mahāyāna." [19]

Thomas' comment cannot, however, be written off summarily. One wonders what he meant about Burnouf's reliance on Tibetan texts. His statement suggests that Burnouf consulted hardly any original texts and, further, that the Tibetan translations upheld a view of nirvāṇa as personal extinction. In fact, the case is the very opposite. Burnouf first discusses nirvāṇa in the *Introduction* in order to illustrate the inadequacies of the Tibetan translations of Sanskrit texts. He wants to establish irrefutably that the Tibetan materials *are* translations, albeit amazingly faithful, from the Sanskrit and that India is the birthplace of Buddhism.[20] He chooses the word nirvāṇa to demonstrate the superiority and historical primacy of the Sanskrit texts because it is "the term that occurs most often in the texts, the most important term of all. . . ." [21]

---

together. And do not think that we promise this noble goal to our efforts in the vain hope of winning a popularity for our works that they cannot have. It is our profound conviction that the study of words without the study of ideas is—if possible—useless and frivolous; while the study of words considered as the visible signs of thought is solid and profound. There is no true philology without philosophy and history. The analysis of the operation of language is also a science of observation. And, if it is not the very science of the human spirit, it is at least the science of the most astounding faculty by means of which man's spirit manifests itself."

18 E. J. Thomas, *The History of Buddhist Thought*, p. 123.

19 Edward Conze, *Buddhist Thought in India*, p. 10.

20 See above, Chapter I, note 9.

21 Burnouf, *Introduction*, p. 16.

Broadly considered, Burnouf declares, nirvāṇa is deliverance or salvation. But deliverance of what kind and from what? Etymology answers that the salvation is at the same time annihilation. Again a question: annihilation of what? "Is it of the conditions relative to existence or of existence itself, of life?" Is it a condition into which a man enters when he has broken the fetters of the external world, a return to man's proper and absolute condition? Is it absorption into God? Into nature? Or, finally, is it nothingness?

One sees that the etymology of the word nirvāṇa answers none of these questions which are themselves nothing other than the expression of very diverse theological systems. It is from the Buddhists' employment of this term—from the definitions that they have given it—that one must seek the explication of these great problems.[22]

Those various theological systems, so called, may be considered as either theistic or atheistic, according to Burnouf. Common to both is the understanding of nirvāṇa as supreme deliverance. In each case, the deliverance entails a fundamental change in the status as individual, a change involving absorption of the individual principle: absorption in the Supreme Being according to the theists, into nothingness according to the atheists.

Let us call the notion of nirvāṇa as release or deliverance the soteriological explanation and the idea of absorption, however conceived, the metaphysical explanation. According to Burnouf, the soteriological explanation is the only clear meaning of nirvāṇa. It is so fundamental, in fact, that the Tibetans translate nirvāṇa only as "release." Burnouf, in turn, translates the Tibetan equivalent literally as "the state of him who is freed from suffering" or "the state in which one is to be found when one is thus released." Schroeder, Csoma, and Isaac Schmidt are cited in support of this translation.[23]

Now, according to Burnouf, the problem is that the Tibetan translation of the term nirvāṇa is not properly a translation at all but rather a commentary. The Sanskrit original seems

[22] *Ibid.*
[23] *Ibid.*, p. 17.

to be far richer in suggestion and implicit meaning than its Tibetan counterpart.

If the word *nirvāṇa* does not tell us what is destroyed in the state of Nirvāṇa, it at least lets us see that there is a destruction. The Tibetan, in saying that Nirvāṇa is the deliverance from suffering, tells us the effect of which Nirvāṇa is the cause, and leaves both this cause and the way in which it acts in the shadows.

Burnouf criticizes the Tibetan "interpretations" on two counts: they say too much and too little. He makes the former accusation because they read more into the word than it says—namely, the effect of nirvāṇa. And he makes the latter accusation also because they pass over the manner in which it is the cause of such an effect. In brief, according to Burnouf, the Tibetans ignore "the true state which this term expresses: annihilation." [24]

Clarification of the meaning of nirvāṇa—beyond its soteriological significance—cannot, then, be found in the Tibetan translations. Burnouf returns to the question of the meaning of nirvāṇa in an appendix to the *Introduction.* There he proposes to "determine according to examples taken from the texts, the significance of the word nirvāṇa. . . ." [25] He quotes Colebrooke's definition according to etymology and the Englishman's conclusion that nirvāṇa is not annihilation but rather unceasing apathy.[26] Burnouf comments:

I do not know on what authority Colebrooke relies to limit the sense of nirvāṇa according to the Buddhists in that way. Although I believe that this is the opinion of some schools, it has not been

[24] *Ibid.* Burnouf stresses that the Tibetan materials provide no assistance in the attempt to discover the original meaning of nirvāṇa. If one should try to reconstruct the Sanskrit original from the Tibetan translation, he goes on, the result would be the term *śokamuktatvam* or *śokamukti. Śoka* corresponds so perfectly to the Tibetan *m̃ya-ṅgan* that the latter term is used in the Tibetan translation of King Aśoka's name. Were we to rely only on the Tibetan translations, Burnouf concludes, we would be led to believe that Aśoka's name was based on the term nirvāṇa.

[25] *Ibid.*, p. 525.

[26] See above, p. 28.

proven to me that it is so for them all, and in particular of the more ancient. Moreover, this question (even supposing that a solution to it may be possible) could only be examined when we have compared the opinions of Northern Buddhists with those prevailing in the South.[27]

The proper understanding of the term nirvāṇa is "extinction" in Burnouf's view. He finds that meaning to be primary whenever the active form of the verbal compound, *nir* + *vā*, is used in non-philosophical discourse. In support of this, he adduces the first-person singular optative active of the causative—*nirvāpayeyam*—employed in the sense of extinguishing the light of a lamp. Extinction is basic to the philosophical meaning of nirvāṇa also, he adds, for "it is to a fire which is extinguished that one compares the nirvāṇa to which one says that a Buddha attains when he dies, thus freeing him from the ties of this world." From the Avadānaśatakam, Burnouf quotes the following passage and offers a translation:

Yāvad vipaśyī samyak saṃbuddhaḥ sakalabuddhakāryam
Kṛtvā indhanakṣayād ivāgnir nirupadhiśeṣe nirvāṇadhātau
parinirvṛtaḥ

Until finally Vipaśyin, the completely perfect Buddha, after having performed the totality of obligations of a Buddha, was, like a fire of which the fuel is consumed, entirely annihilated in the element of nirvāṇa in which nothing remains of that which constitutes existence.[28]

Burnouf is convinced that this passage reinforces all expressions relative to nirvāṇa in the Buddhist texts and that it clearly demonstrates that the dominant sense of nirvāṇa is the idea of extinction.

Burnouf's detailed analysis of that citation does not concern us here.[29] For the present it will be sufficient to observe that he recognizes a distinction between the terms *anupadhiśeṣanirvāṇa* and *sopadhiśeṣanirvāṇa*, and he attempts to fix their precise meaning through a comparison of the Sanskrit

[27] Burnouf, *Introduction*, p. 525.
[28] *Ibid.*, p. 526.
[29] See Chapter IV, below.

and Pali materials. In this matter, as in so many others, Burnouf's early death prevented the completion of the analysis he had planned.

During the remainder of this chapter the reader will be given the opportunity to judge the ways in which Burnouf's ideas about nirvāṇa were utilized—sometimes exploited—by the scholars who wrote about Buddhism in the 1850's and 1860's. It may be said that these writers were concerned mainly with the meaning of his interpretation. As undeniable as it may be that there was no qualified successor to Burnouf's incomplete enterprise, it can be maintained equally that the intimations that nirvāṇa meant "extinction," "utter annihilation," were alarming enough to demand comments. In this regard, Burnouf's own reputation may be accused of assisting the diversion of scholars from any further investigations according to the texts. Whatever he surmised was, in general, felt to be conclusive.

Burnouf says that the base meaning of the prefix-plus-root verbal compound from which nirvāṇa is generated is "extinguish," "extinguishing," "extinction," and so on when used in ordinary, non-philosophic discourse. He further insists that the sense of extinction is peculiarly proper to the philosophic usages. That evaluation obviously predisposes interpreters to infer that the Buddhist nirvāṇa is the absolute nothing. And Burnouf assures his readers that, in any event, nirvāṇa means a fundamental change in the condition of the individual. It is, he writes, a disappearance of individuality by way of absorption—absorption into the Supreme Being or into the void (*śūnyatā*). He would not commit himself beyond saying that nirvāṇa, in the latter instance, would to all appearances be utter annihilation. He wanted to consult more texts before deciding definitely.

Although there are hazards in attempting precisely to formulate opinions that are so difficult to grasp in texts still so incompletely studied as those of Nepal, I believe that on entering the religious life Śakyamuni took with him certain givens that the atheistic Samkhya doctrines furnished. Ontologically, these were the absence of God and the multiplicity and eternity of human souls.

In physics these were the existence of an eternal nature—endowed with qualities, transforming herself, and having the components of those forms which reembody the human soul in the course of its journey through the world. Śakyamuni took from these doctrines the idea that there is no God, as well as the theory of the multiplicity of human souls, that of transmigration, and that of nirvāṇa or deliverance which, in general, belongs to all the Brahmanic schools. But it is not easy to see today what he understood by nirvāṇa, because he did not define it anywhere. In any event, as he never spoke of God, nirvāṇa for him could not have been the absorption of the individual soul in the breast of the universal God as the Brahmanas believed. And, as he scarcely said any more about matter, his nirvāṇa is also not the dissolution of the human soul in the midst of the physical elements.[30]

To many readers, however, it seemed that the proof of Buddhist atheism was all that was lacking in order to prove that the Buddhist nirvāṇa meant annihilation—the absorption or dissipation of the individual into nothing. The impact of the suggestion that nirvāṇa is complete extinction was immediate and profound in Europe. For some time thereafter, the question on the Continent was not "What is nirvāṇa?" but rather "Can one accept the notion that nirvāṇa is in fact nothing?" The negative interpretation carried the day. Either one supported it and judged Buddhism in the light of it, or one refused—usually on a priori grounds—to believe that nirvāṇa could possibly mean annihilation. Philological and historico-critical arguments receded in either case as emotional and "common-sensical" arguments proliferated.

Albrecht Weber

The Buddhist scholarship of Albrecht Weber in Germany provides an impressive contrast to the caution and moderation

[30] Burnouf, *Introduction*, pp. 463–64.

e Burnouf. Speaking before the Academy of Science in 1856, Weber declared that the importance of ı rests principally on its instrumentation of social According to Weber, the Buddha raised himself absolutely against the Brahmanic order. He preached a purely human morality, recognized the rights of all men, and introduced a root-and-branch reform of Indian social institutions.[31]

Insisting that the Aryan invaders of India had been culturally superior to the indigenous populations, Weber declares that the Aryans brought with them a developed belief in the immortality of the soul and the idea of *karman* and *karmaphalam*. In this interpretation, the theory of *saṃsāra* is seen as a tool with which the priestly class stabilizes its authority and exploits the people. With regard to release (*mokṣa*):

> On the whole this [*i.e.*, the Brahmanic idea of *mokṣa*] is the same doctrine as the one Buddhism teaches, although in the latter it seems to be differently applied. That is, it is a matter of total extinction (nirvāṇam) in a primary substance rather than dissolution in a universal spirit. At bottom, however, that amounts to the same thing. In both, it is a question of disengaging the personal consciousness and striving after complete annihilation.[32]

According to Weber, then, it is a matter of strictest indifference as to which of the theories of release one subscribes. Both are annihilation. So

> the greatness of the founder of Buddhism does not consist, as was erroneously thought, in this doctrine which Brahmans had taught before him and which he only accepted—perhaps giving it a new speculative direction. It is entirely the way he taught . . . and to whom.[33]

Weber considers that the question of the precise signification of nirvāṇa is not important at all. But when he discusses

[31] Albrecht Weber, "Über den Buddhismus [Ein Vortrag, im Berliner Wissenschaftlichen Verein, Gerhalten am 1. Marz 1856]," *Indische Skizzen* (Berlin: Dummlers, 1857), pp. 43–44.

[32] *Ibid.*, p. 46.

[33] *Ibid.*, pp. 46–47.

this point, he denounces vigorously the idea and the concept—in German or Indian guise.

The speculative foundations from which his [the Buddha's] teaching proceeds, as the teaching itself, suffers decisively from a lack of rigor and clarity. And one must adjudge it all to be an aberration even though recently in our midst the ingenious but confused philosopher Arthur Schopenhauer has come forth as a new herald of the same thing. Following this thesis of the absolute suppression of the passions, one is led to a quietism hostile to every human activity, to an imbecilic torpor, to the most complete denial of human feelings and endeavors.[34]

The evils of this wild metaphysical doctrine were concealed, according to Weber, by the goodness of the Buddha's method and intentions.

We have before us an extremely peculiar spectacle: a doctrine that rests on the wretchedness and uselessness of earthly, individual life and whose announced goal is the most complete negation of it brings forth in its execution the opposite results! [35]

Weber insists that the democratic spirit of Buddhist universalism encouraged the Buddhists themselves to place a higher value on life and to seek some answer other than nihilism to the question of life's goal.

The frequent allusion to the hereafter is sufficient evidence that the people were little given to strict observance of the doctrine. Actually, it is a question of assuring them of a happy lot in future existences. Nirvāṇa, final deliverance, demands other conditions than the exercise of practical virtues.[36]

Weber's theory of Buddhism's historical development is clear: the Buddha had taught a purely rational doctrine, and his notion of salvation was practically identical with that propounded by the Brāhmaṇas. But he preached to all men and instilled notions of equality and liberty into all who followed him. As the Buddha realized that there was some

[34] *Ibid.*, p. 50.
[35] *Ibid.*, p. 51.
[36] *Ibid.*, p. 55.

dissonance between the way and the goal, he himself instituted a division into religious and lay followers. From the expanding lay segment have come the fantastic notions of paradises and the extravagant tales of the *Jātaka*-s—indeed, the entire Mahāyāna tradition.[37] Thus, the history of Buddhism shows a definite trend away from the original idea of nirvāṇa.

Today it is quite clear that the speculative side of Buddhist dogmatics has undergone many alterations, and that the original nihilistic doctrine of the Buddha himself has been entirely pushed aside to make room for various other principles—even purely monotheistic ones. And nirvāṇa, the final goal, this extinction in the all or—what probably amounts to the same thing—in the nothing is often comprehended merely as a state of beatitude that involves no injury to the personality of those (the Buddhas and Bodhisattvas) who attain it, and even supposes the persistence of consciousness and the most extensive freedom of the will.[38]

Weber represents an historicistic, consciously anti-metaphysical attitude which became increasingly powerful and finally dominant in many branches of Geisteswissenschaft in the nineteenth century. For investigators of this kind, the social—hence historical—aspects of such complex systems as Buddhism were considered much more significant than any specific doctrinal point. The quest for the authentic meaning of nirvāṇa is regarded as trivial.[39]

[37] The importance of the so-called lay traditions in the formulation and development of the Mahāyāna is a notion still prized by several scholars. "The advent of the Mahāyāna consecrated the lay aspirations." Etienne Lamotte, *L'Histoire du bouddhisme indien des origines à l'ère Śaka*, p. 89.

[38] Weber, p. 67.

[39] On this subject—one to which I shall advert more than once again —I have found stimulating and valuable the observations of E. E. Evans-Pritchard. See especially his lectures: "Social Anthropology: Past and Present" (*Marrett Lecture*, 1950); "Religion and the Anthropologists" (*Acquinas Lecture*, 1960); and "Anthropology and History" (*Simon Fund for the Social Sciences Lecture*, 1961)—all three of which are now found in *Essays in Social Anthropology* (Glencoe, Illinois: The Free Press, 1963), pp. 13–28, 29–45, and 46–65.

Jules Barthélemy Saint-Hilaire

Although he shares with Weber the view that nirvāṇa does mean personal annihilation, Jules Barthélemy Saint-Hilaire takes quite a different position vis-à-vis Buddhism. In his eyes, Buddhism is a monstrous enterprise in which every potential service to mankind is sterilized by a pervasive nihilism. According to him, the Buddhist idea of nirvāṇa invalidates the entire structure of Buddhism.

Barthélemy Saint-Hilaire, whom Max Müller honored as the first true historian of Buddhism,[40] was born August 19, 1805. Before he had reached the age of twenty, he had studied Sanskrit informally with his friend Eugène Burnouf.[41] But he did not follow Burnouf in dedicating his life to Indic studies. Rather, he became a journalist and entered wholeheartedly into political life—a bit too enthusiastically it would seem, for he was censored by the government because of his participation in the Journalists' Protest of 1830 and forced to withdraw from public life. At this time he began his *Lebenswerk:* the complete translation into French of the works of Aristotle. The first volume appeared in 1832, and he continued the project for sixty-three years, publishing the final volume in 1895.

In 1837, Barthélemy Saint-Hilaire accepted the chair of Greek and Latin philosophy at the Collège de France, a position which he occupied until political conditions forced his second retirement in 1852. In 1839, before a session of the Académie des sciences morales et politiques, he read a

[40] F. Max Müller, "Buddhism," *Selected Essays on Language, Mythology and Religion*, II, 187. And see Chapter III, below.

[41] Felix LaCôte, "L'Indianisme," *Société asiatique: Livre du centenaire*, p. 224.

Mémoire sur la philosophie sanscrite. Le Nyâya.[42] From that time until 1892, he published articles and reviews on various aspects of Indian religions and philosophies.[43] Most important, by virtue of its scope and influence, was his popular *Le Bouddha et sa religion*, published in 1860.[44]

In a biographical sketch of Barthélemy Saint-Hilaire, L. Feller offers a highly complimentary estimate of the scholarly virtues of this savant.

> Above all—and this is a rare occurrence—his life conformed to his philosophical convictions, and these were more Platonic than Aristotelian. He pushed scruple to the point of criticizing, sometimes harshly, Aristotle's errors. His philosophic ideal was the socratic-platonic doctrine which he defined as: true love of science, that is to say, of eternal things inaccessible to those vicissitudes which try that which is born and that which dies; love of the true sustained by the resolution never to harbor falsehood; temperance, which renders one foreign to greed; and a dread of all meanness.[45]

One must suppose that Buddhism would defy the resolve of a Socrates, for Barthélemy Saint-Hilaire begins *Le Bouddha* with the following statement:

> In publishing this work on Buddhism, I have but one purpose in view: that of bringing out in striking contrast the beneficial truths and the greatness of our spiritualistic beliefs. Nurtured in an admirable philosophy and religion, we do not seek to know

[42] Read at the sessions of September 21 and October 26, 1839. *Mémoires de l'Académie royale des sciences morales et politiques de l'Institut de France* (Paris: Firmin Didot Frères, 1841), III, 147–250.

[43] For a sample of his late critical work, see Barthélemy Saint-Hilaire, review of *A Life of Buddha by Asvaghosha*, trans. S. Beal, *Journal des Savants* (May and June, 1892), 261–73 and 363–75; and his review of *The Zend Avesta*, trans. J. Darmesteter, *ibid.* (August and September, 1892), 465–78 and 533–44.

[44] Barthélemy Saint-Hilaire, *Le Bouddha et sa religion.* Three later editions have also been consulted: the 2d ed. (1862), the 3d ed. (1866), and the English translation—*The Buddha and His Religion*, trans. (from the 3d ed.) L. Ensor (*Sir John Lubbock's Hundred Books*, Vol. XCIV; London, 1895).

[45] *Dictionnaire de biographie française* (Paris, 1951), V, 683a. A complete bibliography of biographical studies will be found at the end of that article.

their value, and we remain ignorant of the great debt we owe to them. . . . I believe that the study of Buddhism . . . will show how a religion which has at the present day more adherents than any other on the surface of the globe, has contributed so little to the happiness of mankind; and we shall find in the strange and deplorable doctrines which it professes, the explanation of its powerlessness for good.[46]

Buddhism is an execrable blot on human history—it would scarcely be possible to misunderstand Barthélemy Saint-Hilaire's sentiments. On occasion he seems ready to award his imprimatur to Buddhist morality. But, partaking in nineteenth-century Europe's dominant optimisms, its love of life, its confidence in the future, and its distinctive interpretations of the Platonic Good and the Aristotelian *eudaimonia*, he is always able to check the temptation to find any unqualified merit in Buddhism. The Buddhist nirvāṇa was his stumbling block.

Nirvāṇa horrified him. Immersed in traditional classical studies, Barthélemy Saint-Hilaire did not participate in the rising wave of anti-metaphysical thought which was engendered by a burgeoning positivism. For him, the *raison d'être* of Buddhism was not its program for the modification of social structures—for example, its reputed anti-caste attitude. It was rather the Buddhist metaphysic. And that metaphysic was plainly nihilistic.

From Burnouf's still-plastic conclusions concerning the meaning of nirvāṇa, Barthélemy Saint-Hilaire fashioned a rigid, dogmatic interpretation: nirvāṇa is annihilation. In a series of articles in the *Journal des Savants* in the 1850's he proclaimed this. And it is the standpoint of *Le Bouddha*—which is merely an aggregate of the previous articles shorn of footnotes—in the 1860's.[47] Aimed frankly at the lay reader,

[46] Barthélemy Saint-Hilaire, *Le Bouddha*, 3d ed., pp. xxix–xxx. Eng. trans., pp. 1–2.

[47] Barthélemy Saint-Hilaire, "De la morale et de la métaphysique du bouddhisme," *Journal des Savants* (May through October, 1854), 270–86, 353–70, 409–26, 484–509, 557–73, 641–59; and *ibid.* (January, February, and April, 1855), 43–59, 115–30, and 243–56. Collected and reprinted as *Du bouddhisme* (Paris: B. Duprat, 1855).

this latter work aroused interest and criticism from several quarters because of its steadfast insistence on the equation: nirvāṇa = néant. Jules Mohl, one of Eugène Burnouf's closest friends and co-workers, found this inflexible interpretation of nirvāṇa to be the weak point in Barthélemy Saint-Hilaire's articles.

In many respects he renders justice to the Buddha and his doctrines, which are examined with a great deal of magnanimity and an evident desire to be impartial. But I believe that the judgment at which he arrives is much too severe; for his entire argument rests on the definition of nirvāṇa, which he takes to be nothingness. He is not the first to adopt this definition, and this is not the place to discuss it in detail. But who could believe for an instant that the absolute nothing could be the goal of any religion, let alone of a religion like Buddhism which preaches above all the purification of the soul, battle against the passions, and the abandonment of the things of this world in order to rise to a higher degree of spiritual perfection? How can one believe that nirvāṇa could be anything other than the goal common to all mysticism: reunion of the soul with God. It is a union of which they all speak—whether Christians, Muslims, or Hindus—in terms drawn from the things of this world; because language furnishes no other expression, and reason can deal only with images and comparisons.[48]

And, six years later, Mohl was no less critical of *Le Bouddha.*

Because he takes nihilism—which we find widespread among the Buddhist sects—to be the Buddha's own doctrine, his judgment is very severe. It is true that this interpretation is that of almost all scholars who are working with these materials today; but this dogma seems so difficult to reconcile with the moral doctrine of the Buddha that one can always appeal to new investigations and to the publication of older and more authentic texts than those which are presently at our disposition. That some later sects have abused certain images and expressions which had served

[48] Jules Mohl, "Rapport sur les travaux du conseil de la Société asiatique, pendant l'année 1854–1855, fait à la séance annuelle de la Société, le 20 juin 1855," *Journal asiatique*, 5ᵉ série, VI (1855), 94–95.

the founder and have constructed on their interpretations systems which are contrary to the primitive doctrine is not such a rare phenomenon in the history of religions that one could not expect to find an example of it in this case. It is much more difficult to believe that a great man like the Buddha preached a metaphysics which would have contradicted his moral theory.[49]

In the second (1862) and third (1866) editions of *Le Bouddha*, Barthélemy Saint-Hilaire met the criticism of Mohl and others in an *avertissement*, the transcription of an address which he had delivered to the Académie des sciences morales et politiques in 1862.[50] The critiques by Obry and Foucaux (outlined below) are directed in the first place at this essay. In order to come to terms with the first of Europe's nirvāṇa disputes, Barthélemy Saint-Hilaire's arguments should be reviewed in detail.

First is the matter of Barthélemy Saint-Hilaire's point of departure. The etymology of the word nirvāṇa is borrowed from Burnouf and Colebrooke.[51] (Although his knowledge of Sanskrit was considerable,[52] Barthélemy Saint-Hilaire always turned to Burnouf as the authority in philological questions.) He agrees that the etymology of the word and the similes in the Buddhist texts—blown-out lamps and so forth—do not answer the question of what nirvāṇa actually is. "This analysis, exact as it is," he says, following Burnouf, "regards only the surface of things, and the expression of the Nirvāṇa thus

[49] Jules Mohl, "Rapport sur les travaux . . . 1860–1861 . . . 29 juin 1861," *ibid.*, 5ᵉ série, XVIII (1861), 119–20.

[50] Barthélemy Saint-Hilaire, "Le Nirvāṇa bouddhique," *Séances et travaux de l'Académie des sciences morales et politiques de l'Institut Impérial de France*, 2ᵉ trimestre, 21ᵉ année, 4ᵉ série, X (Paris: Auguste Durand, 1862), 321–41. Reprinted as the *avertissement* to *Le Bouddha*, 2d and 3d ed. Not included in the English translation.

[51] Barthélemy Saint-Hilaire, *Le Bouddha*, 3d ed., pp. 132–33. Eng. trans., p. 139. The English version is misleading: "to blow *out*" is an ambiguous equivalent for both the Sanskrit root *vā* and the French infinitive *souffler*.

[52] He translated the entire *Sāṃkhyakārikā* ("son travail capital," LaCôte, p. 232): "Premier Mémoire: Sur le Sankhya," *Mémoires de l'Académie des sciences morales et politiques de l'Institut de France*, VIII (1852), 107–560.

understood, if sufficient to represent the image of death, tells nothing of the succeeding state. . . ."[53]

Barthélemy Saint-Hilaire proceeds to cite "authorities" on Buddhism—scholars, missionaries, indeed, anyone who had ventured an opinion—to prove that nirvāṇa must mean absolute annihilation. Müller, Obry, and Foucaux—to mention only three dissenters—were to object to such an evaluation by means of an appeal to certain universals in human nature. Each insisted that any religion positing utter annihilation as its supreme goal would in that very act violate the most obvious givens concerning human nature and human aspirations.

In the face of those arguments based on the conception of a universal human nature, Barthélemy Saint-Hilaire counters that peoples influenced by Indian thought do not fit into such simple schemes. Buddhism, with its patent nihilism, is merely the natural outcome of the history of Indian philosophy. It is, according to him, the inevitable consequence of prolonged brooding on the leitmotiv of Indian speculation: transmigration.

> The prevailing sentiment among the entire population—not only Buddhist but Brahmanic—is an unappeasable horror for life with all its attendant ills. The idea of transmigration ceaselessly pursues them like a terrifying phantom. At any cost the hideous image must be driven off, and all of Brahmanism was applied to finding a means of deliverance. The search was conducted with as much fervor as the Buddha was to have for it later. The only difference is the choice of methods. The goal is absolutely the same.[54]

This understanding of the foundation of Indian thought is the basis and the justification for Barthélemy Saint-Hilaire's interpretation of nirvāṇa as annihilation. Whether he originally investigated the meaning of nirvāṇa from that vantage point would be difficult to determine. But whatever may be the chronology of his theory, it seems very clear that this is logically the center of his argument.

[53] *Le Bouddha*, 3d ed., pp. 132–33. Eng. trans., p. 139.

[54] *Ibid.*, 3d ed., pp. xxiii–xxiv. Compare *Journal des Savants*, January, 1855, pp. 45–46.

This makes compulsive metaphysicians of the Indians. They theorized because they were possessed by the demon called transmigration. Barthélemy Saint-Hilaire had often heard it mentioned that the Buddhist nirvāṇa must refer to the absolute termination of *saṃsāra* through absorption of the individual soul into some divine essence. His arguments against that point of view are several.

In the first place, the Buddha and all the Buddhist texts ignore the existence of a god or divine essence into which an individual soul could be absorbed. Second, those same authorities deny that there exists any soul which could be absorbed. Absorption is obviously out of the question. We notice that these are Burnouf's tentative conclusions expunged of their original moderation.

But Barthélemy Saint-Hilaire moves even further from Burnouf. He next takes careful pains to show that if nirvāṇa were really absorption, it would still be annihilation.

> I confess, moreover, that even in this mitigated form [that is, as absorption], which it does not have, nirvāṇa would seem to me to be so close to nothingness that I should easily confuse the one with the other. Absorption in God—especially the God of Brahmanism—is the annihilation of the personality, that is to say, true nothingness for the individual soul; and I cannot see what is to be gained from imposing this new form on the Buddhist nirvāṇa.[55]

It is important to realize that there are various levels to Barthélemy Saint-Hilaire's criticism and exposition of the Buddhist nirvāṇa. Most obvious is his unfaltering insistence that the Buddhist nirvāṇa is absolute annihilation. That this nihilism is horrible, naïve, and so on, he repeats *ad nauseam*. But he is cautious to point out that it is not at all incredible that millions of men should believe in such a notion.

To a man like Max Müller, as will be examined in some detail below, the very idea of nihilism is not only repugnant but an impossibility. To believe in the currency of so preposterous an idea would be to believe in the existence of a

[55] *Le Bouddha*, 3d ed., pp. v–vi. Compare Albrecht Weber's views above.

radically different variety of humans. With a better-developed sense of the potency of ideas in history, Barthélemy Saint-Hilaire suggests that thoroughgoing nihilism is not merely a possibility but an historical actuality in Buddhism—and this without assuming that Buddhists are not human.

At a deeper level, it would seem that Barthélemy Saint-Hilaire is declaring that Buddhist nihilism is the natural, the logical, the inevitable final step in the development of Indian philosophy and religion.

> Buddhism . . . is not at all the monstrous innovation that we should wish to be able to dismiss. No, it is not a doctrine which could have been formulated spontaneously. India came to it step by step. It is a superior, indeed the definitive, stage in a progressive series. Buddhism did not arise in a single day. Centuries of inquiry and controversy were required to give it birth—as hideous as it is. It issued forth from this as a legitimate and supreme consequence. The Buddha was merely the most logical and audacious of the Hindu philosophers.[56]

The abuse which Barthélemy Saint-Hilaire lavishes on Buddhism is directed, at bottom, to the quest for salvation in Hindu philosophy, a quest motivated by the idea of *saṃsāra.* Of course, Buddhism must differ from Hinduism—this is axiomatic for Barthélemy Saint-Hilaire. And the difference consists in the solution to the problem of *saṃsāra.* The Buddha denies a supreme being, denies the existence of a soul, and denies, as a consequence, that there can be any salvation from the round of rebirths except complete annihilation.

Barthélemy Saint-Hilaire calls many witnesses to support his contention. The argument from etymology is least important. And the testimony of such scholars and missionaries as Burnouf, Gogerly, Spence Hardy, Bigandet, and others is hardly more valuable. (Barthélemy Saint-Hilaire seems intentionally to exploit the susceptibility of a lay audience to a volume of expert opinion.) Even his own contribution to the study of nirvāṇa—namely, that an analysis of Buddhist

[56] *Ibid.*, p. viii.

meditation techniques (the stages of *dhyāna*) clearly shows that the Buddhists aspire to annihilation [57]—is minor in his argument. His most effective point is the historical evolution of Indian thought and the necessity of Buddhist nihilism.

In Barthélemy Saint-Hilaire's discussion of the Buddhist nirvāṇa, one sees a great deal more personal involvement displayed than in the commentaries written by earlier European students of Buddhism. In the following chapter, a similar type of concern will be seen in Max Müller's studies. It will not be short of the mark to declare that the particular emotional impact of annihilation on a scholar's mind becomes a major factor in the interpretation of nirvāṇa and other Buddhist institutions during the hundred years which separate Barthélemy Saint-Hilaire and Müller from us.

Raymond Schwab is consciously embarrassed about Barthélemy Saint-Hilaire. "I confess that I am unable to read the name of Barthélemy Saint-Hilaire with much more composure than, for other reasons, Hugo could. In my eyes, this devotee of Victor Cousin's has a great number of *prudhommeries* on his mind. . . ." [58] Felix LaCôte's evaluation is more informative and sympathetic:

> Seduced by the rationalism of the *sāṃkhya*, which reminded him of Descartes, he was not content to understand and explain it. He judged it, disengaging elements of absolute value from it. . . . And doubtless one can object to a certain narrowness in his dogmatism. Still, for the first time in France, an Indian philosophical system was assessed for its intrinsic merit, as one did those systems of Plato and Aristotle. . . . Carrying the same attitude to Buddhism . . . he only reached a conclusion that was too simplistic. Religious phenomena do not allow themselves to be

[57] *Ibid.*, pp. 134–39. Eng. trans. pp. 140–44. Barthélemy Saint-Hilaire believed that a sort of temporary nirvāṇa was considered by the Buddhists to be attainable in this life during the fourth state of controlled meditation (*dhyāna*), that state constituting, according to him, a transitory annihilation of consciousness. Emphasis on the ecstatic features in Buddhist thought and practice is to be found in the work of Emile Senart and Louis de La Vallée Poussin. See below, Chapter VIII.

[58] Schwab, p. 130, footnote.

explained in a purely rationalist manner: logical probability and psychological truth are of a different order.[59]

To be righteously indignant *or* condescending in response to Barthélemy Saint-Hilaire's comments on Buddhism would be to miss the point entirely. That different stylistic and rhetorical conventions control the formal presentation of scholarly studies fifty or a hundred years later should not suggest to the sensitive reader that there are corresponding differences of sophistication with regard to insight into the subject matter.[60]

All Barthélemy Saint-Hilaire's judgments of Buddhism were buttressed by his deep and informed commitment to the philosophical, emotional, and religious foundations of his Western European society. Classical Greek and Christian traditions, he believed, had sanctified and fructified human life. From his point of view, all Indian thought denied the values fostered and supported by Christianity and the philosophies of ancient Greece. He wrote on Buddhism at length because there were points at issue—in a lively, non-academic sense.[61]

Barthélemy Saint-Hilaire was not reacting merely to the challenges posed by a newly discovered, alien life view. At

[59] LaCôte, pp. 232–33. Compare de Lubac, *La Recontre du bouddhisme*, p. 148, footnote.

[60] Barthélemy Saint-Hilaire was a gifted polemicist, and it would be grossly unfair to discount him as a sensationalist and vulgarizer—as one might be tempted to do in light of his activist, journalistic background.

[61] As M. G. S. Hodgson (University of Chicago) commented, in private discussion with the author, it is fascinating how soon after its first scholarly presentation in the nineteenth century Buddhism aroused the first personal response in Western Europe—a response not to an absurd idolatry but in the sense of an insightful confrontation. In Barthélemy Saint-Hilaire's case, the response was violently negative, obviously in direct defense of the Hellenic-Christian tradition's superiority over all challengers. One finds the issues discussed rather sophisticatedly in terms of the various sources of intercultural misunderstanding and of the inherent likenesses of human nature by the defenders of Buddhism. A significant dimension of the dispute about the meaning of nirvāṇa is that it is part of a much larger debate between Western European communalists and universalists.

the same time—and, one must presume, independently—he was well aware that nihilism, atheism, and the denial of the traditionally accepted "goods" were announcing themselves through various revolutionary spokesmen in his own society. Not the "vain opinions" of Buddhists alone are assaulted in his writings.

Immediately after Barthélemy Saint-Hilaire read his lecture on the Buddhist nirvāṇa (1862), two members of the audience, Ad. Franck and Ad. Garnier, protested against his conclusions. The Buddha announced himself as the incarnation of wisdom, Franck declared baldly; and it follows therefrom that he could not have preached a nihilistic doctrine.

A great deal has been spoken and written recently about the diversity of races. Whatever this difference may be, it would not destroy the general similitude of our faculties and the unity of the human species. The human genre constitutes one and the same family, in which all members are endowed with the same reason, illumined by the same consciousness, and have the same notions of the just and the unjust, of being and nothingness. I cannot admit that three hundred million people live in the hope of their future annihilation and know no other religion than this. No nation, no human race could be reduced to this horrible condition. Otherwise there would have to be, not varieties of the human species, but several humanities with differing faculties, intelligences, and natures.[62]

Franck then argues that history documents the usage of the idea of non-being in various religious and philosophical systems. And, he asserts, unless we are to describe the neoplatonists, the cabbalists, and all Hegelians as nihilists, we must admit that the idea of non-being may be used in a sense sharply distinguishable from annihilation.

In summary, and again confessing my ignorance of Sanskrit, I believe that our learned colleague has forced the sense of the texts he has translated. I believe that historical analogies, the similarity of expressions employed by most of the pantheistic or mystical systems do not allow us to understand nirvāṇa as the

[62] Ad. Franck, *Séances et travaux de l'Académie des sciences morales et politiques de l'Institut Impérial de France*, X (1862), 344.

absolute nothing and to consider Buddhism to be an atheistic religion.[63]

Barthélemy Saint-Hilaire admits that many mysticisms define God, or the universal principle, or what have you in negative terms because of confusion and also perhaps because of the fact that no verbal form can embrace the totality of an infinite existence.

> These are merely subtleties of language and verbal ambiguities which do not modify their profound and enthusiastic belief in a supreme power which they adore and with which they wish to unite in the delusions of ecstasy or which they wish to circumscribe in the formulas of their contradictory logic.[64]

Buddhism, Barthélemy Saint-Hilaire reaffirms, is absolutely atheistic. It does not acknowledge the existence of a god in any form, and believes in man as the highest form of life. Consequently, there is no such thing as Buddhist mysticism.[65] Adolphe Garnier, the president of the academy, sides with Franck: "Human nature instinctively loathes nothingness. There is no rationality in the love of life. One does not love it for this reason or that. One loves it without knowing why and despite the torments with which it may be filled." [66]

Suppose, Garnier continues, that the Buddha did preach a doctrine of annihilation. In that case, it must be mentioned that the practical faith of a sect often differs from the speculations of its priests.

> It is objected that our observations, drawn from general laws of the human spirit, cannot prevail against the facts which we encounter. To the witnesses that are adduced for us we oppose others. For example, we are directed to the works of Foucaux. Very well, I hold of Foucaux himself that he does not understand the doctrine of nirvāṇa in the same way as Barthélemy Saint-Hilaire does. It is often said that one hundred or two hundred million people profess such and such a faith. Have they all been interviewed? Conclusions for all of them are drawn from two or

[63] *Ibid.*, p. 345.
[64] *Ibid.*, p. 349.
[65] *Ibid.*
[66] *Ibid.*, p. 346.

three. Théodore Pavie, Michael Nicholas (very well versed in Sanskrit), and Sir John Bowring, the former governor of Hong Kong—whom I myself have questioned—do not attribute to the Buddhist populations that belief which our learned colleague imputes to them.[67]

For a variety of reasons—some obvious, others opaque—neither argument had the slightest effect on Barthélemy Saint-Hilaire. He published his address unchanged in the second edition of *Le Bouddha*. In the two years which followed, the nirvāṇa-néant equation faced another pair of challengers: Jean Baptiste François Obry and Philippe Edouard Foucaux.

Jean Baptiste François Obry

J. B. F. Obry (1793–1871) begins his *Du Nirvâna bouddhique en réponse à M. Barthélemy Saint-Hilaire* with the following question:

> Is Buddhism going to lose its high position in the esteem of the learned world because its founder employed an obscure term—more frequently than the other school or sect leaders who were his contemporaries and rivals *and without explaining it categorically*—that of nirvāṇa (extinction), to express a state of the soul still more obscure concerning its destiny after a death not followed by transmigration or because six or seven centuries after the Buddha a school of nihilists dared to mix the most audacious and absurd skepticism with his teaching under the pretext of completing it? [68]

He goes on to say that he had posed the same question in 1856 in response to Barthélemy Saint-Hilaire's articles on

[67] *Ibid.*, p. 347.

[68] J. B. F. Obry, *Du Nirvâna bouddhique en réponse à M. Barthélemy Saint-Hilaire*, p. 6. This work was read (presumably not in its entirety) before the Academy of Amiens, March 14 and 28, 1863.

the Buddhist nirvāṇa. In Obry's mind, there had been no real progress in the discussion during the seven intervening years. Barthélemy Saint-Hilaire would not yield—would not even acknowledge criticism—and Obry doggedly refused to cease questioning.[69]

Three points of special interest should be underscored in Obry's initial question. In the first place, Obry fixes intently on the fact that there is no categorical definition of nirvāṇa in the Buddhist texts. That he did not know this fact from firsthand study is beside the point. It is rather that the absence of precise definitions, so called, in the texts has been and continues to be a justification for much of the writing and discussion about nirvāṇa. As noted in my Preface, it is most important to observe how various scholars make use of textual ambiguities—real and imagined—and what significance they attach to them.[70]

Second, notice that Obry has already formulated a thesis in his question—namely, that Buddhist nihilism is entirely the product of later speculation and, consequently, that there is a severe doctrinal discontinuity in Buddhism. The thesis proved popular for some time, especially among those who declared that they wished to take all the data into account: They could grant the nihilism of the *prajñāpāramitā* and *abhidharma* texts and still salvage the Buddha's reputation.

The third and most obvious point follows from the preceding. It concerns the attitude Obry and others display apropos of the alleged nihilism of later Buddhism: "the most audacious and the most absurd skepticism," Obry writes representatively. Again, and to the point of being redundant, the similarity of response to the very idea of nihilism needs

[69] See J. B. F. Obry, *Du Nirvâna indien, ou de l'affranchissement de l'âme après la mort, selon les Brahmanes et les Bouddhistes* (*Mémoires de l'Académie des sciences, agriculture, commerce, belles-lettres et arts du département de la Somme;* Amiens, 1856).

[70] Obry agrees with the accepted etymology of nirvāṇa and also with the judgments of Burnouf, Barthélemy Saint-Hilaire, *et al.* that this etymological explanation cannot illumine the subject per se. See Obry, *Du Nirvâna bouddhique*, p. 61.

stressing. Burnouf's *Introduction* inaugurated an era at least as devoted to reaction and explanation as to scientific investigation of texts and practices. (With this in mind, it will be less easy to discount Edward Conze's statement as recently as 1962 that "numerically speaking, perhaps 5 per cent of the Mahāyāna Sūtras have so far been reliably edited, and perhaps 2 per cent intelligibly translated." [71])

The tenor of Obry's *Du Nirvâna* is succinctly summarized and highlighted in the following:

> Today, as in 1856, I am convinced that it is morally impossible that in Magadha in the sixth century before our era the son of Māyadevī preached the absolute annihilation of virtuous souls until six hundred years later in Galilee the son of Mary could come to preach the Gospel of their eternal beatitude.[72]

In 1855, Barthélemy Saint-Hilaire himself had acknowledged the Buddha's compassion and human virtue, Obry insists.

> Well then, if the Buddha truly was a sage, an ardent lover of mankind, a revealer of good law, a committed apostle—and nothing indicates the contrary—does it not injure his memory to attribute to him almost the following: "My dear disciples, fate condemns you all to revolve eternally in the moving circle of transmigrations which you fear. Well, have faith in my word. I shall deliver all of you from it, but it will mean your annihilation. And what is more, you will only obtain this exemption from rebirths on this condition: that you practice religiously all your life the virtues, the penances, the mortifications, and the austerities that I ceaselessly commend to you in my discourses and that I myself practice in preaching to you from example." [73]

The most indulgent reader's patience may fail him in the course of this passage, but it must be completed in order to illustrate the dimensions of the emotional basis on which Obry grounded his attack. It is of considerable interest to ponder the reasons which led a man nearly seventy years old to contest the statements of one of France's most respected

[71] Conze, p. 200.
[72] Obry, *Du Nirvâna bouddhique*, p. 14.
[73] *Ibid.*, pp. 15–16.

and prolific scholars. I need not emphasize the passion exhibited in the remainder of the statement.

> Is it not to malign the good sense of the Buddhist peoples—who, if they are not exactly like us, are, after all, our own brothers, . . . is it not to do injury to all humanity to pose this strange proposition as an article of Buddhist faith: For twenty-five centuries the faithful and fervent ascetics are forced to practice the rigorous discipline of their master in order to be rewarded with nothingness! [74]

Obry fortifies his insistence on the vital nature of discussions about the true meaning of nirvāṇa by adducing three principal reasons for the study of Buddhism. First, Buddhism is a living religion—a declaration presumably carrying its own set of justifications. Second, as imperfect as they are, major Buddhist conceptions approximate Christian conceptions at many points, and thus, naturally enough, arouse curiosity.[75] Finally,

> the problem disputed among the Brahmins and the Buddhists is universal: human destiny. And it is not without interest to know what the founder of the most widespread religion on our little terrestrial globe thought about this.[76]

To Barthélemy Saint-Hilaire's argument that Buddhism would lose its *raison d'être* if its goal were construed to be the same as that of the Brāhmaṇa-s, Obry counters that the Buddha's new idea concerned who might attain that goal. Brahmanism reserved the attainment of complete salvation to a certain class. And only ascetics within that class could realize the state of non-returning to the cycle of existences. On the other hand, the Buddha, in Obry's interpretation, was far more liberal and humanitarian. And, not content to leave

[74] *Ibid.*

[75] Barthélemy Saint-Hilaire, on the other hand, deplored the idea of finding similarities between Buddhism and Christianity. Those we find fade into insignificance, he said, when we learn more about Buddhism and discover that, at bottom, it is wholly different from Christianity.

[76] Obry, *Du Nirvâna bouddhique*, p. 20.

this point without further comment, Obry declares that the Buddha was proclaiming a "law of grace for all." [77]

Obry next criticized Barthélemy Saint-Hilaire's statement that the Indians hated life with as intense a passion as we—we Europeans—love it. Citations from (translations of) the Vedas, Manu, the Rāmāyaṇa, Mahābhārata, and the memoires of Hiouen-tsang are used to illustrate the intense love of life displayed by Indians through the epochs. Obry also observes that the Buddhist *sūtra*-s often insist on the difficulties which face anyone who tries to abandon the world and its attractions.[78]

And Obry scoffs at Barthélemy Saint-Hilaire's picture of the spectral transmigration doctrine haunting the Indian people. It is the contrary, he insists: transmigration arouses fear in the evil and the impious, but it is rather a consolation to the virtuous.[79] After all, do not the Buddhist scriptures tell of rewards for those who do good? In a not too oblique fashion, Obry is trying to tell his readers that the Buddha, like Saint Paul, was all things to all men. That Obry knew anything more substantial about the Buddhist notion of means (*upāya*) is doubtful.

Liberation, Obry admits, was the goal of many Indian ascetics, but they were far from constituting a majority of the population.[80] Again, it is the Buddha's social gospel, a sort of Indian "liberté, égalité, fraternité," which Obry singles out as the most significant achievement.

Most important of all the charges which Barthélemy Saint-Hilaire brings against Buddhism, according to Obry, are atheism and materialism. Obry's objection to the accusation of Buddhist atheism is complicated and, in the main, untenable.[81] The gist of it is that during the time of the Buddha the notion of an impersonal Brahman was still an esoteric doctrine in India. Obry maintains that absorption into such

[77] *Ibid.*, p. 24.
[78] *Ibid.*, pp. 25–26.
[79] *Ibid.*, pp. 26–27.
[80] *Ibid.*, pp. 28–30.
[81] *Ibid.*, pp. 32–37.

an androgynous world soul was opposed by the Buddha on the same grounds that Barthélemy Saint-Hilaire opposed it: it meant the annihilation of the individual personality.

What Obry stresses with creditable acumen is that both the Buddha and Kapila (see below) had not specified the state in which released souls would exist. Referring to theistic *Sāṃkhyayoga* and aiśvarika (that is, theistic) Buddhism, he asks:

> Will it be said that these two schools revive the principles of their glorious founders Kapila and Śākyamuni? On the contrary, is one not to infer that the schools have only interpreted in a more determinate fashion the solitude (*kaivalyam*) and the void (*śūnyatā*) in which the two leaders respectively placed the released souls? [82]

Continuing to argue from secondary sources, Obry denies that the Buddha himself was not in fact divinized. The texts, he affirms without citing any texts, even the Pali texts, mention epithets which indicate that Śākyamuni had been considered a divinity.[83]

The most serious imputation of all, according to Obry, is Barthélemy Saint-Hilaire's charge that the Buddhists are materialists. Atheism of itself would not imply the annihilation of the soul, but it is quite otherwise with materialism. Here, as in his previous consideration of atheism, Obry relies on a chronology of Indian philosophical systems which was not generally accepted even in his own time. He declares that the founder of the Sāṃkhya, Kapila, was the precursor of Buddha Śākyamuni and, further, that the Jainas were the heirs of the Buddhists.

In his address to the Academy in 1862, Barthélemy Saint-Hilaire also insisted, following Burnouf, that the Sāṃkhyans were earlier than the Bauddhas.[84] In that scheme, he could accord the Sāṃkhyans a legitimate place in the history of Indian speculation. The Sāṃkhya was considered to occupy a stage intermediate between orthodox Brahmanism and Bud-

[82] *Ibid.*, p. 37.
[83] *Ibid.*, pp. 38–40, 211–12.
[84] Barthélemy Saint-Hilaire, "Le Nirvāṇa bouddhique," pp. 325–26.

dhism. The Sāṃkhyans deny the existence of a supreme being —a break with Brahmanic orthodoxy, on the one hand, but an inevitable consequence of meditation on *saṃsāra*, on the other. The Buddha, more courageous than Kapila, denied not only the existence of God but of the soul as well.

Sometime between 1862 and 1866, however, Barthélemy Saint-Hilaire had some second thoughts about this chronology, for in the *avertissement* of 1866 he states that the Buddhists preceded the Sāṃkhyans. His explanation of the development of Indian thought is scarcely disturbed, nonetheless. The Sāṃkhyans, no longer considered a link in the chain of thought which culminated in Buddhist nihilism, become backsliders according to the modified view. They are depicted as rather weak individuals lacking the Buddha's resolution and intent on preserving some status in Brahmanic society. They deny the existence of a supreme being, but they readmit the belief in an eternal soul.[85]

Obry insists on the historical primacy of the Sāṃkhya, and for a very good reason. The Sāṃkhyans believed in the existence of imperishable souls. The Buddha, as a disciple of Kapila,[86] believed likewise. Fortunately, Obry manages to divert attention and step out of this historical quicksand. He demands that Barthélemy Saint-Hilaire be consistent on an issue which makes difficult the clear understanding of Buddhist speculations even today and has probably exercised more scholars—professional and amateur—than any other. If the soul transmigrates to another body, how can it be, as Barthélemy Saint-Hilaire has it, that the soul is not distinct from the body in any way? The soul either transmigrates or does not, Obry maintains confidently. If the soul comes into existence with the body and dies with it, there is no transmigration.[87]

Now, the crux of Obry's argument is that the Buddhists

[85] Barthélemy Saint-Hilaire, *Le Bouddha*, 3d ed., pp. vii–viii.

[86] Some of this confusion stems from a fanciful, though popular, analysis and commentary on the name *Kapilavastu:* "the dwelling place of Kapila."

[87] Obry, *Du Nirvâna bouddique*, pp. 45–47.

are disciples of the Sāṃkhyans. In fact, to be more blunt and hardly less exact, it is obvious that Obry believes that the Buddha and all Buddhists are Sāṃkhyans.[88] And on this estimation, the Mādhyamikas, for example, are not Buddhists at all. They are modernists propounding nihilistic doctrines which are against the basic tenets of bona fide Buddhist thought.

Obry's *Du nirvâna* suffers greatly on account of its extreme length, prolixity, and not infrequent logical lapses. I should say that these are the principal reasons that it is a forgotten text. But it is not fair to accuse Obry of verbosity and let the work go at that. Certainly Foucaux believed that the volume wanted academic rigor, and his own response to Barthélemy Saint-Hilaire is only thirty pages long. Obry's contribution is more on the order of a testament—a passionate and not wholly unreasonable plea for a positive interpretation of nirvāṇa. Not only does it illustrate the impact of Buddhist thought on mid-nineteenth-century Europe, but hidden within the cumbersome manuscript are several statements and citations which have much more than mere antiquarian interest for the Buddhist scholar a hundred years later.

Such a gem is this quotation from C. Schoebel's neglected *Le Bouddha et le Bouddhisme:*

> In Buddhism, all negative terms, even when they are posed as absolutes, have a relative value; and annihilation always relates to nature, to the created thing, to that which has any sort of form. . . .[89]

A sample of the type of statement which Obry would have been well advised to have excluded from his book is the following concerning the vexatious question of *sopadhiśeṣa* and *nirupadhiśeṣa:*

> In the former as in the latter, the thinking principle remains intact by virtue of being simple, pure, immaterial, and indissoluable. The only difference is that, in the one, this principle still has a

[88] *Ibid.*, pp. 51–52.
[89] *Ibid.*, p. 83.

support, a prop, a buttress (*Lingam* according to the Sankhyas, *Upadhi* according to the Buddhists), while in the other it no longer has any other support or reason for its existence than itself. It has become *Svayambhū*, existing in and for itself.[90]

And further,

In orthodox Buddhism, every time the name *Nirvāṇam* is followed by the epithet *Nirupadhiśeṣam*, "in which nothing of aggregation remains"—even with the gloss "in which absolutely nothing remains"—what is meant is that all is annihilated except the pure spirit or the thinking principle.[91]

Throughout, Obry hammers upon a thesis hanging on the dubious thread of the Sāṃkhya's historical priority. Against his hypothesis that nirvāṇa is a positive condition, he considers that the most specious argument is the one dating back to the earliest Portuguese missionaries. Briefly, it is that "the absorption into the neuter Brahma being the annihilation of the human personality, the absorption into the void [that is, *śūnyatā*] ought to be the annihilation of the soul itself." [92] This notion was never more than a conjecture for Burnouf, Obry declares; and Barthélemy Saint-Hilaire had done nothing more imaginative or significant than to ossify it.

Obry's long chapter on the "Rapports du Christianisme et du Bouddhisme sur les doctrines de la vie future" further exhibits the extent to which he is prepared to go to exculpate the Buddha of the charge of nihilism. Dozens of analogies between Buddhism and Christianity are listed with evident relish. Of them one may be mentioned which is both interesting and typical: "Their ascetics think that one must die to the world in order to live in the Buddha in nirvāṇa, just as our mystics teach that one must die to the world in order to live in Christ in Paradise." [93]

To conclude this summary consideration of Obry's work,

[90] *Ibid.*, p. 85.

[91] *Ibid.*, p. 86.

[92] *Ibid.*, p. 125. Obry's discussion of the meaning of *śūnyatā* (*ibid.*, pp. 127–30) is merely a paraphrase from Hodgson's essays, for which latter see above, Chapter I.

[93] Obry, *Du Nirvâna bouddique*, p. 181.

it will be of interest to note his disapproval of Barthélemy Saint-Hilaire's justification for the study of Buddhism. The latter, it will be recalled, believed that Buddhist studies serve one basic purpose: they help us appreciate the abiding values of our own heritage. On the other hand, Obry condemns "the contradictory opinions of two classes of scholars: one of which saw in Buddhism a reflection of Christianity . . . while the other tried to find in it Christianity's rival. . . ." One or the other of these two attitudes characterized the earliest encounters with Buddhism, according to Obry.

Today such narrow and passionate views—equally insupportable—should both disappear in the face of a more impartial and more elevated critique. Nevertheless, the resemblances do remain; and, although similarities in the history of religion do not always presuppose direct contacts, those that have been singled out for review here, principally from the point of view of the Buddhist nirvāṇa, for the most part are of such a character that, in the opinion of A[lbrecht] Weber, it is impossible to believe in the independent production of things so much alike. Why, then, does Barthélemy Saint-Hilaire force himself to set them aside? [94]

Reading Obry's *Du nirvâna*, I was reminded of Plato's portrait of Cephalus in the *Republic*. Both Obry and Cephalus "enjoy discourse" and "stand on 'old age the threshold.'" And it seems that Obry, subsequent to his encounter with the writings of Barthélemy Saint-Hilaire, shares with Cephalus that "fear and foreboding about things that have not troubled him before." [95]

The positive contribution of Obry's work to the advancement of Buddhist scholarship is, of course, negligible. He knew the source materials only by way of translations and paraphrases. He was oblivious to the complex history of Buddhism and to the emergence of several, distinct school positions. And he fails to adduce even one new piece of

[94] *Ibid.*, pp. 156–57.

[95] Plato *Republic*, 330d. Obry does manifest a certain penchant for studies of immortality notions, however. See his "De l'immortalité de l'âme selon les Hébreux," *Mémoires de l'Académie des sciences, agriculture, commerce, belles-lettres et arts du département de la Somme* (Amiens, 1839), pp. 471–648.

evidence in support of his claim that nirvāṇa is a positive state. But Father de Lubac is undoubtedly correct when he says of Obry: "Sometimes he lacks critical acumen, and not all of his arguments are convincing. Yet at least he shows that the opposing thesis is by no means incontestable." [96]

Philippe Edouard Foucaux

The second of Barthélemy Saint-Hilaire's major antagonists on the nirvāṇa question was Philippe Edouard Foucaux. Foucaux's professional competence lay in Tibetan studies, and he is acclaimed as the first to organize the study of Tibetan language and culture in France.[97] In 1864, a year after Obry's book had appeared, Foucaux published his pamphlet "Nirvāṇa." Though he obviously believed that Obry's position could be strengthened by means of a specialist's assistance, his praise of *Du Nirvâna* is warmly positive.

> Obry's new book is very carefully constructed. In it, the author not only calls on the Indian philosophers for aid but on those from every age and country. One sees that he has dealt with his subject with the keenest desire to arrive at the truth. His arguments are always supported by original texts; and those who, after having read his work attentively, do not share his opinion at the conclusion can agree at least that the thesis he combats is far from being proved in a manner which no longer leaves any doubt.[98]

Foucaux launches his critique with a question:

> How can Barthélemy Saint-Hilaire be perfectly sure about the "nirvāṇa equals annihilation" equation which he advances as

[96] De Lubac, p. 178.

[97] LaCôte, pp. 233–34.

[98] Philippe Edouard Foucaux, *Doctrine des bouddhistes sur le nirvâna*, p. 1.

the Buddha's pure doctrine when it is recognized today that the Master left no written work, that for about 250 years his doctrine was perpetuated in an oral tradition, and that it came to be written in Ceylon only at the end of the century preceding our own era and in North India some years after that? [99]

Foucaux's question points up Barthélemy Saint-Hilaire's rather uncritical presentation of the Buddha word. (This is not to say that specific assumptions embedded in Foucaux's question are themselves accurate.) Problems concerning textual authenticity had by no means been solved in the 1860's; in fact, they are still a plague to some and a refuge for others. Yet Barthélemy Saint-Hilaire was too likely to consider that all the important questions had been answered.[100]

We cannot be absolutely certain about what the Buddha himself actually taught, Foucaux protested; moreover, it would be unreasonable to press any point of doctrine further than the Buddhist "doctors" themselves have. And contemporary authorities are to be read more attentively. Barthélemy Saint-Hilaire cites the Reverend Spence Hardy in support of the view that nirvāṇa is annihilation.[101] Foucaux reminds him that Hardy's conclusion was that nirvāṇa was "beyond all reckoning; an incomprehensible mystery." [102]

Burnouf's authority, on which Barthélemy Saint-Hilaire relied so heavily, cannot be ignored; but Foucaux insists that Burnouf had not been committed absolutely to the strictly negative interpretation of nirvāṇa. In support of his claim,

[99] *Ibid.*, p. 2; cf. p. 27.

[100] Barthélemy Saint-Hilaire mentions the state of Buddhist studies in *Le Bouddha*, 3d ed., pp. xx–xxi: "Nothing was known about Buddhism, I shall not say in the last century or the beginning of ours, but even thirty years ago. The original *Tripitaka*, the translations of it into four or five languages of Asia, the commentaries of which it is the object—none had been read. One cannot pretend that even today one knows Buddhism as it will be known in the twentieth century, which is already so close to us. *But in the present state of our studies we can see what is essential to it and what its enterprise has been. . . .*" (My italics.)

[101] *Ibid.*, p. XVI.

[102] Foucaux, p. 4.

Foucaux cites the following passage from Burnouf's *Introduction:*

The word "void," which already appeared in all the texts proving to be the most ancient, *leads me to believe* that Śakya considered that the supreme good was the complete annihilation of the thinking principle. He does not free the spirit—as the Sāṃkhyas have it—by disengaging it forever from nature or—as the Brāhmaṇas say—by returning it to the breast of the eternal and absolute Brahman. He annihilates the conditions of its relative existence by precipitating it into the void; that is to say, *according to all appearances* into annihilation.

After that, it is not at all surprising that this doctrine produced the Pyrrhonism of the Prajñā and the nihilism of such schools as Nāgārjuna's. *But neither this Pyrrhonism nor this nihilism is written out in so many words in the sūtras stemming from the words of Śākya* as they are in the Prajñāpāramitā and in the other works based on it. That is enough to justify the opinion I advanced at the outset of this analysis—namely, that *there is an interval of several centuries between these sūtras considered to be the source of Buddhist metaphysics and the Prajñā or those books which depend on it* as well as the distinction which separates a doctrine which is only in its beginnings from a philosophy which has reached its final development.[103] [Foucaux's italics.]

Three important points about that extended quotation should be kept in mind. In the first place, Foucaux has preserved an adequate degree of context. The statement is representative of Burnouf's views, and it reaffirms the judgment that his understanding of nirvāṇa was moderate and fluid. Second, Burnouf's opinion about Nāgārjuna and the prajñāpāramitā literature was the standard until the great dispute between Louis de La Vallée Poussin and Th. Stcherbatsky. That is to say, no nineteenth-century author attempted to make a case for the Mādhyamikas as non-nihilists. Third, this passage provides support—perhaps the impetus—for Max Müller's "change of mind" on the subject of nirvāṇa's meaning.

In an appendix to Burnouf's *Le Lotus*, Foucaux finds an-

[103] *Ibid.*, pp. 4–5, quoting Burnouf, *Introduction*, pp. 464–65. See also Burnouf, *Introduction*, p. 22.

other statement about nirvāṇa, one tending to confirm that Burnouf's estimate had not become any less tentative in the course of further study of the documents. Again mindful of the context, Foucaux quotes the following:

Here once again I feel no need to depart from the reserve that I have imposed on myself. *Very much on the contrary, each forward step I take makes me see how much in the way of documents I am lacking in order to give definitive conclusions on this point.*[104] [Foucaux's italics.]

Foucaux contests nine points in Barthélemy Saint-Hilaire's argument for the interpretation of nirvāṇa as annihilation. It will be helpful to discuss them in order, indicating the substance of Foucaux's counterpropositions.

1. On the nature and content of the Buddha's dispute with Brahmanism. Barthélemy Saint-Hilaire had insisted that the point at issue between the Buddha and the Brāhmaṇas was the conception of the nature of release. On the contrary, Foucaux maintains, the Buddha's reform was not important because of its philosophy but rather because it destroyed the fabric of Brahmanic ritualism. Not the goal but the way to the goal constituted the Buddha's contribution.

In fact, it is in the manner of practicing the way which leads to eternal salvation that the difference which distinguishes these two rival religions is found. But is it equally certain that it may be in the manner of comprehending final deliverance itself, when we observe that the Brahmins and the Buddhists do not clearly define at any point the nature of the human soul's release after death? [105]

Throughout his discussion—though without explicit reference—Foucaux worries the now familiar set of analogies between Buddhism and the Protestant Reformation which has long attracted investigators. It is the practical reform, the abolition of manifold, rigourously detailed rituals, and the destruction of religious and social exclusivity which are principal in the Buddha's achievement.

[104] Foucaux, p. 5, quoting Burnouf, *Le Lotus*, pp. 817–18.
[105] Foucaux, p. 6.

To say everything in a few words: The doctrine of the Buddha became a religion rivaling the Brahmanic religion rather than remaining a philosophical school as the other systems did. Doubtless it is in this that one must see the cause of the implacable persecution which drove the Buddhists from India.[106]

2. On the Brahmanic conceptions of release from *saṃsāra*. Citing the Chāndogya Upaniṣad—which he believes to be contemporary with the Buddha at the very latest—Foucaux declares that Brahmanism postulated a permanent release from *saṃsāra:* the promise of a state which did not involve utter annihilation of the individual yet assured a condition of non-returning. Barthélemy Saint-Hilaire had written that the logic of the systems whose common center was the belief in transmigration demanded that all Brahmanic salvation schemes be tentative and that only the Buddhist-annihilationist notion be definitive. Foucaux suggests that Barthélemy Saint-Hilaire does not know his Upaniṣads very well, for the theory fails in the face of the data.

3. On the charge of Buddhist atheism. Foucaux counters Barthélemy Saint-Hilaire's assertion that the Buddha did not acknowledge the existence of God in any fashion with citations from Burnouf,[107] Hodgson, the Laṅkāvatārasūtra, and the Abhidharmakośa. His argument is based almost exclusively on Hodgson's elucidation of the Svābhāvika theories of the various modes of matter. There is, according to Hodgson's account, in the Svābhāvika view an immanent intelligence or ordering force in material nature. This Foucaux construes as a sort of god. Foucaux's plea is pretty flimsy in this difficult case; but Barthélemy Saint-Hilaire's blatantly dogmatic statement that the Buddhists do not admit of a god in any guise is successfully challenged.[108]

[106] *Ibid.*, p. 8.

[107] Burnouf, of course, did believe that the Buddhists were atheists; but it is equally true that he did not attempt to "correct" or otherwise modify Hodgson's analysis of Svābhāvika beliefs. His meticulous caution and reserve in presenting conclusions meant that it was likely that the intentionality of his statements would be violated by partisans of various persuasions.

[108] Foucaux, pp. 9–10. It is interesting that Barthélemy Saint-Hilaire did not attempt to soften this contested statement.

4. On the nature of absorption in Brahman according to the Brāhmaṇas. In Barthélemy Saint-Hilaire's account of the history of Indian philosophy, Buddhist nihilism is considered the historical, logical, inevitable climax. Personal annihilation, implicit in the Brahmanic conception of absorption in Brahman, was merely brought out into the open by the Buddha and clearly labeled. (It would seem that Foucaux could have capitalized on some fuzzy reasoning and near contradictions in Saint-Hilaire's presentation at this juncture [see 2, above]. For whatever reason, however, he did not do so.) Barthélemy Saint-Hilaire says that he cannot imagine what would be gained by interpreting nirvāṇa merely as absorption in God. Foucaux wants to turn that statement around. One may wonder, he writes, "what is gained by accusing Buddhism of preaching atheism and adoration of the nothing when it is admitted that the doctrine arrives at the very same result." [109]

Foucaux calls on Hodgson for support:

> The *Svābhāvika* attempts to deify nature are but a sad confusion of cause and effect. But, in a serious religious point of view, I fail to perceive any superiority possessed by the immaterial pantheism of the *Brahmanists* over the material pantheism of the Buddhists.[110]

5. On the charge of Buddhist materialism. Was the Buddha incapable of distinguishing between the soul and body of a man? No, says Barthélemy Saint-Hilaire. Foucaux, agreeing with Obry, insists that a clear distinction is implied in the texts. Grant transmigration, he declares, and you must also grant that there is something that transmigrates.

> Indeed, however rapid may be the passage of the soul from one body to another, there is necessarily an instant when it is in neither the one nor the other. What becomes of the thinking principle in this interval when it finds itself forcibly separated from matter? [111]

[109] *Ibid.*, p. 11.
[110] Hodgson, "Quotations," p. 75, note, as cited in Foucaux, p. 12.
[111] Foucaux, p. 13.

The matter, of course, is not put to rest that easily. We have come to realize that one is not justified in assuming that there must be some substantial entity that transmigrates. But the substantialistic bias dies hard. There have been, and continue to be, uncounted numbers of attempts to circumvent the supposed difficulties inherent in the Buddhist notion that all things, men included, are *anātmaka* (essence-less)—even among Buddhists. As Conze remarks with good cause, though somewhat indelicately,

> Among all the tenets of Buddhism none has occasioned more controversy and misunderstanding than the *anātman* theory, which suggests that nowhere can a "self" be apprehended. The prospect of complete self-extinction, welcomed by the true Buddhist, seems so bleak and arid to many students of the Dharma that they dream up a "true Self" which, they say, will be realized by the extinction of the false, empirical self. This misinterpretation has proved so popular in Europe that one may be tempted to regard it as either an expression of the typical concern of modern Europeans for "individuality" and "personality," or as a remnant of the Christian belief in an immortal "soul." In fact it is not confined to European Christians or ex-Christians. Everywhere, even in India, it voices the murmurings of the unregenerate Adam when faced with the more magnificent vistas of Buddhist thought. Two centuries after the Buddha's Nirvāṇa it gave rise to the sect of the Pudgalavādins.[112]

Foucaux pays no attention to the positive reflex of his own question. Instead, he notes that Barthélemy Saint-Hilaire is obviously wrong when he asserts that no texts indicate the slightest distinction between the ego and the body. He cites one among several texts in which the *anātmaka* idea appears; and, of course, the core of these discussions is that the soul or self is not to be identified with any part of the body.[113]

Foucaux also repeats Burnouf's unfounded judgment that the Buddha must have believed in a multiplicity of eternal souls after the fashion of the Sāṃkhyas.[114] Manifestly uneasy about what the Buddhists actually do think apropos of the soul

[112] Conze, p. 122; and see the note to that passage, p. 280.
[113] Foucaux, pp. 13–14.
[114] See above, pp. 62–63.

or self, Foucaux shifts his emphasis to the meaning of śūnyatā —the void. "If, as Barthélemy Saint-Hilaire would have it, the Buddhists make no distinction between the soul and the body, what do they understand by the divisions of a world with form and a world without form which one would say were borrowed from the Upaniṣads? . . ." [115] Again quoting the Chāndogya Upaniṣad, Foucaux insists that the Buddhists and Brāhmaṇas agree concerning the existence of a formless realm, and even of a state which is void—neither being nor non-being.

> That the Buddhists confused this Brahman which is neither existing nor non-existing with that which they call the void, and that they have suppressed this god who is hardly easy to comprehend in this form, is not at all surprising when the word they use to express the interval between the momentary destruction of the universe and its reconstruction is precisely the same as that employed by the Brāhmaṇas.[116]

The outline of Foucaux's argument could not be more clear. First stating that "the ideas of the Brāhmaṇas concerning the destruction and reconstruction of the worlds are the same as those of the Buddhists," he flatly declares that the meaning of the Buddhist nirvāṇa depends on the interpretation of *śūnya*.[117] (And for an interpretation of *śūnya*, he cites three passages from Hodgson.[118])

6. On Brahmanic charges of Buddhist nihilism and the meaning of the epithet, *nāstika*. Barthélemy Saint-Hilaire had used the Brahmanic charges against the Buddhists as testimony for the latters' nihilism. Foucaux's position is that almost anything the Brāhmaṇas had to say about Buddhists should be discarded as mere polemic. That the Brāhmaṇas called the Buddhists *nāstika*-s meant only that from an orthodox standpoint the Buddhists could be accused of denying the

[115] Foucaux, p. 15.
[116] *Ibid.*, p. 16.
[117] *Ibid.*
[118] *Ibid.*, pp. 17–18, quoting Hodgson, "Quotations," pp. 83 (note) and 73; and "Notices," p. 26. And see pp. 37–40, above.

proper order of things, the Brahmanic scheme of ritual and social institutions.[119]

7. On the Bodhisattva doctrine. How does one explain the return to earth of beings who have attained nirvāṇa? It is difficult to ask Barthélemy Saint-Hilaire that question, for he ignored the point completely. Foucaux points to texts which testify to the belief that Buddhas and Bodhisattvas return to earth after attaining nirvāṇa in order "to render witness to the terrestrial Buddhas or to explain the sense of the law to the faithful." [120] Unaccountably, Foucaux displays as little interest and knowledge in the Bodhisattva theories as Barthélemy Saint-Hilaire. The important point in the Mahāyāna doctrine that the Bodhisattvas have not yet entered nirvāṇa is lost to both.

8. On the prajñāpāramitā literature. Does it provide incontrovertible proof of Buddhist nihilism? Barthélemy Saint-Hilaire had said yes. Foucaux will agree that it is nihilistic, but he immediately specifies that it was composed several hundred years after the Buddha's life and is outside the zones of orthodox Buddhism.[121]

9. On the significance of the idea of transmigration. Much of Barthélemy Saint-Hilaire's argument hinges on a positive answer to this question: does the hatred and fear of a never ending cycle of rebirths necessarily involve a hatred and fear of life itself? Minimizing the significance of the *saṃsāra* notion, Foucaux answers negatively. Certain inescapable facets of life—such as sickness and death—are hated of course. But the despicable aspects of *saṃsāra* are not part of the attainment of new lives, for youth is treasured. Foucaux devotes several pages to illustrating the Indians' love of life, but his treatment is one which mid-twentieth-century readers would discount for the most part as trivial and superficial. Barthélemy Saint-Hilaire's psychological insight, on the other

[119] Foucaux tries to reinforce this point through an appeal to the observation that the term *nāstika* (or its equivalent) apparently was not applied to Buddhists outside India.

[120] Foucaux, p. 20.

[121] *Ibid.*, pp. 21–22.

hand, seems to be more probing if one agrees that the problem which *saṃsāra* delineates was a living, existential concern among the Indians.[122]

In review, the most substantial points in Foucaux's critique are based on the nature of the textual sources available to scholars and the existence of various, divergent interpretations in the different schools of Buddhism. According to him, we cannot know what the Buddha's precise sentiments about nirvāṇa were, for the first texts were composed two hundred

[122] Certain reductionist tendencies in positivist scholarship have contributed to the publication and persistence of a number of misleading statements concerning the dominant themes in the complex Indian civilization. It is especially important that such statements not be repeated uncritically. And, in particular, historians of religions must be doubly careful—as they have not always been—to guard against succumbing to the distorted perspectives which are the inevitable by-products of gross or partial analysis. For how long and to what extent the *saṃsāra*-idea was in fact a *leitmotiv* in India is not yet clear. On this problem see, for example, J. A. B. van Buitenen, "The Indian Hero as Vidyādhara," *Traditional India: Structure and Change*, ed. Milton Singer (Philadelphia: American Folklore Society, 1959), pp. 99–105.

"To a large extent it is true that we are better informed about the religious doctrines and practices, moral ideals, and metaphysical speculations of pre-Muslim India than about any other aspect of the Indian civilization. The authors whose works have come down to us, whether Hindu or Buddhist, largely belonged to a class which was preoccupied with its sacerdotal prerogatives, its pedagogic duties, and its functions as the guardian of a sacred tradition. But, although we must recognize the great significance of their articulate eschatology in our evaluation of the Indian Weltanschauung, the mere mass of evidence for one set of values should not tempt us to overlook the actual importance of different outlooks. While the increasingly prevailing note of quietistic world despair may have set the key, other notes were sounded. Nor should we forget that the Indian looked upon anything that fell short of a conceivable ideal state of being as an occasion for sorrow, and that accordingly the intention of the very notion of sorrow was inflated. In spite of an undeniable plaintiveness about life in general, the Indian's attitude was essentially melioristic; and though the moralists in unison complained about the misery of man's fate to live, there are few indications that the average person's life was more than ordinarily unpleasant. To a point, sorrow was a theological presupposition, comparable to original sin, and one cannot help feeling that it was more dogma than reality. . . ." (*Ibid.*, p. 99.)

and fifty years after his death. It is not possible to infer that the Buddhist goal was at all different from the Brahmanic. There is no manageable consensus among the Buddhist schools on the question of nirvāṇa; therefore, a convenient and possibly trustworthy alternative indication of the founder's attitude is denied us. The Svābhāvika, for example, apparently the oldest North Indian Buddhist school, split into two subsects over the meaning of nirvāṇa, one declaring that it was absolute annihilation, and the other that it was a state of calm in which the individual personality is not destroyed.[123] And Foucaux maintains that it is this latter view which is accepted by both the Tibetan and Chinese Buddhists.

Many of Foucaux's conclusions are patently a priori—a charge which could be leveled at most of his contemporaries. Still, he does evince a definite tendency to run counter to the methodological fashions and preoccupations of his time. He was not seduced by the charms of a search for origins and the fabrication of a scheme outlining evolutionary development. (In fact, that tendentious sort of pseudo-solution to historical problems had little appeal for those scholars who attempted to piece together a knowledge of Buddhism from a variety of texts.) Foucaux firmly states that he does not expect that the original teaching of the Buddha will ever be discovered. If he had had a direct knowledge of the Pali materials, he might have changed his mind. But this seems improbable, for he declares in his conclusion:

> Even if—and this is doubtful—one could demonstrate that the Buddhist doctrine is pure nihilism, it would not follow that all Buddhists in the present adopt this sad doctrine. To declare flatly that Śākya's disciples worship nothingness is not to be

[123] Foucaux, p. 26. Several pages earlier he had summarized the matter reasonably and concisely: "It is necessary to conclude from this [*viz.*, the diversity of school definitions of *nirvāṇa*] that the sects were not in accord among themselves about the sense of the word nirvāṇa. And, as it is impossible in the present state of our knowledge to know exactly which one carried on the most direct tradition of Sakyamuni's teaching, we are forced to say that the definition of nirvāṇa was a question of school." (*Ibid.*, p. 19.)

rigorously exact; because, as we have seen, the definition of nirvāṇa is a question of school according to the Svabhāvikas, who belong to one of the oldest sects.[124]

Such an attitude predisposes Foucaux to write off the importance of the development and modification of Buddhist thought and institutions in time. Unintentionally, Foucaux indicates that he is more than a little worried that the original doctrine of nirvāṇa may have been annihilation. By carefully denying that the original meaning is either important or discoverable, he avoids any occasion for the challenge of an alien idea. So, in adopting a more functionalistic than historical attitude, Foucaux is still in perfect consonance with the anti-metaphysical atmosphere of his age. He neatly sidesteps nirvāṇa as an issue and joins a chorus of other writers who assert that Buddhism is significant because of its social and ritual reforms.

Critical Buddhist studies in France at the end of the 1860's were in practically the same state as Burnouf had left them at his death. His *Introduction* had not been completed. The Pali Canon had not been compared with the Sanskrit and Tibetan recensions. France, where the study of Buddhism was confined to the Mahāyāna, was not producing younger scholars who were concerned about exploring the distinctions and correspondences between the Mahāyāna and the so-called Hīnayāna. In short, France had been the birthplace of Europe's first and—or so it appeared—her last Pali scholar: Eugène Burnouf.

It was otherwise in England. That country's deep involvement in the administrative and economic affairs of Burma and Ceylon sponsored interest in—and opportunities for the investigation of—the cultural history of those societies. And it is from England that the first solid information about the texts and practices of Pali Buddhism comes. In the next two chapters I shall review the conclusions about nirvāṇa (Pali: *nibbāna*) reached by three of the earliest students of the Pali traditions: Max Müller, James D'Alwis, and Robert Childers.

[124] *Ibid.*, p. 28.

[CHAPTER III]

Friedrich Max Müller

It was in the *Times* of April 17 and 20 of this year [1857] that a review appeared by Max Müller of Stanislas Julien's *Voyages des Pèlerins Bouddhistes*. It was afterwards published as a pamphlet, together with a letter on Nirvāṇa called forth by a protest printed in the *Times* of April 24, against Max Müller's view of Nirvāṇa as *utter annihilation*, whereas the writer of the protest maintained that Nirvāṇa meant *union and communion with God*. . . . The article on Stanislas Julien's book was almost Max Müller's first introduction to Buddhism. Pali he had studied at Berlin.[1]

Five years later, in 1862, Müller published an extended essay, "Buddhism," in the *Edinburgh Review*.[2] And in 1869, at the general meeting of the Association of German Philologists in Kiel, he presented a "Lecture on Buddhist Nihilism" (*Buddhistischer Nihilismus*).[3] That is the extent of Müller's pub-

[1] *The Life and Letters of the Right Honorable Friedrich Max Müller*, ed. his wife, I, 202–3. Cited hereafter as *Life and Letters*.

[2] *Selected Essays*, II, 160–223.

[3] *Ibid.*, pp. 292–312.

lished statements on Buddhism and nirvāṇa: only four short works in a voluminous bibliography which spans more than half a century.[4] Still, the authority of Müller's statements cannot be measured merely in fixed ratio to their quantity.

Max Müller was a singularly dominating figure in Indic studies in Western Europe during the latter half of the nineteenth century. Before discussing his views about the Buddhist nirvāṇa, it will be worthwhile to mention some details about the man. Eugène Burnouf was perhaps the first mature European Sanskrit scholar. His early death, however, denied him the reputation he would undoubtedly have been accorded. Not so with Müller, who lived a long and very productive life. He was a giant; and the story of his efforts and accomplishments is important for anyone wishing to understand the development of Indic studies in Europe.

Friedrich Max ("Max" after the leading man in Weber's *Freischütz*) Müller was born December 6, 1823, in Dessau, then capital of the duchy of Anhalt–Dessau. His father, Wilhelm Müller, was a poet—"second in stature only to Goethe as a lyricist," said Heine—librarian to the duke, and master at the Dessau gymnasium. Max's mother, Adelheid, daughter of the Prime Minister, President von Basedow, was an extremely attractive woman and an accomplished musician.[5] Max's childhood was tranquil and happy, however, for only four years. Wilhelm Müller's death in 1827 hurled him, his sister, and especially his mother into a melancholia for many years—a sadness from which not even the serene beauty of the countryside and the warm, creative companionship of such artist-friends as Felix Mendelssohn could rouse them.

Max attended the local gymnasium from his sixth to twelfth

[4] Of course, there are numerous references to Buddhism in Müller's many essays on languages, myths, and religions, as well as in his introductions to several translations. For the purposes of this study, however, they may be considered to be peripheral.

[5] Müller received a great deal of musical instruction from his mother, and he became a pianist of near-professional caliber—by all odds the most competent musician among Indologists of the nineteenth and twentieth centuries.

year, and, at Easter, 1836, he entered the famous Nicolai School of Leipzig (Leibniz's alma mater). He matriculated at the University of Leipzig for the summer term 1841. It was during the term following—winter, 1841–42—that he began to study Sanskrit with Herrmann Brockhaus.[6] Müller received his doctorate from Leipzig September 1, 1843. Then, in 1844, he went to Berlin for additional Sanskrit studies under Franz Bopp, "but more especially philosophy under Schelling."[7] There he also took instruction in Pali, Hindi, and Persian.

Müller left Berlin in late winter, 1845, for France and more Sanskrit. He arrived in Paris on March 10. Ten days later he met Eugène Burnouf.

> Went to Burnouf, spiritual, amiable, thoroughly French. He received me in the most friendly way, talked a great deal, and all he said valuable, not on ordinary topics but on special. I managed better in French than I expected. "I am a Brahman, a Buddhist, a Zoroastrian; I hate the Jesuits"—that is the sort of man. I am looking forward to his lectures.[8]

And for a little more than a year Müller attended those lectures, studying in a small class among whose members were Abbé Bardelli, Jules Barthélemy Saint-Hilaire, and Theodor Goldstücker.

Unquestionably, Burnouf exercised the decisive influence on Müller's career. Again Müller's journal captures Burnouf's magnetism and Max's own enthusiasm:

> [Burnouf is] small, his face decidedly German, only lighted up with a constant sparkle which is distinctively French. I must have seemed very stupid to him when I tried to explain what I really wanted to do in Paris. He told me afterwards that he could not make me out at first. His lectures were on the *Rig-veda*, and opened a new world to me. He explained to us his own researches,

[6] On Herrmann Brockhaus, 1806–77, see Windisch, *Geschichte*, pp. 211–14.

[7] *Life and Letters*, I, 21. The reference is to F. W. Schelling (1775–1854).

[8] *Ibid.*, p. 36.

he showed us new MSS. which he had received from India, in fact he did all he could to make us his fellow-workers.[9]

Young Müller's excitement is unmistakable. The *Ṛgveda was* a new world, and Müller was eager to explore. " 'Either study Indian philosophy or study Indian religion and copy the Hymns and Sāyaṇa,' said Burnouf." [10] Müller chose the latter, a task it was to take him more than twenty-five years to complete! [11]

Unfortunately, I can take no time here to retell Müller's Vedic adventures, even though his struggles with the various manuscripts and his difficulties with publishers are a fascinating chapter in the history of European Indology. Max left Paris and Burnouf in late spring, 1846, and arrived in London on June 11. It was to have been a brief stay. His trip to Oxford later in the summer was to have been for only a few days. Max Müller remained in England, at Oxford, until his death on October 28, 1900.

In all probability (sources are mute on this point) Müller's first serious contact with Buddhist texts came in Berlin when he first studied Pali. I presume that this was done with Franz Bopp, but I have found no details concerning the texts which Müller read. In 1844, at the same time that young Max was learning the language of the Theravāda Buddhist Canon, Eugène Burnouf published his pioneering *Introduction*. Cer-

[9] *Ibid.*

[10] *Ibid.*, p. 11.

[11] Edward Washburn Hopkins insisted that Müller was responsible only for the first few years of the project and should be credited merely with initiating it. For this and several other less than complimentary remarks about Müller's achievements, see Hopkins' ill-considered obituary article "Max Müller," *Nation*, 71 (1900), 343–44, now reprinted in Sebeok, *Portraits of Linguists*, I, 395–99.

Almost thirty years earlier another famous American Sanskritist, William Dwight Whitney, reviewed Müller's first volume of translations from the Veda with equal disdain and even less charity of expression. See William Dwight Whitney, "Müller's Rig-Veda Translation," *Oriental and Linguistic Studies* (New York: Scribner, Armstrong, and Co., 1873), pp. 133–48.

tainly Müller read this work no later than his stay in Paris, although he does not refer to the text until later.

In the preface to his translation of the Dhammapada (1869), Müller freely acknowledged his indebtedness to a number of Buddhist scholars. The fact that he considered himself—somewhat over-modestly to be sure—a "humble gleaner"[12] rather than a savant in Buddhist studies is of some importance. It was to the Veda and the Vedānta that he devoted his most assiduous labors. Let no one imagine that Müller's Buddhist studies were trivial. But it should be kept in mind that some of his failings in the interpretation of Buddhism are directly attributable to the fact that he was not a specialist.

Slightly more than twelve years separate Müller's articles for the *Times* from his paper at Kiel. All the studies were reprinted several times during his life. And because of this latter fact, it might be supposed that any difference of emphasis in the first paper vis-à-vis the fourth would have disappeared during the course of successive revisions. This does not seem to be the case, however. Only an occasional footnote differentiates a first edition from those subsequent. Consequently, the papers may be analyzed in chronological order with some profit.

The essays do, in fact, constitute a single fabric. To borrow from the terminology of musical composition, one could liken the four to the movements of a scherzo-less symphony. The first two essays state the thematic material and establish a mood which is maintained throughout. The third expands on the initial themes and develops them in moderate variations. Finally, the *Buddhistischer Nihilismus* restates the themes and boldly resolves them in a conclusion which Müller did not recast though he researched and wrote for another thirty years. There are progress and dialectic in the four papers, and it may seem that there is a radical change of opinion manifest

[12] *Lectures on the Science of Religion*, p. 152.

in the final one. In fact, however, the essential harmony of all four is not disturbed.

The First Encounter

Max Müller's interest in Buddhism centered on the following four aspects:

Buddhism as a system of ethics. It was this concern which led him to ask and re-ask questions about coincidences and historical connections between Buddhism and Christianity.

Buddhism in its socio-historical context—that is, in its relation to *Brāhmaṇa*-ism.

Buddhist atheism.

Nirvāṇa: Buddhism and nihilism.

To understand both what Müller comprehended in the term nirvāṇa and how he worked with that knowledge, one must assess his interest in Buddhism as an historical fact. In such an evaluation, it will be enlightening to underscore his general attitude toward Buddhist phenomena. Or, to put it another way, we want to observe what Müller expected from Buddhism—what he would let Buddhism mean.

Early in "Buddhist Pilgrims" Müller gives a capsule account of his definition of religion. It is quoted here in full because of the illumination which it provides for understanding his work.

No doubt there existed in the human mind, from the very beginning, something, whether we call it a suspicion, an innate idea, an intuition, or a sense of the Divine. What distinguishes man from the rest of the animal creation is chiefly that ineradicable feeling of dependence upon some higher power, a consciousness of bondage from which the very name "religion" was derived. "It is He that hath made us, and not we ourselves." The presence of that power was felt everywhere, and nowhere more clearly and strongly than in the rising and setting of the sun, in the change of day and night, of spring and winter, of birth and death. But although the Divine presence was felt everywhere, it was impossible in that early period of thought, and with a language incapable of expressing anything but material objects, to conceive the idea of God in its purity and fullness, or to assign to it an adequate and worthy expression. Children cannot think the thoughts of men, and the poets of the Veda could not speak the language of Aristotle. It was by a slow progress that the human mind elaborated the idea of one absolute and supreme Godhead: and by a still slower process that the human language matured a word to express that idea.[13]

It seems never to have occurred to Müller that the poets of the Veda might very well have found Aristotle's language incapable of expressing their intentions. He was convinced in 1857—and remained so throughout his life—that the history of religion was inextricably bound up with the history of language. Conceptual thought structures can develop only, so he believed, as language modifies and becomes capable of expressing thought constructs with greater precision. The process is envisioned as a reciprocal flow in which thought struggles to expression and language, on its part, provides new forms (or in certain instances thwarts thought activity by creating shadow existences which obfuscate realities).

The meaning of "idea" in the above passage is elusive, but what Müller is suggesting is clear enough. The history of religion, in that view, is a ladder whose rungs are the ever more perfect expressions of the idea of God, expressions which are formulated through the complex interplay of thought and language. Here is evolution in an unmistakable form. From his vantage point at the top, Müller depicts the upward struggle of men attempting to articulate religious experience. The very fact that man has never been satisfied with the conception of his own awareness of divine reality is the motive force in the history of religion. And, according to Müller, the history of religion is the progress of religion, for truth lies in the

[13] *Selected Essays*, II, 237–38.

comprehension and conception of one god. A teleological formulation intertwines with evolution.

The basic content of religious experience is a constant which is grounded on what Müller was later to call a "perception of the infinite." [14] The experienced content is explored and elucidated in the course of human history. Apparently Müller thought that at each stage in the history of religion the expressions and ideas tend to be more satisfactory, to do greater justice to the underlying experience. All goes smoothly if language is healthy. When the expressions themselves become the objects of attention, however, the process is inhibited. Language is subject to a disease, and that disease is myth.

I dwell on these points at some length because they provide certain clues as to the way in which Müller would approach Buddhism and Buddhist terminology. Where we should be inclined to say that religious language as such, within its own particular historical and spiritual context, is always adequate and adequate absolutely, Müller insists that it is adequate only because the particular society, like a child, has no other means through which to express its experiences. That religious significations ossify and often disappear through rationalizations which ostensibly seek to give them a more perfect articulation is nowhere suggested by Müller.

Müller says quite rightly that Buddhism emerged from a definite cultural situation and consequently is explicable—in certain measure—in terms of that particular *Zeitgeist*. That Buddhism was both a reaction to and a consequence of *Brāhmaṇa*-ism is also true to some extent. However, Müller could not imagine and would not accept the significance of Buddhism as an independently existing phenomenon.

He emphasizes that the rise of Buddhism was a social and political event of the first importance. And it is the ethics of Buddhism that he finds attractive. *Siddhārtha Gautama*, the Buddha, cut through the Brahmanic noose which was strangling the moral and spiritual life of India. That activity was

[14] *Lectures on the Origin and Growth of Religion* (London: Longmans, Green, and Co., 1880), pp. 1–51, especially pp. 22–27.

what Müller found to be of lasting value in the Buddha's reform. The precepts of the Buddha and the disregard for class barrier and privilege—these were the Buddhist achievements.

All the essentials of Buddhism—except two—were assimilated facilely into Müller's over-all view. The problems connected with the imputed Buddhist atheism and the vexing nirvāṇa greatly annoyed him. In *Buddhistischer Nihilismus* (to leave the chronological frame for a moment), he reviewed the conclusions reached concerning Buddhism by several other scholars and travelers. The consensus was high praise for the ideals and prescriptions of the Buddha. Müller continued:

> But then, on the other hand, it appears as if people had only permitted themselves to be so liberal in their praise of Buddha and Buddhism, because they could, in the end, condemn a religion which, in spite of all its merits, culminated in Atheism and Nihilism. Thus we are told by Bishop Bigandet: "It may be said in favor of Buddhism, that no philosophicoreligious system has ever upheld, to an equal degree, the notions of a savior and deliverer, and the necessity of his mission, for procuring the salvation of man, in a Buddhist sense. The role of Buddha, from beginning to end, is that of a deliverer, who preaches a law designed to secure to man the deliverance from all the miseries he is laboring under. But by an inexplicable and deplorable eccentricity, the pretended savior, after having taught man the way to deliver himself from the tyranny of his passions, leads him after all, into the bottomless gulf of total annihilation." [15]

Müller freely admitted that the good bishop's

> language may have a slightly episcopal tinge, yet we find the same judgement, in almost identical words by the most eminent scholars who have written on Buddhism. The warm discussions on this subject, which have recently taken place at the Académie des Inscriptions et Belles-Lettres of Paris, are probably known to many of those who are here present; but better still, the work of the man whose place has not yet been filled, either in the French Academy, or on the Council Board of German Science—the work of Eugène Burnouf, the true founder of a scientific study of

[15] *Selected Essays*, II, 294–95.

Buddhism. Burnouf, too, in his researches arrives at the same result, namely that Buddhism, as known to us from its canonical books, in spite of its great qualities, ends in Atheism and Nihilism.[16]

More than a decade earlier, Müller had read Barthélemy Saint-Hilaire's series of articles on Buddhism in the *Journal des Savants*. And it would seem certain that his former classmate's conclusions about Buddhist atheism and nihilism were among the major causes which prompted Müller to write a review of Julien's translation and to devote considerable energy to the solution of the nirvāṇa dispute. Barthélemy Saint-Hilaire's statements offended Müller's sentiments and condemned several of his cherished theories. In a very real sense, all Müller's investigations were conducted in response to Barthélemy Saint-Hilaire's judgment (quoted by Müller in his "Buddhist Pilgrims"):

> Buddhism has no God; it has not even the confused and vague notion of a Universal Spirit in which the human soul, according to the orthodox doctrine of Brahmanism, and the Sankhya philosophy, may be absorbed. Nor does it admit nature, in the proper sense of the word, and it ignores that profound division between spirit and matter which forms the system and the glory of Kapila. It confounds man with all that surrounds him, all the while preaching to him the laws of virtue. Buddhism, therefore, cannot unite the human soul, which it does not even mention, with a God, whom it does not know better. Nothing remained but to annihilate the soul; and in order to be quite sure that the soul may not reappear under some new form in this world, which has been cursed as the abode of illusion and misery, Buddhism destroys its very elements, and never gets tired of glorying in this achievement. What more is wanted? If this is not the absolute nothing, what is Nirvāṇa? [17]

Naturally enough, I would argue, Müller wanted to find out for himself.

The Buddhism he encountered constituted a many-faceted

[16] *Ibid.*
[17] *Ibid.*, pp. 252–53.

problem. It presented an ethical system in which mercy and compassion were the key attitudes. It set forth a code of behavior rich in its implications for social welfare even though austere in its asceticism.

> And yet, all this self-sacrificing charity, all this self-sacrificing humility, by which the life of Buddha was distinguished throughout, and which he preached to the multitudes that came to listen to him, had, we are told, but one object, and that object was final annihilation. It is impossible almost to believe it, and yet when we turn away our eyes from the pleasing picture of that high morality which Buddha preached for the first time to all classes of men, and look into the dark pages of his code of religious metaphysics, we can hardly find another explanation. Fortunately, the millions who embraced the doctrines of Buddha, and were saved by it from the depths of barbarism, brutality, and selfishness, were unable to fathom the meaning of his metaphysical doctrines. With them the Nirvāṇa to which they aspired, became only a relative deliverance from the miseries of human life; nay, it soon took the bright colours of a paradise to be regained by the pious worshipper of Buddha. But was this the meaning of Buddha himself? [18]

That final question was the important one for Müller. In 1857, it appeared to him that the popular beliefs of Buddhist millions did not correspond wholly to the doctrine of the Buddha himself. Müller declared that the so-called four verities [19] enunciated by the Buddha do not directly "define Nirvāṇa, except by cessation of all pain." But, as he probed to understand the Buddha's teaching with regard to the elimination of pain and the cause of pain, he espied darker aspects

[18] *Ibid.*, pp. 249–50.

[19] Found in the so-called Sermon of the Turning of the Wheel of the Law (*Dharmacakrapravartanasūtra;* Pali: *Dhammacakkapavattanasutta*), they are, "the noble truth concerning suffering . . . the noble truth concerning the origin of suffering . . . the noble truth concerning the destruction of suffering . . . the noble truth concerning the way leading to the destruction of suffering." For a recent and exact translation, see Erich Frauwallner, *Die Philosophie des Buddhismus* (Berlin: Akademie-Verlag, 1958), p. 11.

of nirvāṇa. The "eightfold path" [20] he took to be a simple moral code. It could, he ventured, be followed without necessarily abandoning belief in a higher being.

Buddhists, however, trace the cause of suffering through the "twelve-linked chain of interdependence (*pratītyasamutpāda*)." [21] As Müller understood this notion, the key link was ignorance. The evil of pain lies with ignorance. Eradicate ignorance, and pain will cease. The Buddhist formulation did not link ignorance directly to pain, though; rather, it linked ignorance to existence and then existence to pain. So, to eliminate pain, ignorance *and* (consequently) existence must be eliminated. This, Müller sighed, was history's most tragic instance of throwing out the baby with the bath water.

> Such a religion, we should say, was made for a madhouse. But Buddhism was an advance, if compared with Brahmanism; it has stood its ground for centuries, and if truth could be decided by majorities, the show of hands, even at the present day, would be in favour of Buddha. The metaphysics of Buddhism, like the metaphysics of most religions, not excluding our own Gnosticism and Mysticism, were beyond the reach of all except a few hardened philosophers or ecstatic dreamers. Human nature could not be changed. Out of the very nothing it made a new paradise; and he who had left no place in the whole universe for a Divine Being, was deified himself by the multitudes. . . .[22]

Somehow, right thinking and the inclinations of mankind had triumphed over the madness of metaphysics. This, then, was Max Müller's purview of Buddhism. He acknowledged and warmly accepted the Buddhist ethic. He praised the tolerance implicit in Buddhism through its equal treatment of all men. But nirvāṇa mystified him. The understanding he had attained about it at this stage came principally from Burnouf and Barthélemy Saint-Hilaire. Nirvāṇa apparently meant annihilation. Very few Buddhists understood that,

[20] "This is the noble eight-membered way: right opinion, right thought, right speech, right business, right activity, right aspiration, right vigilance, right concentration." *Ibid.*

[21] Translated closely as "conditioned co-production" by Conze, *Buddhist Thought in India*, pp. 156–58.

[22] *Selected Essays*, II, 250.

Müller was convinced; but, though uneasy, he was prepared to defend the word of Burnouf's interpretation.

The Letter on Nirvāṇa

The opportunity for such a defense came immediately after the publication of Müller's review. A Francis Barham of Bath vigorously opposed Müller's interpretation. In a letter printed in the *Times* four days after the second part of Müller's essay had appeared, Barham adduced the judgments of Néander, Creuzer, and the Abbé Huc [23] to show, in Müller's words,

> that the Nirvāṇa in which the Buddhists believe, and which they represent as the highest goal of their religion and philosophy, means union and communion with God, or absorption of the individual soul by the divine essence, and not as I tried to show in my articles on the "Buddhist Pilgrims," utter annihilation.[24]

"The Meaning of Nirvāṇa" was published also as a letter to the *Times*'s editor. Müller begins it by challenging the authority of the three experts whom Barham had called to support his position.

> Now with regard to Néander and Creuzer, I must observe that their works were written before the canonical books of the Buddhists composed in Sanskrit had been discovered, or at least before they had been sent to Europe and analysed by European scholars. Besides, neither Néander nor Creuzer was an Oriental scholar, and their knowledge of the subject could only be second-hand.[25]

[23] On the Church historian, August Néander, see a brief account in G. P. Gooch, *History and Historians in the Nineteenth Century* (new ed.; Boston: Beacon Press, 1959), pp. 491–93. For Georg Friedrich Creuzer (1771–1858), classicist and philosopher, see Schwab, *La Renaissance orientale*, pp. 234–39 *et passim*.

[24] *Selected Essays*, II, 280.

[25] *Ibid.*, p. 281.

Müller remained silent for the moment about Abbé Huc.[26] The point was that Müller would not allow amateurs to cloud issues in Oriental studies. However much he was in sympathy with Barham's or Creuzer's or Néander's view, he did not know of a single Buddhist text which would support a positive interpretation. (It would be well to keep in mind that during this period Müller himself had practically no direct knowledge of Buddhist texts.) Personal preferences were irrelevant, said Müller; the facts of the case must decide.

Nonetheless, I am reminded of a statement which Müller made earlier in 1857. In a letter to his close friend Baren Bunsen he wrote:

> I do not yet despair of discovering the chord by which the dissonance of the *Veda* and the *Zendavesta* and the Chinese *Kings* will be brought into unison with the key-note of the Bible. There can be nothing inharmonious on earth and in history; the unresolved discords in the East must find their solution, and we dare not leave off till we have discovered the why and the wherefore.[27]

Beyond doubt, the Buddhist nirvāṇa was the most strident of those dissonances, and Müller took heart from the fact that the meaning of the term was not troublesome merely for his European contemporaries.

> The discussions on the true meaning of Nirvāṇa are not of modern date, and . . . at an early period different philosophical schools among the Buddhists of India, and different teachers who spread the doctrine of Buddhism abroad, propounded every conceivable opinion as to the orthodox explanation of this term. Even in one and the same school we find different parties maintaining different views on the meaning of Nirvāṇa.[28]

The best place to start if one is interested in the meaning of nirvāṇa, Müller suggests, is with an etymological analysis.

[26] Later he was to observe: "The late Abbé Huc pointed out the similarities between Buddhist and Roman Catholic ceremonials with such naïveté that, to his surprise, he found his delightful *Travels in Tibet* placed on the *Index*. . . ." *Ibid.*, p. 168.

[27] *Life and Letters*, I, 198.

[28] *Selected Essays*, II, 282.

Every Sanskrit scholar knows that Nirvāṇa means originally the blowing out, the extinction of light, and not absorption. The human soul, when it arrives at its perfection, is blown out, [Here Müller adds a note: " 'Calm,' 'without wind,' as Nirvāṇa is sometimes explained, is expressed in Sanskrit by Nirvāta. . . ."] if we use the phraseology of the Buddhists, like a lamp; it is not absorbed, as the Brahmins say, like a drop in the ocean.[29]

At this point, Müller's argument turns somewhat cloudy. He advances a doubt that "the term Nirvāṇa was coined by Buddha." Rather, he asserts, the term nirvāṇa appears also in the Brahmanic literature and there in the general sense of *mokṣa.*

Unless, however, we succeed in tracing this term in works which can be proved to be anterior to Buddha, we may admit that it was invented by him to express that meaning of the *summum bonum* which he was the first to preach, and which some of his disciples explained in the sense of absolute annihilation.[30]

Müller could well have stated that more felicitously. He stresses that it is impossible to be absolutely sure that nirvāṇa as a technical term was first used by the Buddha. But to be at all systematic while investigating nirvāṇa from this standpoint, three distinct problems must be solved.

Was the term itself in use before the Buddha's time?

What was the specific content which the Buddha assigned to nirvāṇa? How arbitrary or idiosyncratic was this usage if one assumes that the term itself was borrowed?

Finally, if it is possible, the meaning which nirvāṇa had for the Buddha should be compared with the explanations and modifications proposed by later Buddhists.

At this juncture in his Buddhist studies, in 1857, Müller realized that the answer to the first question above should be a qualified yes. That is to say, in all probability the word nirvāṇa *was* used prior to the Buddha's time. Yet, Müller also realized that strict proof of this would be impossible in the absence of texts which could be placed definitely before the earliest

[29] *Ibid.*, p. 283.
[30] *Ibid.*, p. 284.

Buddhist documents. It seems obvious that Müller would like to assume that the Buddha was the first to use nirvāṇa in a technical or school sense. This assumption would allow us to maintain that the varying interpretations of the term in the later literature—from *mokṣa* use in the Brahmanic texts to the sense of complete annihilation in certain Buddhist speculations—indicate that either the Buddha's own employment of the term was not at all radical or, on the other hand, that it was so radical as to be incomprehensible. Whatever the intrinsic worth of such a proposition may be, it does illustrate one of the reasons that the search for the original words of the Buddha has proved so attractive to so many.

Materials which we possess for a study of the content of the term nirvāṇa in Buddhist thought are no more to be considered transcripts of the Buddha's "sermons" than the Gospel accounts are of the words of Jesus. The so-called canonical collections in Pali and Sanskrit Buddhism would not permit a clear distinction between actual statements of the Buddha and later interpretations without making use of the most recent methods of *Formsgeschichte*—methods which, for the most part, are still inaccessible to Buddhist scholars. (And it is, of course, true that we do not have at our disposal any critical apparatus delicate enough to place legitimate quotation marks around any passages in those texts.) Müller insisted that the original teaching of the Buddha, in the absence of earlier or more authentic documents, must be seen through the refractory of the canon. "Nirvāṇa, as taught both in the metaphysics of Kaśyapa and in the Prajñāpāramitā of the Northern Buddhists, is annihilation, not absorption." Müller's conclusion in 1857 is a faithful echo of the statement made by Burnouf thirteen years earlier.

> Buddhism, therefore, if tested by its own canonical books, cannot be freed from the charge of Nihilism, whatever may have been its character in the mind of its founder, and whatever changes it may have undergone in later times, and among races less inured to metaphysical discussions than the Hindus.[31]

[31] *Ibid.*, pp. 284–85.

Particular attention should be paid to what Müller means by "Nihilism." He does not mean "annihilationism." Rather, he is referring to the Buddha's "denial of the divinity of the gods." The Buddha's supposed atheism *is* nihilism.

Therefore, if Nirvāṇa in his mind was not yet complete annihilation, still less could it have been absorption into a Divine essence. It was nothing but self-ness, in the metaphysical sense of the word —a relapse into that being which is nothing but itself. This is the most charitable view which we can take of the Nirvāṇa, even as conceived by Buddha himself, and it is this view which Burnouf derived from the canonical books of the Northern Buddhists. Mr. Spence Hardy, who in his works follows exclusively the authority of the Southern Buddhists . . . arrives at the same result.[32]

Theories, Practices, and Texts

The third of Müller's essays on Buddhism (1862) shows little change in his views. He still believed that nirvāṇa could not possibly mean the absorption of the individual into the divine. And he would not dispute the fact that certain canonical Buddhist texts established that nirvāṇa means "annihilation." His concern at this time centered on the importance which should be assigned to that established meaning. Metaphysically, nirvāṇa was annihilation or, at best, selfness. But what was the importance of metaphysics after all?

The most important element of the Buddhist reform has always been its social and moral code, not its metaphysical theories. That moral code, taken by itself, is one of the most perfect which the world has ever known. On this point all testimonies from hostile and from friendly quarters agree.[33]

[32] *Ibid.*, p. 289.
[33] *Ibid.*, p. 207.

In that spirit, Müller participated wholeheartedly in the Ritschlian, anti-metaphysical attitudes which were to root themselves firmly in the European scholarly world during his lifetime. (In this connection, one may recall the fact that Müller prepared and published a translation of Kant's *Kritik der Reinen Vernunft.*) Unfortunately, Müller does not specify precisely what he means by "metaphysics." The exact sense, of course, must be grounded solidly on Kant. But because Müller's own view is rather vague and simplistic, about all that can be said definitely is that for him metaphysics was a vain intellectual enterprise.

According to the metaphysical tenets, if not of Buddha himself, at least of his sect, there is no reality anywhere, neither in the past nor in the future. True wisdom consists in perceiving the nothingness of all things, and in a desire to become nothing, to be blown out, to enter into the state of Nirvāṇa.[34]

Müller was appalled. Again he turned to a point which truly concerned him: the exploration of the meaning that a nirvāṇa conceived as utter annihilation would have for practicing Buddhists.

Whether the belief in this kind of Nirvāṇa—*i.e.* in a total extinction of being, personality, and consciousness—was at any time shared by the large masses of the people, is difficult either to assert or deny. We know nothing in ancient times of the religious convictions of the millions. We only know what a few leading spirits believed or professed to believe. That certain people in modern and ancient times have spoken and written of total extinction as the highest aim of man cannot be denied. . . . Under clouds of madness, such language is intelligible: but to believe, as we are asked to believe, that one half of mankind had yearned for total annihilation would be tantamount to a belief that there is a difference in kind between man and man.[35]

Once more Müller took solace in the fact that divergent interpretations of nirvāṇa abounded in the various Buddhist schools. "With the modern Buddhists of Burmah, for instance, Nigban, as they call it, is defined simply as freedom from old

[34] *Ibid.*, p. 219.
[35] *Ibid.*, pp. 220–21.

age, disease, and death." [36] That perturbing question—what was Gautama's intention with regard to nirvāṇa?—troubled Müller less. He was close to fashioning an answer. True, "in one portion of the Buddhist Canon the most extreme views of nihilism are put into his [the Buddha's] mouth." [37] But Müller relies more and more on the fact that the canon itself is later than the Buddha. He had pointed to this in 1857, and in 1862 he stressed it further by showing an instance of inconsistency in the canonical accounts: *after*—or so the canon chronology would have it—speaking in nihilistic terms, the Buddha tells of sending miracles to the world subsequent to his attainment of the highest nirvāṇa. Can the extinct send miracles?

In order to obtain the reference for this seeming contradiction, however, Müller jumped from a very cursory and incomplete examination of the Pali traditions and some statements in the Abhidharma texts to the Saddharmapuṇḍarīka-sūtra of the Buddhist Sanskrit tradition.[38] A closer examination of the Pali texts (which was not to come until his work on the Dhammapada) would have yielded further and more substantial insights—for example, the shadings of meaning which nirvāṇa assumed and the occasions of the Buddha's refusal to discuss nirvāṇa. Instead of devoting attention to closer textual analysis, however, Müller concludes his third article by appealing again to the universalist sentiment.

If we may argue from human nature, such as we find it at all times and in all countries, we confess that we cannot bring ourselves to believe that the reformer of India, the teacher of so perfect a code of morality, the young prince who gave up all he had in order to help those whom he saw afflicted in mind, body, or estate, should have cared much about speculations which he knew would either be misunderstood, or not understood at all, by those whom he wished to benefit; that he should have thrown away one of the most powerful weapons in the hands of every religious teacher, the belief in a future life, and should not have seen that, if this

[36] *Ibid.*, p. 221.

[37] *Ibid.*

[38] *Ibid.*, p. 286. James D'Alwis, *The Nirvāṇa of the Buddhists* [*Buddhist Nirvāṇa: A Review of Max Müller's Dhammapada*].

life was sooner or later to end in nothing, it was hardly worth the trouble which he took himself, or the sacrifices which he imposed on his disciples.[39]

That mighty sentence echoes Müller's constantly and fervently held conviction that the Buddha could not have preached a supreme good which meant the utter annihilation of the individual. Müller was unnerved by the institution, the structure of the Buddhist establishment, just as he was dissatisfied with the institutional development and organization of the Church. Max Weber and Adolf von Harnack were to approach the discussion of continuity between religious innovator and the structure which crystallizes following the "death" of the founder in a manner which would have been most congenial to Müller.[40]

Resolution

In 1869, Müller asked directly if it were "possible to distinguish between Buddhism and the personal teaching of Buddha." He assured his audience that the same question was asked at least as early as the reign of King Aśoka. "The question is only whether such a separation is still possible for us." The answer which circumstances forced him to give was less than pleasant.

[39] *Selected Essays*, II, 222–23.

[40] On 26 July 1895, in a letter to a Mr. Dharmapala, Müller wrote: "You should endeavour to do for Buddhism what the more enlightened students of Christianity have long been doing in the different countries of Europe: you should free your religion from its latter excrescences, and bring it back to its earliest, simplest, and purest form, as taught by Buddha and his immediate disciples. If that is done, you will be surprised to see how little difference there is in essentials between the great religions of the world. And this must be done with perfect honesty." *Life and Letters*, II, 350–51.

My belief is that all honest inquirers must oppose a No to this question. Burnouf never ventured to cast a glance beyond the boundaries of the Buddhist canon. What he finds in the canonical books, in the so-called "Three Baskets," is to him the doctrine of the Buddha, similarly as we must accept, as the doctrine of Christ, what is contained in the four Gospels.

Still the question ought to be asked again, and again, whether, at least with regard to certain doctrines or facts, it may not be possible to make a step further in advance, even with the conviction that it cannot lead us to results of apodictic certainty.[41]

We should not give up hope, Müller says with determination. The question should be asked repeatedly and always apropos of specific details. He adds the proviso that there is only a limited exactitude to be expected in any event. Here Müller grapples with a problem which greatly upsets him. In the face of his obvious personal involvement, it is important to emphasize that he does not lose his scholarly self-control. He approaches the subject with considerable caution and reserve. And there is no reason to reject his preliminary line of reasoning a priori merely because it is a priori with him.

If, as happens frequently, we find in the different parts of the canon, views not only differing from, but even contradictory to each other, it follows, I think, that one only of them can belong to Buddha personally, and I believe that in such a case we have the right to choose, and the liberty to accept *that* view as the original one, the one peculiar to Buddha, which least harmonizes with the later system of orthodox Buddhism.[42]

Several valid objections may be raised with regard to that methodological statement. In the first place, when confronting a phenomenon as puzzling as nirvāṇa, one finds it all too easy to conclude that any two statements about it are contradictory. (It may be added that this evaluation could be productive of substantial insight into what nirvāṇa is all about. However, such seeds require cultivation.) Second, if it were shown that two statements are in contradiction, strictly so called—a proof requiring careful examination of their textual relationships—

[41] *Selected Essays*, II, 300.
[42] *Ibid.*

this should not at all convince us that only one of them, if either, actually belongs to the Buddha himself. Also, what could justify the establishment of a single criterion to separate authentic statements from contributions made by Buddhist traditionalists?

Rights and liberties are beside the point. What is directly to the point is that Müller's suggestion—despite its flaws—is a solid advance over Burnouf's and Barthélemy Saint-Hilaire's positions. That this is the case becomes clear if one considers similar problems which have occurred in the course of scholarly study of the earliest Christian Church.

Maurice Goguel, in his study *Jesus and the Origins of Christianity*, noted that "critics of the nineteenth century, who were not greatly concerned with the problem of tradition, had too much confidence in a purely literary type of criticism; they were too ready to believe that the most ancient records were the most historical." [43] Both Burnouf and Barthélemy Saint-Hilaire were critics of that kind, and there is hardly a scholar in the history of Buddhist studies who has not fallen prey at some point to this historico-critical trap. Now, in discussing criteria which can assist the historian in determining the authenticity of statements attributed to Jesus, Goguel offers one which bears a striking resemblance to Müller's suggestion. "Every time we find, attributed to Jesus or recommended by him, an attitude which is contrary to that which is current in the very earliest form of the Church, there is room to suppose that we are in the presence of an historical fact." [44]

Sixty years separate Müller's and Goguel's respective statements, and the latter is much more tentative—consequently making the reader more comfortable—than Müller's. Nonetheless, we may credit Müller with holding a critical technique which was in advance of his era. Perceptive though Müller's research principle was, there were no guarantees that it would

[43] Maurice Goguel, *Jesus and the Origins of Christianity*, trans. Olive Wyon (2 vols.; New York: Macmillan, 1933), I, 204.

[44] *Ibid.*, p. 206.

provide true answers rather than preferred ones. And it cannot be stressed too often that phenomena which do not lend themselves to discursive categories inevitably inspire diverse and ambiguous statements. In such a situation, paradox will assume all the characteristics of actual contradiction.

Müller, to continue, asks his new question of two special topics: atheism and nihilism. The answer to the first is immediate and brief. There are no contradictory statements concerning the gods. He notes metaphors and other poetic images which refer to the gods; but those are to be taken for what they are and not interpreted literally. Müller concludes that the Buddha was an atheist insofar as that may be determined from the Buddhist texts. Whatever existence the Buddha allowed the gods was merely a shadow existence. They were less than divine—not proper gods at all.

But whilst we have no ground for exonerating the Buddha from the accusation of Atheism, the matter stands very differently as regards the charge of Nihilism. Buddhist Nihilism has always been much more incomprehensible than mere Atheism. A kind of religion is still conceivable when there is something firm somewhere, when a something, eternal and self-dependent, is recognized, if not *without* and *above* man, at least *within* him. But if, as Buddhism teaches, the soul after having passed through all the phases of existence, all the worlds of the gods and of the higher spirits, attains finally Nirvāṇa as its highest aim and last reward, *i.e.* becomes quite extinct, then religion is not any more what it ought to be—a bridge from the finite to the infinite, but a trap-bridge hurling man into the abyss, at the very moment when he thought he had arrived at the stronghold of the Eternal.[45]

The metaphysical portions of the Buddhist canon, Müller insists once again, *do* explain nirvāṇa as the absolute nothing,

Burnouf adds, however, that this doctrine, in its crude form, appears only in the third part of the canon, the so-called Abhidharma, but not in the first and second parts, in the Sutras, the Sermons, and the Vinaya, the ethics, which together bear the name of Dharma or Law. He next points out that, according to some ancient authorities, this entire part of the canon was designated as

[45] *Selected Essays*, II, 301–2.

"not pronounced by Buddha." These are, at once, two important limitations. I add a third, and maintain that sayings of the Buddha occur in the first and second parts of the canon, which are in open contradiction to this Metaphysical Nihilism.[46]

Müller proudly supports that assertion with quotations from the Dhammapada. Eighteen passages are cited to show positions which would have been untenable under the assumption that the Buddha believed nirvāṇa to be absolute annihilation.[47] Müller emphasizes as strongly as before that nirvāṇa means extinction—a signification supported by its etymology. But

> Nirvāṇa may mean the extinction of many things—of selfishness, desire, and sin, without going so far as the extinction of subjective consciousness. Further, if we consider that Buddha himself, after he had already seen Nirvāṇa, still remains on earth until his body falls prey to death; that Buddha appears to his disciples even after his death, it seems to me that all these circumstances are hardly reconcilable with the orthodox metaphysical doctrine of Nirvāṇa.[48]

In the preface to his translation of the Dhammapada—revised in the summer of 1869—Müller declares that

> if we look in the Dhammapada at every passage where Nirvāṇa is mentioned, there is not one which would require that its meaning should be annihilation, while most, if not all, would become perfectly unintelligible if we assigned to the word Nirvāṇa the meaning which it has in the Abhidharma or the metaphysical portions of the canon.[49]

Dhammapada, verse 21, calls reflection the path of immortality (*amṛta*, *amata*) and heedlessness the way of death, according to Müller. The medieval Pali commentator Buddhaghosa, he notes, equates *amṛta* and nirvāṇa. "This was also Buddha's thought," Müller declares, citing Dhammapada, verse 23. The Buddha could not have meant nirvāṇa as nothingness in the strict sense. "Would such expressions have been used by the founder of this new religion, if what he called

[46] *Ibid.*, pp. 302–3.

[47] In order of citation: Vss. 160, 323, 21, 23, 134, 184, 369, 203, 285, 225, 368, 381, 114, 374, 411, 97, 383, and 218.

[48] *Selected Essays*, II, 303.

[49] *Lectures on the Science of Religion*, pp. 180–81.

immortality had, in his own idea, been annihilation?" Furthermore, Müller insists, "Nirvāṇa occurs even in the purely moral sense of quietness and absence of passion." [50]

His summary judgment concerning the Dhammapada is that it offers "a conception of Nirvāṇa, altogether irreconcilable with the third part of the Buddhist canon." Then he schematizes his conclusions. Nirvāṇa must be seen at three different levels of interpretation:

Nirvāṇa understood as "the entrance of the soul into rest, a subduing of all wishes and desires, indifference to joy and pain, to good and evil, and absorption of the soul in itself and a freedom from the circle of existences from birth to death, and from death to a new birth." [51] This, Müller states, is the general understanding among Buddhists today, and it is also the view of the Buddha and his disciples.

Nirvāṇa understood as a gross paradise. This is the view of a large number of uneducated, poorly trained Buddhists.

And, finally, "Only in the hands of the philosophers, to whom Buddhism owes its metaphysics, the Nirvāṇa, through constant negations, carried to an indefinite degree, through the excluding and abstracting of all that is not Nirvāṇa, at last became an empty Nothing, a philosophical myth." [52]

Ernst Cassirer has encapsulated Müller's views on language and myth as follows:

For him, myth is neither a transformation of history into fabulous legend nor is it fable accepted as history; and just as certainly it does not spring directly from the contemplation of the great forms and powers of nature. What we call myth is, for him, something conditioned and negotiated by the agency of language; it is, in fact, the product of a basic shortcoming, an inherent weakness of language. All linguistic denotation is essentially ambiguous—and in this ambiguity, this 'paronymia' of words lies the source of all myths.[53]

[50] *Selected Essays*, II, 304.

[51] *Ibid.*, pp. 305–6. Compare *Lectures on the Science of Religion*, p. 184.

[52] *Selected Essays*, II, 306.

[53] Ernst Cassirer, *Language and Myth*, trans. Susanne K. Langer (New York: Harper & Brothers, 1946), pp. 3–4.

In a review of Müller's *Lectures on the Science of Language*, Whitney remarked caustically, "It seems as if Professor Müller were

In this sense, then, that Buddhist nirvāṇa which is conceived as the absolute annihilation of all modes of existence for an individual personality is a myth. It is a myth grounded in the ambiguity of the very word *nirvāṇa*. And there is a measure of irony in this of which Müller was presumably never aware. For him, nirvāṇa-as-annihilation is a myth: a name without a reality that corresponds to it. For the Buddhist, "self" is a myth: a name, a convention to which no thing corresponds. From remarkably similar attitudes regarding the weaknesses of language, Müller and the Buddhists reinforce two radically different conclusions. And one cannot suppose that this paradox would surprise a Buddhist.

In summary, Müller's resolution of the problem of nirvāṇa—ineffable, indescribable experience—is simple enough: either one must believe that the Buddha taught both an exoteric and an esoteric doctrine, or one must accept that view of nirvāṇa as the original which "corresponds best with the simple, clear, and practical character of Buddha." Reacting against the, for the most part, negative statements of his beloved teacher Burnouf and the more emphatic tirades of his former classmate Barthélemy Saint-Hilaire, Müller struggled and finally proved to his own satisfaction that the simple declaration "Nirvāṇa is annihilation" cannot be advanced categorically. In that, whatever the weaknesses in his own position may be, he has convinced many others as well.

Father Henri de Lubac insists that Müller's approach was not scholarly in the strictest sense.

---

attempting to persuade us that such words as *nothingness*, *non-existence*, *extinction*, were words only, which, as having no idea beneath them, ought never to have been suffered to creep into the vocabularies; and that those who dread and those who court extinction are equally the dupes of a congeries of meaningless articulations. We shall be prepared to rejoice at his success, and to use our utmost influence to have all words of the sort marked in the dictionaries as 'obsolete,' in order to [*sic*] their total omission later. He will thus at a blow annihilate—we beg pardon, put out of existence—no, extinguish—well, we may at least be permitted to say, reduce to a state of irretrievable pastness, a host of religious and philosophical systems" (William Dwight Whitney, "Müller's Lectures on Language," *ibid.*, p. 260).

By some sort of intuition . . . Max Müller advanced the opinion that the Buddha had not been able to preach nothingness. If the canonical books say that he did, they do not represent the primitive doctrine. This is a bold hypothesis, founded on psychological probabilities; but the author should have recognized that it did not have the support of the very texts he himself knew.[54]

To some extent that criticism is just. A more serious and less fair charge is reserved for a footnote:

Moreover the opinion of Max Müller is a bit irresolute. He had begun by holding as a popular deviation that which he was later to interpret as a revindication of the human soul and as the teaching of the Buddha.[55]

Müller's Buddhist essays reveal continuity and integrity in his consideration of the nirvāṇa question, however; and this cannot be dismissed so lightly.

[54] De Lubac, *Le Rencontre du bouddhisme*, p. 177.
[55] *Ibid.*, footnote 95.

[CHAPTER IV]

James D'Alwis and Robert Caesar Childers

Barthélemy Saint-Hilaire's sternly uncompromising interpretation of nirvāṇa aroused vigorous challenges from J. B. F. Obry, Ph. Ed. Foucaux, and Max Müller, among others. Yet, despite certain undeniable insights manifested on both sides of that earliest stage of the European nirvāṇa controversy, the arguments faded—especially in France—without having attained academic respectability. Disdaining to dialogue with his critics, Barthélemy Saint-Hilaire remained adamant in his evaluation, dying in 1895 convinced of the correctness of his view. Obry, whose work on nirvāṇa had been more confessional than scholarly, died in 1871, having written all that was in his mind and heart on the subject eight years before. Foucaux continued to work directly with the Tibetan and Buddhist Sanskrit documents, and in 1885 he wrote again about nirvāṇa. Reviewing F. G. Ayuso's *El Nirvāṇa buddhista en sus relaciones con otros sistemas filosóficos*, Foucaux condemned the Spanish scholar's failure to bring forth any new evidence for a negative interpretation of nirvāṇa. But on his own side, Foucaux himself restated arguments and conclusions almost a generation old.[1]

It is both striking and alarming that throughout the later 1800's Barthélemy Saint-Hilaire and Foucaux were able to adhere so closely to conclusions formed in mid-century. Striking because of the fact that so much new material was being made accessible through the research efforts of a growing number of qualified students. And it is alarming to observe respected scholars who took no serious notice of that new information, using it neither to modify nor to reinforce conclusions already drawn.

One of the most significant developments in Europe's study of Buddhism—and, it may be argued, one which has determined in great measure the course of that study until the present day—took place in the final third of the nineteenth century: the beginning of a systematic attempt to publish texts and translations of the entire Pali Buddhist Canon. During the first two generations of scientific Buddhist scholarship, Western Europe's attention had been focused on the Northern Buddhist traditions. In no small part this was due to the limitations of the resources which Hodgson had provided. Through Burnouf's efforts, however, those Northern materials had been sampled and one critical point had been

[1] F. G. Ayuso, *El Nirvāṇa buddhista en sus relaciones con otros sistemas filosóficos* (Madrid, 1885) as reviewed by Ph. Ed. Foucaux, "Un mémoire espagnol sur le Nirvāṇa bouddhique," pp. 321–33. Foucaux reiterates his arguments that the Buddha did not categorically deny the existence of the soul and that the meaning of nirvāṇa is a question of school definitions. His estimate of Ayuso's efforts is particularly low:

"Ayuso's memoir does not bring much illumination to the already much discussed question of Nirvāṇa. He leaves it almost where it was in the time of Eugène Burnouf—that is to say, some forty years ago. Written in Spanish, his study will have the advantage, however, of placing before those of his countrymen who read neither English nor German nor French a sketch of Buddhism which in Catholic Spain has scarcely any chance of making converts such as Buddhism has made in England, Germany, America, and even France." (P. 333.)

underscored: an investigation into the Pali Buddhist texts must precede any attempt to present a cogent and reliable study of Buddhist thought.

Now, it is difficult to imagine a tradition more alien to most nineteenth-century Europeans than the bewildering phantasmagoria of fancies, ideas, and doctrines constituting the Mahāyāna in its broadest sense. The Pali tradition, on the other hand, seemed to promise a more concise, older, and less fantastic presentation of Buddhism. Buddhist origins especially interested Europeans, and so, in the 1870's, after more than thirty years of dedicated effort on the part of the earliest Pali students, scholarly attention shifted emphatically to the Pali sources.

In particular, the attention to Pali sources was apparent in England. The work of Max Müller may be seen as an attempt to continue Burnouf's program in a modest way—at least with regard to the nirvāṇa question. Relying on one text from the Pali collection—the Dhammapada—Müller had tried to resolve the question of the original significance of the term. But shortly after the publication of his conclusions, embodied in the lecture *Buddhistischer Nihilismus* (1869), two Pali scholars attacked his thesis that the original Buddhist nirvāṇa doctrine had not postulated the annihilation of the individual.

The present chapter will be devoted to a study of the refutations of Müller's theory which were presented in the early 1870's by James D'Alwis and Robert Caesar Childers. Both men represent the beginnings of a distinct Pali era in European Buddhist studies. They may also be called the first important fieldwork students of Buddhism (in the company of Spence Hardy), for their knowledge was the product of many years of study and association with the living tradition of Buddhism in Ceylon. D'Alwis was "an eminent Ceylonese student of Buddhism," said Hermann Oldenberg; [2] and

[2] Hermann Oldenberg, *The Buddha: His Life, His Doctrine, His Order*, trans. William Hoey, p. 268. Repeated inquiries have failed to disclose sufficient biographical details for even a brief sketch. For me at this writing, D'Alwis *is* his critical volume.

Childers was a member of the Ceylon Civil Service and later professor of Pali and Buddhist Literature at University College, London.

James D'Alwis

Müller believed that he had solved the question of nirvāṇa through demonstrating the practical, anti-metaphysical character of earliest Buddhism. That assertion had been advanced cautiously by Burnouf, and Müller tried to provide the documentation necessary for its acceptance.[3] He insisted that the earlier portions of the Buddhist Canon do not define nirvāṇa as absolute annihilation. In 1871, James D'Alwis published his *Buddhist Nirvāṇa*, in which he strongly criticized those conclusions.[4] D'Alwis' concern was to demonstrate conclusively that the Pali Canon does indeed interpret nirvāṇa consistently as personal annihilation.

A long-time resident missionary and student in Ceylon, D'Alwis explains the events leading up to his *Buddhist Nirvāṇa* in the preface. Early in 1860's, he begins, there had been an animated public discussion in Ceylon about the meaning of the Buddhists' nirvāṇa. D'Alwis states that he studied the problem carefully at the time (though he did not enter the popular discussion of it) and concluded that Buddhist nirvāṇa signified absolute annihilation. This interpretation he found corroborated by Burnouf, Müller, and others.[5]

In March, 1870, D'Alwis received a copy of Müller's Dhammapada. Müller's earlier essays, "Buddhist Pilgrims"

[3] See above, Chapters II and III.

[4] James D'Alwis, *Buddhist Nirvāṇa: A Review of Max Müller's Dhammapada*. The preface is dated 10 June 1870 at Kossēmulla.

[5] *Ibid.*, p. v.

and "The Meaning of Nirvāṇa," had supported D'Alwis' views —or so he believed. In the new work, to D'Alwis' "great surprise", Müller "had reversed himself".

> The interest I felt in reading it, and the earnestness with which I examined the new doctrine, were not less than my previous surprise. Actuated, indeed, by the same honesty of purpose with which a distinguished Oriental Scholar has stated the change which his views had undergone by subsequent researches, I have gone into the entire question *de novo*, and the result is embodied in the following Review.[6]

Buddhist Nirvāṇa is more than a mere review of Müller's Dhammapada, however, for in it D'Alwis attempts to defend a nihilistic interpretation of nirvāṇa on the basis of the entire Pali Buddhist Canon, the Tripiṭaka (Pali: Tipiṭaka). D'Alwis lists five arguments which Müller had advanced in support of an affirmative interpretation and then presents a general refutation of each through an appeal to the Pali texts. Briefly stated, here, according to D'Alwis, are the five props of Müller's conclusions:

> It is inconceivable that one-half of mankind should have adopted Buddhism if its supreme good were actually absolute annihilation.
>
> Nihilistic statements about nirvāṇa occur only in the Abhidhamma portion of the canon—not in the other two collections, the Sutta and Vinaya.
>
> The Abhidhamma is no authority on matters of original Buddhist doctrine, because it is demonstrably more recent than both the Sutta and Vinaya Piṭakas.
>
> The Buddha saw his disciples, and taught and conversed with them after he had attained nirvāṇa; therefore, it would be absurd to insist that nirvāṇa is annihilation.
>
> Finally, the synonyms and epithets of nirvāṇa in the Dhammapada—as well as those in the other books of the Sutta and Vinaya—may be more reasonably construed in every case as signifying some sort of positive state rather than total extinction.[7]

On the contrary, D'Alwis writes, nirvāṇa is utter extinction. It *must* be utter extinction. Consider the Buddhist Canon, he

[6] *Ibid.*, p. vi.

[7] *Ibid.*, pp. vi–vii. Compare pp. 20–21.

goes on; it unequivocally declares that neither a supreme being nor an immortal soul exists. These two denials constitute "the foundation for the Buddhist doctrine of Nirvāṇa; and . . . therefore there could be no condition of the soul after the final 'destruction of the elements, and the germs of existence,' or Nirvāṇa." [8]

The central statement in D'Alwis' book, then, is that the possibility of a postmortem existence is denied by the Buddhists because of their rejection of both God and soul. Neither D'Alwis' thesis nor his personal reaction to the consequences is novel. He finds this conclusion every bit as repugnant as Barthélemy Saint-Hilaire and Müller had previously. The nirvāṇa doctrine of the Buddhists, says D'Alwis—apparently without humour—is "soul-harrowing." The Buddhists are artificial creatures, for their most important articles of belief are contrary to basic, natural human propensities.

Some Buddhists believe in a supreme creator god, D'Alwis acknowledges; but these are, after all, merely nominal Buddhists who know little if anything about genuine Buddhism as elucidated in the texts. By voicing a belief in the existence of a creator god, the pseudo-Buddhist merely demonstrates his communality with all men. He "gives utterance, from 'an ineradicable feeling of dependence on a Superior Being.' " But, D'Alwis continues,

> That . . . is not a Buddhistical notion. In the case of the Buddhist, as in that of any Atheist, it is not derived from instruction. It is not taught to him. It is implanted in the very soul of man. It is intuitively impressed on his mind. It is "the manifestation of God Himself, hidden in the depths of his conscience." The evidence, moreover, of design, which we everywhere perceive, produces the notion of an absolute Supreme Being; and that evidence is as much patent to the wild savage as it was to Socrates or Paley.
>
> Though the fool in his heart said—"There is no God,"—yet no one knows better than himself that it is a "lie"; for the self-same man in the transports of joy, in the anguish of his affliction or pain, or in the perils of danger or distress, vehemently, though

[8] *Ibid.*, p. vii. Compare p. 31.

intuitively, appeals to—call him by whatever name you please, Superhuman Being, or Almighty,—he appeals to—"God." The wild savage, who dances over the fire which he has kindled to cook the flesh of his fellow man, and the enlightened Buddhist who holds life as sacred, and does not drink a drop of water without purifying it of all animal life, are both conscious of—it may not be Almighty God, but—a first cause. And this peculiarity which, as remarked by the first writer under review, "serves to distinguish man from the beast," is also the characteristic of the Buddhist, like that of all other religionists, who, not having at their command the expressive words of the poet, exclaim, on a sudden emergency of fear or distress, by designating "The first cause," with a name, with which they are by no means unfamiliar, viz: God. Just as we are writing, the proceedings of a murder case at Kandy reveal that a Buddhist priest, in the agonies of death, invoked the help of "God." This then does not derive its authority from Buddhism as it is taught, or Buddha's personal teaching, but emanates from that spark of the creative power which lies buried within the very depth of our souls, and which bursts forth into a blaze under the influence of sudden joy or agonizing pain. The declaration, or the exclamation itself, must therefore be accepted as the spontaneous outburst from one's entire being, proving to our mind the near communion which ever exists between the Creator and his creatures.[9]

Müller (and several others) declares that if we are to suppose that one-half of mankind yearns for extinction, we must be prepared to admit that there are radical differences among men, differences which would invalidate all efforts to speak of man. "Not so exactly," D'Alwis counters,

We do not believe that naturally there is this "yearning" in a single human being. Even in the case of the Buddhist, and therefore of "half of mankind," the desire is not a natural one, nor does it arise from "a difference in kind between man and man," but it is the result of the cause laid down in his religion, the necessary consequence of "the danger," which Gotama's doctrine "of *Bhāva*," and of transmigration, unfolds. That "naturally" the mind is averse to, and therefore has a "horror" for, Nirvāṇa, we can easily understand. As there is in us an "ineradicable feeling" of the existence of one supreme absolute Being, so there is alike consciousness of man being possessed of a neverdying soul. It would

[9] *Ibid.*, pp. 13–15.

seem to be an impulse of that very principle implanted in man, and between which and the Creator there seems to be a mysterious communion. . . . At all events, it is a secret whispering of those "ministering spirits," of whom St. Paul speaks in his Epistle to the Hebrews (i, 14);—and we apprehend, it is that which renders the doctrine of the destruction of the soul a subject both distasteful to the mind, and difficult of comprehension. It therefore produces a yearning for existence, and gives a relish rather "to be" than "not to be." Buddha knew the fact, and he stated it thus.[10]

Both Müller and D'Alwis are repelled by what they believe is the patent nihilism of the Abhidhamma. Müller insists that this is not found in original Buddhism. The Abhidhamma, he declares, is the product of meddling, muddy-headed metaphysicians, neither part of the Buddha's message nor consonant with it. Such a conclusion is unacceptable to D'Alwis.

Granting that nihilism is a loathsome doctrine, D'Alwis nonetheless insists that the Buddha's understanding of human existence and its concomitant suffering, old age, and death made the notion of complete extinction the only possible goal—the only way out. Relying to a great extent (and somewhat uncritically) on the Sinhalese Buddhist tradition, D'Alwis maintains that the Tipiṭaka is an organic whole. The Abhidhamma portions are integral with the Sutta and Vinaya, he declares, going so far as to insist—without substantiation—that the entire canon had been committed to writing before Mahinda's mission to Ceylon.[11]

Burnouf, who had been Müller's authority for the general dating of the Abhidhamma, is severely criticized by D'Alwis. Drawing references from the historical text the *Dīpavaṃsa*, D'Alwis suggests that the schismatic Vajjians (the *Vṛjin* or *Vajjiputtaka* monks who may have been proto-Mahāyāna-ists and most certainly were participants in the *pudgala* heresy) were the only Buddhists to deny that the Abhidhamma was the "word of the Buddha" (*buddhavacanam*). Their tradition must have been Burnouf's authority. Asserting that the Tibetan Abhidharma is identical with the Pali version and that

[10] *Ibid.*, pp. 22–23.
[11] *Ibid.*, pp. 8–9. Compare p. 42.

the Tibetans consider that the Abhidharma is authentic, D'Alwis concludes that Burnouf had relied on non-orthodox testimony. "Or," he adds wryly, "the Abhidharma, to which Burnouf's authority refers, did not mean the third basket of the Canon. . . ." [12]

D'Alwis' declaration that the Buddhist Canon must not be fractured in a search for "original" Buddhism is a heroic one. At a time in the history of European scholarship when the search for origins had captivated so many investigators, he is a most solitary figure. His chief argument for the authenticity of nirvāṇa-as-nihilism in the Buddha's message is based on the traditions of the Southern Buddhist Community—a living tradition that he had observed at first hand. And, to be sure, he was not so uncritical as to maintain that the canon consisted solely in *buddhavacanam*.

> A close and critical examination of the works of Buddhism in Ceylon will enable such scholars as the writer before us to separate the "wheat" from the "chaff"; and if we are not mistaken, Buddhists themselves in this Island, for weighty reasons, have already rejected much of the fiction which has found its way into their religious and historical books. It is indeed possible, according to hints given by Buddha himself, to separate his genuine doctrines from the greater part, if not the whole, of what has been long accepted as "the logia.". . .
>
> The three Baskets do not contain entirely the words of Gotama. None of them are free from additions; and the discourses themselves shew that they are not without omissions. All the Legends, until we come to the words of Gotama, which are generally expressed in the first person, and with the designation of the party addressed, are chiefly in the language of the compilers.[13]

We may well consider these feeble criteria indeed for establishing the authentic word of the Buddha; but D'Alwis

[12] *Ibid.*, p. 45. In a footnote (p. 28) D'Alwis quotes Müller: " 'Burnouf adds that this doctrine [namely, nirvāṇa as annihilation] appears in its crude form in . . . [the] Abhidhamma, but not in the first and second parts . . . [namely, the] Sūtras . . . [and the] Ethics which together bear the name Dharma. . . .' " Then D'Alwis objects: "There is some error here; for dharma is the name for the Sūtra and Abhidharma, contradistinguished from the Vinaya." It is doubtful that D'Alwis had read Burnouf's *Introduction.*

[13] *Ibid.*, pp. 16–18.

is more intent on overcoming a further argument. If he is allowed the truth of his insistence that the Buddhist Canon should be evaluated as a whole, there still remains the question of its consistency. Müller declared that wherever nirvāṇa is described outside the Abhidhamma, we may well read it as some order of positive experience.

Any contradictions which Müller or other students believed to exist in the canon on the topic of nirvāṇa are purely imaginary, D'Alwis asserts. Throughout the Tipiṭaka, nirvāṇa clearly does mean extinction. Any scholar who is unsure of this point, he says, is merely unable to decipher the texts: he does not know either the Pali language or the Buddhist tradition well enough.

"The transition from the Sanskrit to the Pāli is, perhaps, easy," D'Alwis avows carefully. "Yet its study is beset with many difficulties." [14] In 1870, the principal handicap was the lack of a reliable Pali dictionary. "Beginners are apt to consult Sanskrit dictionaries to ascertain the sense of Pāli words." And this, he warns, is a doubtful recourse for at least four reasons: in many instances different meanings are assigned to the verbal roots in the two languages; Pali contains neologisms; Pali compounds often are to be analyzed differently from Sanskrit compounds; and extra-Sanskritic conventions apply in the general usage of many Pali vocables.

Most important for D'Alwis is the fourth point: that words found in Sanskrit and Pali

> have, owing to local circumstances, and the differences of religion, different significations. In order, therefore, critically to understand Pali religious terms, which are technical terms, it is essentially necessary that we should be intimately acquainted with Buddhism.[15]

In effect, D'Alwis accuses Müller of trying to solve the problems in Buddhism with Brahmanic answers. That is an impossible course, he declares, for the basic conceptions of the two are radically opposed.[16]

[14] *Ibid.*, p. 2.
[15] *Ibid.*, p. 3.
[16] *Ibid.*, p. 4.

In a manner which would have been most congenial to Burnouf, a scholar was pleading, almost unnoticed, for strict interpretive tenets as the indispensable condition to confronting an alien tradition. Other than his insistence that Buddhism borrowed extensively from the Brahmanic vocabulary and then fabricated its own technical vocabulary from those borrowed words, D'Alwis pays almost no attention to the evaluation of Buddhism as a revolt against Brahmanic ritualism, authority, and social stratification—themes which had captivated not only a number of his precursors but also many of his successors. Rather, he considers Buddhism as a specifically soteriological revolt and seeks to understand it as it understands itself.

Buddhism can be understood only through the texts. Textual interpretation depends on an understanding of Buddhism. But it is a spiral, not a circle, that D'Alwis is trying to sketch. The close interrelationship of idea and linguistic expression demands that the interpreter deal with both, that he refer conclusions about one aspect to the other for verification. The goal is an ascending degree of understanding of each. There is no Buddhist scholar who is not also a Pali scholar; equally, no Pali scholar who is not a Buddhist scholar.

According to D'Alwis, the words of the Pali Canon must be construed in their primary sense in most cases. There are two exceptions: when the context makes it clear that the writer intended another meaning, and when the words involved have a specific technical signification and are obviously being used conventionally in a technical context.[17] Admit that the Buddha consistently denied the existence of an eternal soul and a supreme creator god, D'Alwis says, and you must admit also that the Buddha's nirvāṇa is absolute annihilation. That is the context for any description or discussion of nirvāṇa, and that context makes it clear that the Buddha borrowed words and not meanings from the Brahmanic vocabulary.

[17] *Ibid.*, p. 30. Compare p. viii.

Perhaps his clarification of the significance of context is D'Alwis' greatest single contribution to Buddhist studies. He chastises Müller for disregarding context in the matter of the Dhammapada. The latter had assured his audience that the text was a distinct entity, perfectly comprehensible in itself. Quite the opposite, D'Alwis retorts, the Dhammapada is "a collection of scraps of poetry from the Tipiṭaka" and "can be misread by not understanding the context." [18]

To stress D'Alwis' insistence that scholars confront the entire canon as a consistent whole and leave the subject at that could be misleading, especially in light of his emphasis that the collections were assembled hierarchically. Moreover, he is convinced that this stratification within the canon helps explain any apparent contradiction between statements about nirvāṇa in the Abhidhamma and those in the Sutta and Vinaya.

It is worthy of notice, that the Abhidhamma contains a compilation of the abstruse doctrines of Buddha, delivered to men of learning, or, as the Comment says, to devas; and that the Sutta consists of his desultory ordinary sermons to the masses, or individuals of common capacity, or low standing, or limited learning.[19]

D'Alwis' estimate of the Buddha's purpose and techniques deserves complete quotation, for it further underlines the fact that he interprets the canonical harmony from an Abhidhammic tonic.

Buddha knew, as we have already shewn, that his doctrine of annihilation was distasteful generally to the masses. He knew, moreover, the difficulty which people generally experienced in mastering the subject. His sole object was therefore, it would seem, to inculcate on the minds of his hearers the danger of bhāva, and the means necessary to avert that danger; and—no matter what Nirvāṇa was, whether "a relative Not," or "a positive Nothing"—to depict in glowing terms the end, as the victory obtained over Desire, Sin, and Ignorance. We are therefore no more surprised to find that a Teacher, who, like Gotama, was so "practical" in all his dealings, failed to enter into an elaborate explanation of nihilism to the masses, than we are disappointed at

[18] *Ibid.*, p. 29.
[19] *Ibid.*, p. 33.

a Christian missionary preaching "Christ and the crucified," without entering into an explanation of the mystery of His holy incarnation.[20]

The examples from the Sutta and Vinaya collections which D'Alwis adduces in support of his contentions need not be listed here.[21] His summation, however, presents an interesting account of what he takes to be the salvation message common to all sections of the canon:

> Now, when "the germ of existence" has been "destroyed," "the oil of human passions," has been "fully exhausted"; when "no new fuel" has been added to "the fire of existence" which is mouldering in the hearth, and when the last crackling sparks of existence itself have been "blown out" or "extinguished," we have indeed yet to learn that Gotama had, or could have, any other conception of Nirvāṇa, but that of "Nothing" "the Nothing"—the "total extinction of being," or Nihilism.[22]

Almost as an afterthought, D'Alwis adds that the repulsive nirvāṇa-nihilism doctrine could not have been introduced so openly in the Abhidhamma if it did not have any basis in the actual teachings of the Buddha. The atmosphere in the Saṃgha would have prevented the introduction, let alone the acceptance, of a spurious six-volume collection, he writes.[23]

D'Alwis observes that the Buddha was quite aware of the difficulties attending the discussion of his doctrines: " 'They are profound, difficult, hard to be understood, etc. etc.' " Müller, having hit upon a statement in which the Buddha states that the "ideas of being and non-being do not admit of discussion," declared that he had found important additional proof that nirvāṇa could not mean the unqualified annihilation of being. (Müller did not persevere on this point. Hermann Oldenberg was the first carefully to examine the nature and significance of the Buddha's reticence. See below, Chapter VI.) Without doubt, D'Alwis casually responds, the doctrine

[20] *Ibid.*

[21] Transliterated texts and D'Alwis' translations are given, *ibid.*, pp. 33–39.

[22] *Ibid.*, pp. 40–41.

[23] *Ibid.*, p. 43.

of nirvāṇa is difficult, but this is due to the fact that it is next to impossible to say anything about nothing. "All that can be said of Nihilism must be in the positive language of Something, considered as the result of some cause." [24] Consequently, he warns, the translator must be on the watch for metaphorical and allegorical usages in the texts.

The words used in such description can therefore only be taken, according to explanation, either in a metaphorical sense, or as conveying the nature of the result of the extinction of being, considered with reference to the cause or danger of existence.[25]

And, too, D'Alwis insists, it is not nirvāṇa that is hard to comprehend, but rather the doctrine of nirvāṇa; for such a doctrine runs contrary to the natural inclinations of men. In fact, according to D'Alwis, herein lies one of the most significant failures in the Buddha's technique; because the

Master had laboured a proof of the doctrine for the benefit of the masses, who, like Dhammapāla, could not, against their natural instincts, divest themselves of the notion of a soul, nor understand what *abhāva* meant, nor comprehend how that "sansāra, the end of which is not known," could be demolished. The Doctrine of Gotama which declares Nirvāṇa to be nihilism, was therefore, doubtless, "profound"; and, we should say, owing to the adoption of already existing phraseology for its exposition in a different sense, he rendered that doctrine still more "difficult of comprehension." [26]

As the final substantiation for his dual claim that nirvāṇa is nothingness and that careful attention must be given to the usages and contexts in the Buddhist Canon, D'Alwis lists forty-five synonyms for nirvāṇa which are found in the *Abhidhānappadīpikā*.[27]

[24] *Ibid.*, p. 53.
[25] *Ibid.*, p. 54.
[26] *Ibid.*, p. 127.
[27] *Ibid.*, pp. 130–37. (Mogallana's *Abhidhānappadīpikā* was probably compiled in the twelfth century.) The terms may be listed here in the order D'Alwis presents them; including in parentheses the page and column in the *Pali Text Society's Pali-English Dictionary*, ed. T. W. Rhys Davids and W. Stede, where treatment of each will be found and, in fifteen instances, the reference in *A Critical Pāli Dic-*

It may be remarked that nearly all the words for *nibbāna* radically convey no quality or attribute of Nirvāṇa or Nothing; for "nothing has no inherent quality.". . . So, it would seem, we are to understand by Nirvāṇa,—not a condition of existence after

---

tionary, Vol. I, ed. V. Trenckner, Dines Anderson, Helmer Smith, and Hans Hendriksen. I have marked an asterisk beside those terms in dispute among the authorities cited.

1. *mokkha* (*PTSD:* p. 541b).
2. **nirodha* (*PTSD:* p. 371a).
3. **nibbāna* "from *ni–vā vagati* bandhanesu 'to go,' 'move,' 'bind,'—'non-moving,' 'motion arrested,' = 'the destruction of life's motion to and fro,' 'the demolition of sansāra,' 'annihilation,' 'nihilism.' In the Sanskrit it signifies 'liberation from existence,' 'gone out as fire.'—Wilson. Thence the Brāhmans apply it for 'eternal happiness, emancipation from matter, and reunion with the Deity.' Gogerly . . . traces nibbāna to *ni–vāna*, 'desire'; and defines it to be 'complete freedom from desire,' = 'complete cessation of existence.' The Siṇhalese word *nivāna* is used simply in the sense of 'blowing out' (as fire) exactly as in the passage, 'Nibbanti dhīrā yathāyam padīpo.'—'Such sensible persons are blown out like this lamp' = *Ratana Sutta;* or as in the passage, Pajjotass'eva nibbānan vimokkho asi chetaso, 'the mind expired like the extinction of a burning light.' —*Parinibbāna Sutta.*" (*PTSD:* pp. 362a–65a)
4. *dīpa* (*PTSD:* p. 323b).
5. *taṇhakkhaya* (*PTSD:* pp. 294a–95a, especially "B.2.c.").
6. **pāra* (*PTSD:* p. 454a).
7. *tāṇa* (*PTSD:* pp. 298b–99a).
8. *lena* (*PTSD:* pp. 586a).
9. *arūpa* (*PTSD:* pp. 78b and 574a–75a; *CPD:* p. 433a).
10. *santa* (*PTSD:* pp. 675b–676b).
11. *sachcha* [*sacca*] (*PTSD:* p. 668a).
12. *anālaya* (*PTSD:* p. 32b, and see p. 109b; *CPD:* p. 167a).
13. *asaṅkhata* [see no. 44 below] (*PTSD:* p. 664a; *CPD:* p. 491b).
14. **siva* (*PTSD:* p. 711b).
15. *amata* (*PTSD:* p. 73a; *CPD:* pp. 387b–88a).
16. *sududdasa* (*PTSD:* p. 714b).
17. **parāyaṇa* (*PTSD:* p. 421a).
18. **saraṇa* (*PTSD:* p. 697b).
19. *anītika* (*PTSD:* p. 33b; *CPD:* p. 178a).
20. **anāsava* (*PTSD:* p. 32a; *CPD:* pp. 168b–69a).
21. *dhuva* (*PTSD:* p. 342b).
22. *anidassana* (*PTSD:* p. 358a [for *nidassana*]; *CPD:* p. 173a).
23. *akata* (*PTSD:* pp. 181a–82a; *CPD:* p. 3a).
24. *apalokita* (*PTSD:* p. 52b; *CPD:* p. 280b).
25. **nipuṇa* (*PTSD:* p. 52b).
26. *ananta* (*PTSD:* p. 46b; *CPD:* p. 151a).

final death, but the result which it is said, the destruction of bhāva has upon a being liable to indefinite transmigration. It may farther be remarked that their allegorical sense is just the same as when St. Paul spoke of death, as being "rest"—rest, not with a view to what the soul may or may not after death enjoy in heaven, but—rest, with reference to the "labours," and the troubles of this very life.[28]

At this point, D'Alwis actually seems to run perilously close to saying what Müller said with regard to the epithets of nirvāṇa. It is here, however, that he elucidates an aspect of nirvāṇa which had escaped the notice of earlier scholars except Burnouf and Spence Hardy. Müller based part of his argument on the fact that the texts clearly state that the Buddha appeared to his disciples after having attained nirvāṇa. True and false, D'Alwis answers.

So that Buddha, after attaining all that was necessary to entitle him to the lot of Nirvāṇa, remained on earth till death, is indeed a fact. A misapprehension alone on this subject has created much of the difficulty in understanding the doctrine of Nirvāṇa; and that misapprehension results from the Buddhist doctrine of Nir-

---

27. *akkhara* (*PTSD:* p. 2b; *CPD:* p. 11b).
28. *dukkhakkhaya* (*PTSD:* pp. 324b–26b, especially p. 326a).
29. *avyāpajjha* (*PTSD:* 86a, 654a; *CPD:* p. 485ab).
30. *vivaṭṭa* (*PTSD:* pp. 594ab, 637a).
31. **khema* (*PTSD:* p. 239a).
32. *kevala* (*PTSD:* p. 226b).
33. *apavagga* (*PTSD:* p. 53a; *CPD:* p. 281a).
34. *virāga* (*PTSD:* p. 634a).
35. *paṇita* (*PTSD:* pp. 403b–4a).
36. *achchuta* [*accuta*] (*PTSD:* p. 8a, and see p. 270b; *CPD:* p. 34b).
37. **pada* (*PTSD:* p. 408ab).
38. *yogakkhema* (*PTSD:* pp. 558b–59a).
39. *para* (*PTSD:* 418b–19a).
40. *mutti* (*PTSD:* p. 537b).
41. *santi* (*PTSD:* p. 676b).
42. *visuddhi* (*PTSD:* p. 640b).
43. *vimutti* (*PTSD:* 632ab).
44. *asaṅkhatadhātu* (see above, no. 13).
45. *suddhi* (*PTSD:* p. 719a).
46. *nibbuti* (*PTSD:* p. 366a, and see above, no. 3).

[28] D'Alwis, p. 129.

vāṇa being different from every other religious notion of final happiness. The *summum bonum* of all religions is attained *after death*, because that result is a *positive* happiness; but the *relative* happiness of Buddhist Nirvāṇa is one which is acquired in this very life (Dhammapada, v. 89), before death, and not beyond the grave.[29]

If D'Alwis includes Christianity among "all religions," we may wonder whether he was such a distinguished missionary after all. But that need not detain us here. There are two, let us say, modes of nirvāṇa, D'Alwis continues, and Müller is oblivious to the distinction.

We need only remark that the Nirvāṇa which Gotama attained before death, and which, according to Buddhism, man must procure in this very life . . . is sav'upādisesa nibbāna, or "nirvāṇa with a remnant of the elements of existence." This lot is called Nirvāṇa, from there being no impediment from thence to the consummation of reality itself; and, as Müller says, it "means the extinction of many things—of selfishness, desire, and sin, *without going so far as the extinction of consciousness, and even existence.*" [30]

It should be noted also that this is not that stage of *dhyāna* to which Barthélemy Saint-Hilaire referred, although

It would also seem to be a condition in which "all wishes and desires are subdued; in which there is indifference to joy and pain, to good and evil; and a freedom from birth in the circle of existence"; and although all the causes which led to the last birth before the attainment of sav'upādisesa nibbāna have been destroyed by the achievement of this condition of existence; yet there is in it a "remnant," of Upādi. That remnant is Existence itself; and its final destruction by death constitutes, what is called, par excellence, the Nirvāṇa, or anupādisesa Nibbāna, or parinibbāna, or Nihilism.[31]

D'Alwis is thus among the first scholars to call attention to a distinction between *sopadhiśeṣanirvāṇa* (nirvāṇa accompanied by a remnant of *upadhi*) and *nir-(an-)upadhiśeṣanirvāṇa*

[29] *Ibid.*, p. 50.
[30] *Ibid.*, p. 52.
[31] *Ibid.*

(nirvāṇa without a remnant of *upadhi*).[32] And this distinction in its turn was shortly to become the subject of further controversy. (See below, Chapter VI.)

Three contributions in particular stand out in D'Alwis' presentation, and their importance is not limited to applications in the study of Buddhist traditions:

The insistence that the integrity of a given body of texts must not be violated by scholars in their attempts to discover a doctrine both primitive and consistent.

The demonstration that the study of an alien tradition in its own language(s) involves a constant need to refer to specific context—to the uses of words and terms in new, metaphorical, allegorical, or technical senses.[33]

The demand that a scholar, whatever his own convictions may be, not approach the study of ideas at variance with his own with a view toward redeeming or exculpating the other tradition.

It is doubtless true enough that the word "nirvāṇa," its synonyms and epithets, veiled more than D'Alwis could

[32] Spence Hardy, who went to Ceylon as a Wesleyan missionary in 1825, may have been the first European to comprehend this distinction. (It is not clear to what extent he may have been influenced by D'Alwis.) See Hardy, *The Legends and Theories of the Buddhists Compared with History and Science*, pp. 169–77. "Upádisésa signifies the five khandhas; and it is so called because only the five khandhas are left, without any attachment or desire. It is said to be sawupádisésa, as having the five khandhas. This is the state of the rahat, and is one view of Nirwána." (P. 173.) Hardy consistently held that nirvāṇa was extinction according to the Buddhists. See also his *Eastern Monachism* (London: Williams and Norgate, 1860), pp. 280–309; and *A Manual of Budhism* [*sic*] (2nd ed.; London: Williams and Norgate, 1880), pp. 409–14.

[33] D'Alwis disputes (pp. 55–61) the validity of examples which are cited by Müller from the Dhammapada in order to prove that nirvāṇa is not complete extinction. The discussion of the words *mata* and *amata* is representative. Müller defines the words, respectively, as "mortal" or "mortality" and "immortal" or "immortality." D'Alwis takes issue, saying that the words must be translated as "death" and "non-death," because the concept of immortality is perfectly distinct from that of non-death in the "Oriental Mind." D'Alwis devotes more than 30 pages (pp. 68–100) to a direct critique of Müller's translation of the Dhammapada. His recurring objection is that Müller is over-literal in his readings.

understand. And it is apparent that a good deal of his "pulpit rhetoric" handicaps his presentation, and suggests, in addition, that many of his conclusions were no less a priori than Müller's. Still, he offers methodological advice that is still serviceable. Despite the fact that he did not fully realize the nature and importance of the ties connecting Buddhism to its Indian origins, he exhibited a deeper understanding of its historical and ideological unity perhaps than Burnouf, Müller, or Barthélemy Saint-Hilaire—scholars who were more sensitive to the similarities between Buddhism and other Indian speculative enterprise. And, if one agrees with Rudolf Otto that "the task of comparative religion is not completed by the demonstration of similarities, its finer work then begins," [34] D'Alwis' efforts constitute a distinct advance in critical Buddhist studies.

Robert Caesar Childers: The Logical Goal of Buddhism

Robert Caesar Childers publicly discussed the meaning of nirvāṇa on three occasions. In *Trübner's Review* (July–October, 1870) he first advanced his opinion that nirvāṇa means utter annihilation.[35] The following year he presented a paper to the Royal Asiatic Society in which he repeated his conclusions and provided additional textual support.[36] And a full statement on nirvāṇa is found in his *A Dictionary of the Pali Language*.[37] His interpretation does not vary, and

[34] Rudolf Otto, *Mysticism East and West* (New York: Collier, 1960, 1962), p. 183.

[35] I have been unable to locate a complete copy.

[36] Robert Childers, "Notes on Dhammapada, with special reference to the question of nirvāṇa," pp. 219–30.

[37] Robert Childers, *A Dictionary of the Pali Language*, pp. 265a–74b.

the three publications may be treated as a single discussion.

That discussion is composed of two related subdiscussions: a vigorous attempt to demonstrate that nirvāṇa is extinction, and an explanation of the apparent discrepancy of the interpretation of nirvāṇa in the Pali Canon.

"Existence is suffering." This is the first of the four Ariyasaccāni, or Sublime truths, upon which the religion of Buddha is founded. But a creed which begins by saying that existence is suffering, must end by saying that release from existence is the highest good, and accordingly we find that annihilation is the goal of Buddhism, the supreme reward held out to the faithful observer of its precepts.[38]

In his communication to the Royal Asiatic Society, Childers stresses especially the following passage from the Dhammapada:

jighacchāparamā rogā, saṅkhārā paramā dukhā,
etam ñātvā yathābhūtam nibbānam paramam sukham/

"As hunger is worse than any disease, so existence is worse than any pain; to him who has realized this truth extinction is the greatest bliss." If any proof is wanted that the author of Dhammapada believed Nirvāṇa to be annihilation of being, it is surely here. When he says in the same breath that existence is the acme of suffering, and that Nirvāṇa is consequently the highest bliss, it follows logically and inevitably that Nirvāṇa must be the cessation of Existence.[39]

One could not possibly ignore Childers' emphasis in the above passages: "must," "logically," "inevitably," and so on. This sort of passionate intensity in the name of logic warrants a comment. It is obvious that Childers is not alone in this matter. His attitude is confirmed in the work of many other Buddhist scholars who zealously applied their own standards of consistency to the elucidation of Buddhist thought. This tendency reminds me of those boorish individuals by whom many of us are afflicted from time to time: the sentence completers, those abrupt and quick-tongued persons who are

[38] *Ibid.*, p. 265b. Compare Childers, "Notes," p. 220.
[39] "Notes," p. 219.

ever impatient with the tempo of meditative discourse. Something of that smugly confident attitude is to be seen in the confrontation between Europeans and Pali Buddhism.

Western Europeans, impressed from the outset by what they took to be a congenial rationalism in early Buddhism, were confident that their own canons of reason and logic (not always securely held or consistently employed) could be applied to the Pali texts without any modifications. "It is the scale that makes the phenomenon." [40] Measured by Barthélemy Saint-Hilaire, D'Alwis, and Childers, nirvāṇa is annihilation. It is annihilation because it must be. "It is certain, however," E. J. Thomas remarks wisely,

> that this is a conclusion which the Buddhists never drew. . . . It is not really to the point to say that the Buddhist premises tended to this conclusion. The only real question is what conclusion did the Buddhists draw and what for them was the logical inference.[41]

Thomas, in fact, singles out both D'Alwis and Childers as "investigators who would commit the Buddhists, in spite of all their efforts, to a one-sided dogmatism, and make them assert not what they themselves inferred, but what others thought they should do." [42] The point is not whether one subscribes to the particulars of Thomas's own interpretation of nirvāṇa, but rather to realize the ways in which rigid and naïve hermeneutical procedures may distort the phenomena they purport to interpret.

To return to Childers's arguments, then, it is clear that his own idea of the logic and coherence of Buddhism as a system is the key to understanding his conception of the Buddhist nirvāṇa. Barthélemy Saint-Hilaire had insisted that the goal of Buddhism could not be the same as the goal of the Hindus. Childers says almost the same thing:

[40] Henri Poincaré as quoted by Mircea Eliade, *Patterns in Comparative Religion*, trans. Rosemary Sheed (New York: Sheed and Ward, 1958), p. xi.

[41] Thomas, *The History of Buddhist Thought*, p. 128.

[42] *Ibid.*, p. 129.

There is probably no doctrine more distinctive of Çākyamuni's original teaching than that of the annihilation of being. To suppose that the Buddhist Nirvāṇa is the blissful repose of Hinduism is to suppose that Çākyamuni on a leading question of religious philosophy, that of a Future State doctrine, would content himself with borrowing from the creed which it was his mission to subvert. In point of fact we find that while he adopted many of the technical terms of Hinduism he almost always gave them a widely different or at least greatly modified meaning. . . .[43]

Certainly the essential content of Childers's interpretation of nirvāṇa is clear at this point, and I shall not re-present the textual materials with which he documents his case (Childers's scholarship has a definite courtroom flavor about it). Before I pass to a consideration of the second part of his discussion, however, it will be interesting to notice the manner in which he disposes of the suggestion that nirvāṇa is some sort of paradise.

An ordinary Buddhist if questioned by a European as to the reward of a virtuous life will generally answer by depicting the sensuous joys of the Kāmavacaradevaloka which is the reward he immediately looks to; the questioner then is apt to come hastily to the conclusion that this blissful state is the famous Buddhist Nirvāṇa, and proclaim to the world that the modern view of Nirvāṇa makes it a sort of paradise of sensual delights. In some Buddhist countries the doctrine of Nirvāṇa appears to have participated in the general degradation that the whole religion has undergone in those countries, and which has produced such monstrosities as the Adi Buddha, the Dhyani Buddha, the worship of Amitabha and Avalokiteçvara, the doctrine of the perdition of women, and many other fantastic modern innovations.[44]

Such a dismissal of the Mahāyāna and the accompanying though implicit glorification of the austere purity and genuineness of the Pali tradition seriously handicapped efforts to realize Burnouf's goals. The French scholar had died before he could explore the Pali Canon and compare it with the Sanskrit and Tibetan sources. Ironically, Pali scholarship, which was to have cleared away the remaining obstacle to

[43] Childers, *Dictionary*, p. 267a.
[44] *Ibid.*, p. 268ab.

the completion of Burnouf's program, actually presented an even more formidable barrier: the attitude that real Buddhism exists only in the Pali tradition.

The second point with which Childers deals in his discussion of nirvāṇa is the apparent contradiction among various descriptions in the Pali Canon. In some places it seems obvious that nirvāṇa is complete annihilation, the absolute extinction of existence no matter how attenuated. But in other passages it would seem that nirvāṇa is rather some type of blissful, passionless state which does not entail the complete annihilation of the individual. According to Childers, the fact that a nirvāṇa controversy existed in Western Europe was to be explained in terms of the two types of descriptions of nirvāṇa supported by the texts. "According to the relative importance attached by them to these expressions scholars have variously held Nirvāṇa to be a state of blissful immunity from human passion, or the total extinction of being." [45]

Müller, in the *Buddhistischer Nihilismus*, explained "the apparent coexistence of two irreconcilable doctrines of Nirvāṇa" in terms of historical stratification in the texts. Childers rejected this explanation for the same reason D'Alwis had. The "fatal objection" to Müller's theory, according to Childers, is "that the doctrine of the Abhidhamma is identical with that of the other two Pitakas, and that the expressions relative to Nirvāṇa used in the Abhidhamma, are in reality taken from or authorised by the Vinaya and Sūtra Pitakas." [46]

Childers cuts through the problem by declaring that both types of nirvāṇa descriptions refer to one and the same phenomenon. The descriptives refer to different aspects or moments of a single, ultimate experience, he writes. The question and the controversy dissolve. Nirvāṇa is not either peace and sanctified passionlessness or absolute annihilation in an exclusive disjunction. Rather, it is *both* bliss and annihilation successively. "The word Nirvāṇa is used to designate two different things, the state of blissful sanctification called

[45] *Ibid.*, p. 265b.
[46] *Ibid.*

Arhatship, and the annihilation of existence in which Arhatship ends." [47]

At one point, Childers acknowledges that Müller's 1869 lecture was "the first attempt to grapple seriously with the difficulties of the question," although he quickly adds that Müller's conclusions cannot be accepted.[48] Childers' own solution was first presented in 1870, and he declares that D'Alwis' writings corroborate it. Spence Hardy, however, is singled out as the first to solve the so-called problem of the two nirvāṇas. According to Childers, Hardy's *Manual of Buddhism* (1866) "clearly gives the true solution to the question of Nirvāṇa." [49] The only complaint Childers registers about the work of D'Alwis and Hardy is that both of them "dismissed this part of the question in a few lines, apparently quite unaware of its extreme importance."

Common to both D'Alwis and Childers is the insistence that nirvāṇa is attainable in this life. According to them, the understanding of this fact resolves any so-called contradictions in the texts. Certain men can shatter the bonds of *saṃsāra* during their earthly life by means of discipline—mental and physical. Once arrived at this state of passionless sanctification, they are not subject to temptations of mind or flesh. By definition, they cannot backslide. On the other hand, neither do they disappear immediately; rather, they live out their normal life span. With death, the aggregate which was their earthly identity fractures, and they are completely annihilated.

Childers lists five reasons in support of his claim that *arahatta* (arhatship) is called nirvāṇa.

"The ideas of Arhatship and of the annihilation of being are inextricably bound up together, there being no annihilation without Arhatship, and no Arhatship that does not end in annihilation. . . ." [50]

"Both Nirvāṇas involve the idea of annihilation. . . ."

"In a great number of instances the use of the word Nirvāṇa

[47] *Ibid.*, p. 266b.
[48] *Ibid.*, p. 265b.
[49] *Ibid.*, p. 274ab.
[50] *Ibid.*, pp. 267b–68a for these five points.

involves the designation of both Arhatship and annihilation."

"When we consider how slender is the tie that binds the Arhat to existence we can understand how easily the word Nirvāṇa might be extended to include Arhatship."

"To say that an Arhat has attained Nirvāṇa is merely to say that he has made sure of Nirvāṇa. . . ."

Now, Childers insists that the terms *savupādisesanibbāna* and *anupādisesanibbāna* refer, respectively, to arahatta and to the final nirvāṇa. *Upādi*, according to him, designates the *khandha*-s (Sanskrit: *skandha*-s), the five compounds of elements thought by Buddhists to make up any sentient existence. Childers' analysis of these compounds describing nirvāṇa is, then, "the nirvāṇa accompanied by a remnant, namely the five constituent element-compounds of any particular existence" and "the nirvāṇa unaccompanied by that remnant."

"From another point of view," Childers adds, "the two Nirvāṇas are distinguished as *kilesanibbānam* or *kilesaparinibbānam*, 'the extinction of human passion,' and *khandhanibbānam* or *khandhaparinibbānam*, 'the extinction of being.' "[51]

In his summary statement, Childers indicates that he believes there is a certain amount of doctrinal development apparent in the Pali Canon, but that such development merely involves extension and clarification which is in perfect accord with the original meaning of nirvāṇa.

The term Nirvāṇa . . . was originally limited to the extinction of being, but by the operation of causes like those . . . enumerated came to be extended so as to include Arhatship, and the terms *savupādisesanibbānam* and *anupādisesanibbānam* were afterwards coined to distinguish the two Nirvāṇas when logical pre-

[51] *Ibid.*, p. 267b. At p. 268a, Childers criticizes the view that the words *nibbāna*, *parinibbāna*, and *mahāparinibbāna* signify three degrees of nirvāṇa. *Parinibbāna*, he says, "means merely Nirvāṇa, or the attainment of Nirvāṇa, and *mahāparinibbāna* means nothing more than the death of Buddha." In his article on *parinibbāna* (*ibid.*, p. 344a), however, he states that the term *parinibbāna* "is used only of the attainment of *Khandhanibbāna* or the annihilation of being." On this problem, see Thomas, p. 121, footnote; and Thomas, "Nirvāṇa and Parinirvāṇa," *India Antiqua*, pp. 294–95.

cision was required, or where the context did not clearly determine which Nirvāṇa was meant.[52]

I shall have occasion (Chapter VI, below) to analyze the complicated problem of the meaning of *upādi*, for Hermann Oldenberg challenged Childers's interpretation and thereby demonstrated that the meaning of nirvāṇa was far from being satisfactorily resolved. But if Childers did not, as he had hoped, provide a definitive answer to the questions about nirvāṇa, he did hammer home one view of considerable importance for the future study of non-Western traditions.

Although expressions like "extinction is bliss" may sound strange or even ridiculous to us, who have from our earliest infancy been taught that bliss consists in eternal life, to a Buddhist, who has always been taught that existence is an evil, they appear perfectly natural and familiar: *this is a mere question of education and association;* the words "extinction is bliss" convey to the mind of a Buddhist the same feeling of enthusiastic longing, the same consciousness of sublime truth, that the words "eternal life is bliss" convey to the Christian. [My italics.] [53]

That relativist and environmentalist view is a far cry from Müller's insistence on the psychological impossibility involved in postulating a type of man who could ardently wish for his own annihilation. Even D'Alwis declared that the human mind was naturally averse to extinction. But after years of living among practicing Buddhists, D'Alwis was convinced that such a doctrine was a living actuality in Buddhism.[54] Childers seems to have been the first European Buddhist scholar to ignore any consideration of innate ideas common to all humans. As such, he represents the first flowering of European positivism within Buddhist studies.

[52] Childers, *Dictionary*, p. 268a.
[53] *Ibid.*, p. 273b.
[54] See above, pp. 133–35.

[CHAPTER V]

Interlude: Schopenhauer, Wagner, and Nietzsche on Nirvāṇa

Some men never heard of the Asiatick writings, and others will not be convinced that there is anything valuable in them. . . . We all love to excuse, or to conceal, our ignorance, and are seldom willing to allow any excellence beyond the limits of our own attainments: like the savages, who thought that the sun rose and set for them alone, and could not imagine that the waves, which surrounded their island, left coral and pearls upon any other shore.[1]

Sir William Jones published that observation in 1771. It seems—sadly—still applicable. Through the closing decades of the eighteenth century and the beginning of the nineteenth, however, the co-workers and heirs of Jones's own enterprises gathered coral and pearls from many other shores. And, by the early 1800's, it was increasingly true that insularity in European intellectual life existed rather more because of the

[1] Sir William Jones, *Grammar of the Persian Language*, as cited in Arberry, p. 79.

native recalcitrance of the "learned savages" than because of a paucity of materials. *La Renaissance orientale* had begun.

While my study is primarily concerned with the efforts and accomplishments of several successive generations of scholars of Buddhism, it will not be out of place at this point to glance at a dimension of their influence beyond their effects on one another. In few respects may the specialist be divorced from the broader and deeper context of his social and intellectual environments. And no study such as this one could pretend to any sort of balance if it ignored entirely the extent to which discoveries and interpretation by specialists penetrated the milieu of the non-specialist as well as the nature of appropriations and syntheses which took place.

Now, limited space prohibits any attempt at a detailed account of non-specialists' estimates of the Buddhist nirvāṇa. Still, in this chapter I shall make an effort to illustrate some attitudes and potencies. This will be done through cursory exposition of selected aspects of the work of three famous and creative non-specialists: Arthur Schopenhauer, Richard Wagner, and Friedrich Nietzsche. Instead of offering a full treatment of the life and works of each, I shall speak to some specific questions and offer observations. On the one hand, these remarks may supplement other and more complete critical studies after the manner of footnotes or anecdotes; and, on the other hand, they may help delimit parameters which evaluative studies of alien cultural influences on creative achievements must acknowledge.

Arthur Schopenhauer

Probably no nineteenth-century European notable has been linked more closely or more frequently with Indian thought than Arthur Schopenhauer (1788–1860). Neither he nor India has benefited unequivocally from such popular association—Schopenhauer the pessimist; Schopenhauer the irrationalist; Schopenhauer the *vedāntī;* Schopenhauer the crypto-Buddhist. The more tolerant of his critics excuse him as a symptom of his era. Will Durant, for example, exhibiting a penchant for catchy, often vacuous statements, writes:

> As the decay of Greece brought the pallor of Stoicism and the hectic flush of Epicureanism upon the cheeks of Hellas, so the chaos of the Napoleonic wars brought into the soul of Europe that plaintive weariness which made Schopenhauer its philosophic voice. Europe had a terrible headache in 1815.[2]

About Schopenhauer's open admiration for Indian thought, there cannot be the slightest doubt. In the preface to *Die Welt als Wille und Vorstellung*, he declares that his treatise presupposes on the part of the reader only a complete knowledge of Kant's philosophy. If, in addition, the reader is familiar with Plato's writings, so much the better.

> But if he has shared in the benefits of the *Vedas*, access to which, opened to us by the *Upanishads*, is in my view the greatest advantage which this still young century has to show over previous centuries, since I surmise that the influence of Sanskrit literature will penetrate no less deeply than did the revival of Greek literature in the fifteenth century; if, I say, the reader has also already received and assimilated the divine inspiration of ancient Indian wisdom, then he is best of all prepared to hear what I have to say to him. It will not speak to him, as to many others, in a strange and even hostile tongue; for, did it not sound too conceited, I might assert that each of the individual and disconnected utterances that make up the *Upanishads* could be derived as a consequence from the thought I am to impart, although conversely my thought is by no means to be found in the *Upanishads*.[3]

[2] Will Durant, *The Story of Philosophy* (New York: Pocket Books, 1954), pp. 343–44. Durant made the comment in 1924.

[3] Arthur Schopenhauer, *The World as Will and Representation*, trans. E. F. J. Payne (2 vols.; Indian Hills, Colorado: Falcon's Wing Press, 1958), I, xxiii–xxiv. I cite from Payne's excellent translation throughout.

That important and often cited statement appeared in the first edition of *Die Welt* in 1818. Buddhism is not mentioned. This is not to say that Schopenhauer had no acquaintance with Buddhism at that time; but one should remember that neither Colebrooke nor Hodgson had yet presented their papers to Europe. Their researches were to find an attentive audience in Schopenhauer, and it is of some importance to outline his own "discovery" of India.

In 1807, two years after his father's death, Schopenhauer abandoned the beginnings of a promising commercial career and turned to classical Greek and Latin studies at Gotha. He was shortly embroiled in controversy, and, following a quarrel with one of his tutors, he transferred from Gotha to Weimar, remaining there until 1809. Attaining his inheritance (and a consequent financial independence which was to be his—except for one brief crisis—for the rest of his life), Schopenhauer left Weimar for the University of Göttingen. There he entered courses in medicine, but was soon introduced to the philosophy of Kant and Plato, who were unquestionably the preeminent influences on the formation of his own philosophy. And it was in order to hear the lectures of Fichte, presumably the most prestigious Kantian of the time, that Schopenhauer left Göttingen in 1811 and moved to the University of Berlin.

Fichte and Friedrich Schleiermacher, two outstanding figures in Berlin, impressed Schopenhauer only negatively.[4] By 1813 he had had his fill of Fichte, Schleiermacher, and the surging Prussian nationalism which had been kindled by the defeat of Napoleon. Leaving Berlin, he took refuge in Rudolstaadt, where he completed his dissertation. This he submitted to Jena (rather than to Berlin) and, after its

4 " 'Pompous, obscurantist, and long-winded,' " Schopenhauer is reported to have written of Fichte in his notebook. And he took violent exception to Schleiermacher's view that philosophy must be grounded in religious faith. See Patrick Gardiner, *Schopenhauer* (Harmondsworth, Middlesex: Penguin Books, 1963), p. 14. For biographical information and several insights into Schopenhauer's thought, I am indebted to this fine critical study. Also see R. K. Das Gupta's interesting "Schopenhauer and Indian Thought," pp. 32–40.

acceptance, financed its publication from his own resources.

Bolstered by that accomplishment—and, one suspects, in search of praise which he felt was due him—Schopenhauer returned to Weimar and his mother's intellectual circle late in 1813.[5] Apparently, Goethe commented favorably on his book, but for some reason Schopenhauer was restless. In 1814 he stormed forth to Dresden, where for the next four years he indulged himself as a *bon vivant* and wrote *Die Welt.* Few works give more oblique indication of the nature and extent of divertissements enjoyed by their authors than this tract.

During those final months at Weimar, in 1813–14, Schopenhauer was introduced directly to Indian antiquity. And Friedrich Maier was the individual whom he credited for this revelation and who directed him to read Anquetil du Perron's Latin translation of fifteen Upaniṣads.[6]

Maier (1772–1818) was a significant contributer to the formative period of so-called German romanticism, though literary historians scarcely notice him. Perhaps more than any other individual in the final decade of the eighteenth century and in the early years of the nineteenth, he was responsible for the introduction and acceptance into German intellectual circles of the results of the earliest phase of Sanskrit scholarship. A place must be reserved for him as

[5] Gardiner, pp. 14–15.

[6] There is no information available to me concerning Schopenhauer's contacts with Maier before that fateful reading assignment. We may presume some interchanges earlier, perhaps during Schopenhauer's first Weimar period, 1807–9. And his association with Goethe and Schlegel—both of whom knew Maier well—further supports the assumption that he knew something about India before reading the Upaniṣads. On Schopenhauer's first encounter with Indian thought, consult R. K. Das Gupta, "Schopenhauer and Indian Thought," pp. 35–36.

The history of this translation is an interesting vignette in itself. Du Perron translated—first into French and then into Latin—from the Persian rendering of fifteen Upaniṣads which had been completed in 1657 by Dara Shukoh, the mystical-eclectic son of the Mughal Emperor Shāh Jahān. See S. M. Ikram, *Muslim Civilization in India*, ed. Ainslee T. Embree (New York: Columbia University Press, 1964), pp. 187–88; and Schwab, *La Renaissance orientale*, p. 58 *et passim.*

one of the founders of serious Indic studies in Germany. Not a Sanskritist, Maier is important rather because of his consuming interest in the mythology of nations and his knowledge of English.

Much of the pioneering work of the first English Indologists —men such as Jones and Wilkins—was made accessible to Continental, particularly German, readers by way of retranslations. Maier, a committed student of mythology, avidly read the materials presented by the English and the members of the Bengal Society during the late 1780's and 1790's. In 1791, Forster had set a pattern by translating Jones's English rendering of the *Śakuntalam* into German. (The impact of that retranslation on Herder and Goethe is common knowledge.) Maier followed Forster's precedent, and in 1802 published two retranslations of his own: the complete *Bhagavadgītā* and the *Gītagovinda.*[7] Through those versions, his own essays on classical Indian mythology and poetry, and his sincere enthusiasm for the full range of discoveries made by Jones and others, Maier touched not only Schopenhauer, but Goethe, Schiller, Novalis, Schelling, Schlegel, and Schleiermacher as well.[8]

Picking apart the philosophy of any thinker and then offering forth fragments as if they were kernels is a precarious undertaking. But, mindful of the pitfalls which may attend such enterprises, I must make some generalities about Schopenhauer's system in order to pursue the inquiry concerning the influences of Indian thought. Above all, it will be necessary to stress the importance of Kant's influence on Schopenhauer. Put another way, I can well imagine Schopenhauer's work without Indian content (or examples), but there is no Schopenhauer without Kant.

What can I know? What ought I to do? What may I hope? —Kant's enunciation of the entire interest of reason. A measure of the importance Schopenhauer attached to those

[7] On Maier's life and works, see Schwab, pp. 64–65, 220–24 *et passim;* and Windisch, *Geschichte*, pp. 56, 204.

[8] Schwab, pp. 59, 64–65 *et passim.*

questions is patent in his insistence that his own system was both metaphysics and ethics, neither of which, he declared, could be separated. For the most part, Schopenhauer preserved Kant's delineation of phenomenal and noumenal realms. And he agreed with Kant's declarations concerning the determining character of the categories of space and time for personal sensibility, for the possibility of perceiving and conceiving.

It is the psychological introspection, Schopenhauer's dead reckoning on the subject of the will, that distinguishes his contributions and sustains the integrity of his theories. Important in Schopenhauer's conception are Kant's notions about moral intuition—the sui generis capacity in men for the discrimination of good and evil in general. According to the Kantian idea, the will is a something unconstrained in its freedom by the mechanisms of necessity imposed on phenomena. As something free, the will in Kantian or Schopenhauerian terms is a thing in itself. Any acts of that will, however, are phenomena.

Schopenhauer proceeds much further than his master. He asserts that all phenomena—all that is space- and time-conditioned—are in fact the objectifications or the acts of will. And, according to Schopenhauer, the will is not merely *a* thing in itself: it is *the* thing in itself, *advaita*. Schopenhauer's statements about the processes involved in apprehending the will are not consistent, for there is a vacillation between intuition, in which the phenomenon (the act) somehow perceives the unmanifest, noumenal thing in itself by means of mystical procedures, and inference, through which the nature and dimensions of the unmanifest are deduced from the patterns in the manifest particulars.[9]

[9] Gardiner's comments, pp. 302–3, are pertinent: "Since he had accepted in its essentials the Kantian doctrine that all objective experience must be ordered and structured in a particular manner, incorporating this within his own theory of the 'world as idea,' it appeared to him that what he had to say must in some manner pertain to what lay beneath the veil of appearances—in other words, that it must concern the realm of the 'thing-in-itself.' But he had already treated the 'delusive' *principium individuationis* as providing the neces-

It has been reported that one of the many things that irritated Johanna Schopenhauer about the behavior of her son was his "morbid tendency to brood over the misery of things." [10] Schopenhauer himself later insisted that the twin realizations of transitoriness and the inevitability of death were the prime sponsors of those questions which a man may address to the world—its nature and his place in it. Suffering and misery in life were, in short, the occasions for metaphysical and ethical inquiry. From this point on, the analogies between Schopenhauer's philosophy and the Indian, particularly the Buddhist, speculations are striking.

In its constant ethical and soteriological drive, Schopenhauer's presentation is in absolute accord with the Buddhist outlook.

> The person is mere phenomenon, and its difference from other individuals, and exemption from the sufferings they bear, rest merely on the form of the phenomenon. . . . According to the true nature of things, everyone has all the sufferings of the world as his own; indeed, he has to look upon all merely possible sufferings as actual for him, so long as he is the firm and constant will-to-live, in other words, affirms life with all his strength.[11]

What is needed, according to Schopenhauer, is an awakening. Man suffers "so long as his eyes are not opened by a better knowledge." Awake, then,

---

sary conditions, not merely of all knowledge as ordinarily conceived, but of thought and communication as well; our concepts represent or 'reflect' what is originally given in phenomenal experience, and are wholly derivable from this. Hence (I think) the indeterminacy which surrounds his notion of the 'mystical,' and the confusing expansion and contraction of the limits bounding the domain of possible experience, which are so recurrent and disconcerting a feature of his system. Hence, too, the difficult passages concerning the transcendence of individuality and liberation from the restrictive conditions of everyday cognition stated to occur in certain forms of consciousness, and the extreme importance accorded to 'genius' and to simple direct vision as contrasted with the pedestrian practically-oriented understanding afforded by the procedures of common sense and science."

[10] *Ibid.*, p. 12.

[11] Schopenhauer, I, 353.

The tormented person would see that all the wickedness that is or ever was perpetrated in the world proceeds from that will which constitutes also *his* own inner being, and appears also in *him*. He would see that, through this phenomenon and its affirmation, he has taken upon himself all the sufferings resulting from such a will, and rightly endures them so long as he is this will.[12]

Thus there is suffering, and thus also suffering is to be accounted just. Schopenhauer declares that "vivid knowledge of eternal justice . . . demands the complete elevation above individuality."[13] A specific program for attaining such an elevation is not forthcoming. Instead, Schopenhauer insists that this insight is not accessible to the majority of men. Then he relates the way in which India described and communicated parallel realizations about the nature of being, existence, and suffering. Direct expression of the truth about "Being" was limited by the Indians to the Vedas (Schopenhauer is thinking strictly of the Upaniṣads), access to which was limited to *dvija*-s ("initiates"). Even there, he avers, expression was direct only "insofar as concept and language comprehend it, and insofar as their method of presentation, always pictorial and even rhapsodical, allows it."[14] The quintessential statement: *tattvamasi* ("you are 'that' ").

The popular presentation of this insight, according to Schopenhauer, was a translation into myth,

A substitute for it which was sufficient as a guide to conduct through figurative description in the method of knowledge according to the principle of sufficient reason. . . . This is the object of all religious teachings, since these are all the mythical garments of the truth which is inaccessible to the crude human intellect. . . . It has the great advantage of containing absolutely no elements but those which lie before our eyes in the realm of reality, and thus of being able to support all its concepts with perceptions. What is here meant is the myth of the transmigration of souls. This teaches that all sufferings inflicted in life by man

[12] *Ibid.*, p. 354.
[13] *Ibid.*, p. 355.
[14] *Ibid.*

on other beings must be expiated in a following life in this world by precisely the same sufferings.[15]

Not only does the myth explain punishment; it also explains reward. Most important, however, is the fact that "the highest reward . . . can be expressed by the myth only negatively in the language of this world, namely by the promise, so often recurring, of not being born any more. . . ." [16] It is here that Schopenhauer first directly acknowledges Buddhism and the Buddhist nirvāṇa.

The Buddhists, admitting neither Vedas nor castes, express it: "You shall attain to Nirvāṇa, in other words, to a state in which there are not four things, namely, birth, old age, disease, and death." [17]

From the perception of justice, however framed, proceeds a concomitant impulse to virtue. And virtue is action in accordance with an understanding of noumenal oneness in the face of phenomenal plurality. It consists of action which is just, "the intention not to go so far in the affirmation of one's own will as to deny the phenomena of will in others by compelling them to serve one's own will." [18]

In virtue and justice there is yet an affirmation of the will to live. The final, highest stage is achieved in "the transition from virtue to asceticism." Eventually, the virtuous person finds that

It is no longer enough for him to love others like himself, and to do as much for them as for himself, but there arises in him a strong aversion to the inner nature whose expression is his own phenomenon, to the will-to-live, the kernel and essence of that world recognised as full of misery. He therefore renounces precisely this inner nature, which appears in him and is expressed

[15] *Ibid.*, pp. 355–56. It would be interesting to contrast in detail the attitudes towards myth held by Schopenhauer and Max Müller.

[16] *Ibid.*, p. 356.

[17] *Ibid.*

[18] *Ibid.*, p. 370.

by his body, and his action gives the lie to his phenomenon, and appears in open contradiction thereto.[19]

Man, the phenomenon, not only can know the will, the thing in itself, he can deny it. Difficulties multiply exponentially. The will can be renounced, thwarted, emasculated. Yet, how the will, through its phenomena (its ideas or representations), can will its own extinction is obscure. And the obscurity is not lost to Schopenhauer. He confesses the difficulty which philosophy encounters at his juncture, but he steadfastly insists that he has not merely constructed some fable (or does he mean "myth"?).

What I have described here with feeble tongue, and only in general terms, is not some philosophical fable, invented by myself and only of today. No, it was the enviable life of so many saints and great souls among the Christians, and even more among the Hindus and Buddhists. . . . Different as were the dogmas that were impressed on their faculty of reason, the inner, direct and intuitive knowledge from which alone all virtue and holiness can come is nevertheless expressed precisely in the same way in the conduct of life. For here also is seen the great distinction between intuitive and abstract knowledge, a distinction of such importance and of general application in the whole of our discussion, and one which hitherto has received too little notice. Between the two is a wide gulf; and, in regard to knowledge of the inner nature of the world, this gulf can be crossed only by philosophy. Intuitively or *in concreto*, every man is really conscious of all philosophical truths; but to bring them into his abstract knowledge, into reflection, is the business of the philosopher, who neither ought nor can do more than this.[20]

There is a definite terminus to strictly philosophical activity; and it is here, at the point of the free denial of the will. It is not for philosophy to prescribe a recipe for the denial. Nor can it describe what comes after. Only the incommunicable insight of the mystic remains.

If, however, it should be absolutely insisted on that somehow a positive knowledge is to be acquired of what philosophy can express only negatively as denial of the will, nothing would be left

[19] *Ibid.*, p. 380.
[20] *Ibid.*, p. 383.

but to refer to that state which is experienced by all who have attained to complete denial of the will, and which is denoted by the names ecstasy, rapture, illumination, union with god and so on. But such a state cannot really be called knowledge, since it no longer has the form of subject and object; moreover, it is accessible only to one's own experience that cannot be further communicated.

We, however, who consistently occupy the standpoint of philosophy, must be satisfied here with negative knowledge, content to have reached the final landmark of the positive. If, therefore, we have recognized the inner nature of the world as will, and have seen in all its phenomena only the objectivity of the will, and if we have followed these from the unconscious impulse of obscure forces up to the most conscious action of man, we shall by no means evade the consequence that, with the free denial, the surrender of the will, all those phenomena are also now abolished. . . . No will: no representation, no world.[21]

Schopenhauer readily concedes that "before us there is certainly left only nothing." That the prospect repels us is merely the mark of our unregeneracy, our clinging to life, our affirmation of the will to live. "Those who have overcome the world," Schopenhauer's *jina*-s, provide unambiguous testimony, he insists, that this nothingness is to be welcomed, not feared. In a now-familiar statement which reads as a direct challenge to such men as Max Müller and Barthélemy Saint-Hilaire, Schopenhauer declares:

We have to banish the dark impression of that nothingness, which as the final goal hovers behind all virtue and holiness, and which we fear as children fear darkness. We must not evade it, as the Indians do, by myths and meaningless words, such as reabsorption in *Brahma*, or the *Nirvāṇa* of the Buddhists. On the contrary, we freely acknowledge that what remains after the complete abolition of the will is, for all who are still full of the will, assuredly nothing. But also conversely, to those in whom the will has turned and denied itself, this very real world of ours with all its suns and galaxies, is—nothing.[22]

Seldom during the century and a half since those words were written have the meaning of nirvāṇa and the motive

[21] *Ibid.*, pp. 410–11.
[22] *Ibid.*, pp. 411–12.

forces undergirding classical Indian speculation been approached more closely by Westerners. The parallels between this creative philosophical effort and much of the Indian *mokṣa* literature are remarkable.

Neither homologies nor analogies, however, constitute identities. And it would be unreasonable to maintain that Schopenhauer's system is only a translation of terms and concepts from India into a more or less Kantian framework. Schopenhauer, writing when scientific Indological research was in its infancy, simply did not have access to sufficient Indian materials to have borrowed a system. We must assign independence to his achievement.

Schopenhauer did not know Sanskrit, let alone Pali. And, although we can presume that he had ample opportunity, apparently he made no effort to learn either language. A text that remained within easy reach and to which he turned frequently was du Perron's translation of the "major" Upaniṣads. In some degree, his lack of interest in pursuing original studies in the material to which he was so dispositionally and philosophically sympathetic is puzzling. Yet, as a philosopher, it was not—nor perhaps could it have been—in his makeup either to forsake his own type of inquiry for textual investigations or to add such an accomplishment to his repertoire.

Certainly Schopenhauer's enthusiasm for the results of Indological research did not diminish. (His article, "Sinologie," and the bibliographical data which it contains witness his unabated interest.[23]) In 1844, a new edition of *Die Welt* appeared, augmented by a voluminous appendix of essays. The first edition had received scanty attention, and it is obvious that Schopenhauer was dismayed and angry that his magnum opus had very nearly been ignored.

It is particularly in the supplement to *Die Welt* that some critics choose to level the charges of racism and anti-Semitism at Schopenhauer. But, while not disputing the fact that

[23] Arthur Schopenhauer, "Sinologie," *Uber den Willen in der Natur*, Vol. III of *Arthur Schopenhauers sämtliche Werke*, collected by Paul Deussen (Munich: R. Piper & Co., 1912 [originally published in 1836, 2nd ed., 1854]), pp. 409–19, especially pp. 410–12.

Schopenhauer's writings played some role in the development of certain attitudes which were to have such dire consequences for Germany and the world, I should insist that his intention was completely different. Of the utmost importance to Schopenhauer was that a philosopher concern himself with real problems, matters vitally affecting men wherever and whenever they are. The very historical actuality of Buddhism assured him that he was not inventing philosophical fables. In the dispute between European communalists and universalists over what was to be made of the Buddhist nirvāṇa, he added a new dimension, suggesting—though few listened—that there were valid ethical and philosophic insights other than those enshrined in Western Europe's societal and spiritual establishment.

Schopenhauer begins the supplement rhetorically:

> If I wished to take the results of my philosophy as the standard of truth, I should have to concede to Buddhism pre-eminence over the others. In any case it must be a pleasure to me to see my doctrine in such close agreement with a religion that the majority of men on earth hold as their own. . . . And this agreement must be yet more pleasing to me, inasmuch as in my philosophizing I have certainly not been under its influence. For up till 1818, when my work appeared, there were to be found in Europe only a very few accounts of Buddhism, and those extremely incomplete and inadequate, confined almost entirely to a few essays in the earlier volumes of the *Asiatic Researches* and principally concerned with the Buddhism of the Burmese. Only since that time has fuller information about this religion reached us, chiefly through the profound and instructive articles of that meritorious member of the St. Petersburg Academy, I. J. Schmidt, in the records of his academy, and then in the course of time through several English and French scholars. . . . Unfortunately, Csoma Korosi, that steadfast and assiduous Hungarian, who, in order to study the language and sacred writings of Buddhism, spent many years in Tibet and particularly in Buddhist monasteries, was carried off by death just as he was beginning to work out for us the results of his investigations. But I cannot deny the pleasure with which I read in his preliminary accounts several passages taken from the Kahgyur itself. . . .[24]

[24] Schopenhauer, *The World*, II, 169.

In the spirit of a latter-day Marcion, Schopenhauer directs attacks against the Old Testament and Judaism. But this is not anti-Semitism. Rather, it is an attempt to stress the ascetic temperament of Christianity, for he dares to say:

> The true spirit and kernel of Christianity, as of Brahmanism and Buddhism also, is the knowledge of the vanity of all earthly happiness, complete contempt for it, and the turning away to an existence of quite a different, indeed an opposite, kind. This, I say, is the spirit and purpose of Christianity, the true "humour of the matter"; but it is not, as they imagine, monotheism. Therefore, atheistic Buddhism is much more closely akin to Christianity than are optimistic Judaism and its variety, Islam.[25]

Through additional, closer scrutiny of Buddhism, Schopenhauer seems to have come closer than most of his contemporaries and many of his successors to the strictest notion of transmigration according to the Buddhists.

> The proper and, so to speak, esoteric doctrine of Buddhism, as we have come to know it through the most recent researches . . . teaches not metempsychosis, but a peculiar palingenesis resting on a moral basis. . . . Yet for the great mass of Buddhists this doctrine is too subtle; and so plain metempsychosis is preached to them as a comprehensible substitute.[26]

Schopenhauer, of course, devotes considerable attention to restating the theme: denial of the will to live. Death merely —a death which only halts a phenomenal existence still affirming the will—that death is not enough. The Indians, Schopenhauer asserts, mythologize at this point, saying that this affirmation inspires *saṃsāra*. Denial of the will is *nirvāṇa*. It is other than mere death. And again Schopenhauer takes up the question concerning the condition or state that follows such a denial of the will. The recurring problem to which he speaks is whether that so-called condition is nothing —whether, in short, it is justifiable to call such terms and theories nihilistic.

[25] *Ibid.*, p. 444.
[26] *Ibid.*, pp. 502–3.

To die willingly, to die gladly, to die cheerfully, is the prerogative of the resigned, of him who gives up and denies the will-to-live. For he alone wishes to die *actually* and not merely *apparently*, and consequently needs and desires no continuance of his person. He willingly gives up the existence that we know; what comes to him instead of it is in our eyes *nothing*, because our existence in reference to that one is *nothing*. The Buddhist faith calls that existence *Nirvāṇa*, that is to say, extinction.[27]

A familiar and crucial epistemological point is confronted at this juncture; and Schopenhauer, almost alone of nineteenth-century commentators on Buddhism, stresses that it is impossible to frame a conceptual evaluation of this newly free condition.

We lack concepts for what the will now is; indeed, we lack all data for such concepts. We can only describe it as that which is free to be or not to be the will-to-live. For the latter case, Buddhism describes it by the word *nirvāṇa*. . . . It is the point that remains for ever inaccessible to all human knowledge precisely as such.[28]

Schopenhauer also suggests that the vedānta descriptions that refer to *mokṣa* as (re)union with Brahman say more than could possibly be said meaningfully.

The Buddhists with complete frankness describe the matter negatively as *Nirvāṇa*, which is the negation of this world or of *Samsara*. If *Nirvāṇa* is defined as nothing, this means only that *Samsara* contains no single element that could serve to define or construct *Nirvāṇa*.[29]

The principal statements by Schopenhauer which relate to the Buddhist nirvāṇa are now before us. What remains—and is within our scope here—is a summing up of the more important factors to be dealt with in assessing the influence of Buddhism on his thought and estimating his interpretation of nirvāṇa. The influence of Buddhism on the formative—that is to say, earliest—stages of his speculations is negligible. Schopenhauer's own disclaimers in this regard are doubtless

[27] *Ibid.*, p. 508 and footnote.
[28] *Ibid.*, p. 560.
[29] *Ibid.*, p. 568.

to be accepted: he had no access to the materials, and he conducted a philosophical enterprise which excluded him by definition from doctrinal influences of whatever kind. The latter point may be mooted at length. The former is decisive and incontrovertible.

We are left, however, with the suggestions of such critics as Schwab and Hecker that the *vedānta* did influence Schopenhauer's early thought and more significantly than the Buddhist materials.[30] Without in any way denying the capital importance of the discovery of the Upaniṣads in his intellectual development, I must repeat that Schopenhauer's systematic presentations and the investigations which underlie them are basically independent. Inspiration is complex, and the most one may say is that Indian materials altogether were but one contributor among many others.

Schopenhauer's concept of will cannot be equated with Śaṅkara's *Brahman*. In his sense of urgency, his concern to find a cure for the mankind he supposed to be afflicted by ignorance and deluded selfishness, he is rather closer to the program of the earliest Buddhist community. And this is illustrated in the key statement in *Die Welt:*

> That great fundamental truth contained in Christianity as well as in Brahmanism and Buddhism, the need for salvation from an existence given up to suffering, and death, and its attainability through the denial of the will, hence by a decided opposition to nature, is beyond all comparison the most important truth there can be.[31]

Perhaps a distinction should be made between "influence" and "determine," for, while no aspect of Indian or Buddhist thought determined the course of Schopenhauer's philosophy, it is certain that a definable influence is present. This latter is seen in his tenacious hold on the notion that ethic and metaphysic may not be divorced. It is also apparent in his discussion of the transition from virtue to asceticism. And through his entire presentation, the historical presence of the

[30] See, for example, Schwab, pp. 447–55, 513.

[31] Schopenhauer, *The World*, II, 628.

fact of a Buddhism, of millions of practicing Buddhists, functions to support, illustrate, and confirm his own understanding of human existence.

It is obvious that Schopenhauer was primarily impressed by the psychologico-ethical implications of Indian speculations. And it was to have been expected that he would become more and more interested in Buddhism, for his energies were directed to the search for the appropriate conduct of life—the organization and ultimate transcendence of moral existence—without presupposing a heavenly lawgiver. Equally patent is the soteriological thrust of his system. Decision and freedom to decide are the basis of salvation. It is within the frame of psychological analysis (in a non-clinical sense)—in which Schopenhauer first probed the determining role of the extra-rational in non-philosophical experience and then called factors of reason to play in that freedom exhibited in willing the denial of the will—that his signal achievement resides. It would be eminently more accurate, then, to call him, not the philosopher of pessimism nor the philosopher of the irrational, but rather the philosopher of freedom through reason. And, insofar as they could tolerate the appellative "philosopher," most Buddhists could be given the same designation.

Richard Wagner—Buddha als Heldentenor?

Richard Wagner, 1813–83, was born about the time that Arthur Schopenhauer was being introduced to Indian lore through the Upaniṣads. The role played by Indian thought in the unfolding of Schopenhauer's philosophy is undeniable though neither determinative nor always admitting of precise specification. Clearly, he relies on it more and more for data to support his system in the face of a Western European community that was disinterested where not actually hostile. In the case of Wagner, possible influences from Indian and Buddhist thought may be even more difficult to gauge, for it is to be measured in his art and in his discussions of art.

It will not be enough to note that Wagner sketched a Buddhist opera, although in itself that fact is sufficiently interesting and important to justify a brief essay. Rather, it will be necessary to confront Wagner as a gifted musical innovator, to see him as an artist in search of new and valid modes of expression, and to estimate Buddhist and Indian influences not merely as they provide new images and myths but as they contribute an entirely new intellectual and emotional context for his work.

About Wagner's early life, his education, and his first musical successes—*Rienzi* (1842), *The Flying Dutchman* (1843), *Tannhäuser* (1845), and *Lohengrin* (1850)—there is little to be said which would serve the purposes of this discussion. The critical period is the decade (1849–59), of his residence in Zurich—the period Wagner called his hegira. During those ten years he began and nearly completed the *Ring* cycle and commenced his *Tristan und Isolde.* Also, this was the period of his greatest output of essays, letters, and criticism. It was the time of the birth and flowering of his famous romance with Mathilde Wesendonck. And, for our purposes most important of all, it was during this decade that Wagner discovered Schopenhauer and Buddhism.

> [I] . . . had finished a fair copy of the *Rheingold* score by the 26th of September [1854]. In the peaceful quietness of my house at this time I first came across a book which was destined to be of great importance to me. This was Arthur Schopenhauer's Die Welt. . . .[32]

We are told that the house was peacefully quiet because Wagner's wife Minna was away in Weimar. He makes it clear also that he had not stumbled on the Schopenhauer vol-

[32] Richard Wagner, *My Life* (2 vols.; New York: Dodd, Mead and Company, 1911), II, 614.

ume. It had been recommended to him, he writes, and he read it first with mixed reactions about its worth.

Like every man who is passionately thrilled with life, I too sought first for the conclusions of Schopenhauer's system. With its aesthetic side I was perfectly content, and was especially astonished at his noble conception of music. But, on the other hand, the final summing-up regarding morals alarmed me, as, indeed, it would have startled anyone in my mood; for here the annihilation of the will and complete abnegation are represented as the sole true and final deliverance from those bonds of individual limitation in estimating and facing the world, which are now clearly felt for the first time. For those who hoped to find some philosophical justification for political and social agitation on behalf of so-called "individual freedom" there was certainly no support to be found here, where all that was demanded was absolute renunciation of all such methods of satisfying the claims of personality. At first I naturally found his ideas by no means palatable, and felt I could not readily abandon that so-called "cheerful" Greek aspect of the world, with which I had looked out upon life in my Kunstwerk der Zukunft.[33]

One suspects that Wagner's memory indulges here in a more colorful and dramatic recollection than an exact one, but it is doubtless true that Schopenhauer did not sit too well with him on first reading. However that may be, Wagner credits his own insight into the significance of *Die Welt* to the tutoring of the poet Herwegh.

As a matter of fact, it was Herwegh who at last, by a well-timed explanation, brought me to a calmer frame of mind about my own sensitive feelings. It is from this perception of the nullity of the world—so he said—that all tragedy is derived, and such a perception must necessarily have dwelt as an intuition in every great poet, and even in every great man. On looking into my *Nibelungen* poem I recognised with surprise that the very things that now so embarrassed me theoretically had long been familiar to me in my own poetical conception. Now at last I could understand my Wotan, and I returned with chastened mind to the renewed study of Schopenhauer's book.[34]

[33] *Ibid.*, pp. 615–16.
[34] *Ibid.*, p. 616.

During the autumn of 1854, Wagner was at work on the music for *Die Walküre*. Still alone in his house, he relaxed by taking long walks.

As usual with me when hard at work on my music, I felt the longing to express myself in poetry. This must have been partly due to the serious mood created by Schopenhauer, which was trying to find ecstatic expression. It was some such mood that inspired the conception of a *Tristan und Isolde*.[35]

Of the *Tristan* story, Wagner insisted that "it was its all-pervading tragedy that impressed me so deeply that I felt convinced it should stand out in bold relief, regardless of minor details." Doubtless, elements from his own interpretation of Schopenhauer were at work also. In any case, Wagner was by that time totally captivated by Schopenhauer, and puts this down unequivocally in a letter to Franz Liszt (December 16, 1854).

I have of late occupied myself exclusively with a man who has come like a gift from heaven, although only a literary one. This is Arthur Schopenhauer, the greatest philosopher since Kant, whose thoughts, as he himself expresses it, he has thought out to the end. The German professors ignored him very prudently for forty years; but recently, to the disgrace of Germany, he has been discovered by an English critic. All the Hegels, etc., are charlatans by the side of him. His chief idea, the final negation of the desire of life, is terribly serious, but it shows the only salvation possible. To me of course that thought was not new, and it can indeed be conceived by no one in whom it did not pre-exist, but this philosopher was the first to place it clearly before me. If I think of the storm of my heart, the terrible tenacity with which, against my desire, it used to cling to the hope of life, and if even now I feel this hurricane within me, I have at least found a quietus which in wakeful nights helps me to sleep. This is unconsciousness, total non-existence. Freedom from all our dreams is our only final salvation. . . . As I have never in life felt the real bliss of love, I must erect a monument to the most beautiful of all my dreams, in which, from beginning to end, that love shall be thoroughly satiated. I have in my head Tristan and Isolde, the

[35] *Ibid.*, p. 617.

simplest but most full-blooded musical conception; with the "black flag" which floats at the end of it I shall cover myself to die.[36]

Schopenhauer's "great fundamental truth" has become for Wagner a soporific! But this interesting letter is more than a showpiece for Wagnerian exuberance. Among the more important insights it affords, one is especially important. It centers on Wagner, the willful artist. By the end of autumn in 1854, Wagner had swallowed Schopenhauer's material whole, not excluding the latter's bitter tirades against those who had ignored him. It is clear, however, that Wagner had by no means digested all that Schopenhauer said. He appropriated a major idea—denial of the will—and affixed it to his own *lebensphilosophie*. That idea, though, was not to interrupt his work. He would build this monument; then he would seek extinction—"Freedom from dreams" not now, but later. And in a critical phase which was to follow (and to which I shall advert shortly), he will attempt to correct Schopenhauer's views so that they more nearly accord with his own. In effect, he will try to be a Schopenhauer for Schopenhauer's Kant.

Through Schopenhauer we are to presume that Wagner confronted Indian and Buddhist allusions for the first time. His earliest statement about Buddhism is found in another letter to Liszt, this one dated June 7, 1855. Again it is the will of life which holds Wagner's fascinated attention—that and the saint's triumph over the will through negation and asceticism.

This act of "negation of will" is the true characteristic of the saint, which finds its last completion in the absolute cessation of personal consciousness; and all consciousness must be personal and individual. But the saints of Christianity, simple-minded and enveloped in the Jewish dogma as they were, could not see this, and their limited imagination looked upon that much-desired stage as the eternal continuation of a life freed from nature. Our judgment of the moral import of their resignation must not be influenced by this circumstance, for in reality they also longed for the cessation of their individual personality, i.e., of their

[36] *Wagner on Music and Drama*, ed. Albert Goldman and Evert Sprinchorn (New York: E. P. Dutton & Co., 1964), pp. 271–72.

existence. But this deep longing is expressed more purely and more significantly in the most sacred and oldest religion of the human race, the doctrine of the Brahmins, and especially in its final transfiguration and highest perfection, Buddhism. This also expounds the myth of a creation of the world by God, but it does not celebrate this act as a boon, but calls it a sin of Brahma which he, *after having embodied himself in this world*, must atone for by the infinite sufferings of this very world. He finds his salvation in the saints who, by perfect negation of the "will of life," by the sympathy with all suffering which alone fills their heart, enter the state of Nirwana, i.e., "the land of being no longer." Such a saint was Buddha. According to his doctrine of the migration of souls every man is born again in the form of that creature on which he had inflicted pain, however pure his life might otherwise have been. He himself must now know this pain, and his sorrowful migration does not cease, until during an entire course of his new-born life he has inflicted pain on no creature but has denied his own will of life in the sympathy with other beings. How sublime, how satisfying is this doctrine compared with the Judaeo-Christian doctrine, according to which a man . . . has only to be obedient to the Church during this short life to be made comfortable for all eternity, while he who has been disobedient in this short life will be tortured for ever.[37]

Wagner "saves" Christianity by explaining that its corrupt present state is due to the influences of "narrow" Judaism. And, according to him, Christianity is redeemable because it is really Buddhism. "Modern research has succeeded in showing that pure and unalloyed Christianity was nothing but a branch of that venerable Buddhism which, after Alexander's Indian expedition, spread to the shores of the Mediterranean." [38]

Later in the summer of 1855, Wagner first read material on Buddhism which had been written by a specialist. He was still recovering from the effects of his four-month stay in England the preceding spring—or so he laments—and was often forced to abandon his work (the orchestration of *Die Walküre*) and retire with his books.

[37] *Ibid.*, p. 277.
[38] *Ibid.*, pp. 277–78.

Burnouf's *Introduction à l'histoire du Bouddhisme* [*sic*] interested me most among my books, and I found material in it for a dramatic poem, which has stayed in my mind ever since, though only vaguely sketched. I may still perhaps work it out. I gave it the title of *Die Sieger.* It was founded on the simple legend of a Tschandala [= *Caṇḍāla*] girl, who is received into the dignified order of beggars known as Clakyamouni [*sic*], and, through her exceedingly passionate and purified love for Ananda, the chief disciple of Buddha, herself gains merit. Besides the underlying beauty of this simple material, a curious relation between it and the subsequent development of my musical experience influenced my selection. For to the mind of Buddha the past life (in a former reincarnation) of every being who appears before him stands revealed as plainly as the present; and this simple story has its significance, as showing that the past life of the suffering hero and heroine is bound up with the immediate present in this life. I saw at once that the continuous reminiscence in the music of this double existence might perfectly well be presented to the emotions, and I decided accordingly to keep in prospect the working out of this poem as a particularly congenial task.[39]

Dated late the following spring, May 16, 1856, the sketch for *Die Sieger (The Conquerors)* has been preserved in Wagner's memorabilia. I reproduce it here in full.

—The *Buddha* on his last journey. —*Ananda* given water from the well by Prakriti, the Tchandala maiden. Her tumult of love for *Ananda;* his consternation.—

Prakriti in love's agony: her mother brings *Ananda* to her: love's royal battle: Ananda, distressed and moved to tears, released by Chakya (the Buddha)—

Prakriti goes to *Buddha,* under the tree at the City's gate, to plead for union with *Ananda.* He asks if she is willing to fulfil the stipulations of such a union? Dialogue with twofold meaning, interpreted by *Prakriti* in the sense of her passion; she sinks horrified and sobbing to the ground, when she hears at length that she must share Ananda's vow of chastity. *Ananda* persecuted by the *Brahmins.* Reproofs against Buddha's commerce with a Tchandala girl. Buddha's attack on the spirit of Caste. He tells of Prakriti's previous incarnation; she then was the daughter of a haughty Brahmin; the Tchandala King, remembering a former existence as a Brahmin, had craved the Brahmin's daughter for

[39] Wagner, II, 638.

his son, who had conceived a violent passion for her; in pride and arrogance the daughter had refused return of love, and mocked at the unfortunate. This she had now to expiate, reborn as Tchandala to feel the torments of a hopeless love; yet to renounce withal, and be led to full redemption by acceptance into Buddha's flock. —*Prakriti* answers Buddha's final question with a joyful Yea. Ananda welcomes her as sister. *Buddha*'s last teachings. All are converted by him. He departs to the place of his redemption.[40]

As an independent composition, *The Conquerors* progressed no further than that sketch. Asked about the work two decades later, Wagner responded that its essence had been pressed into his *Parsifal*.[41] It is not altogether clear, however, what essence he had in mind. Suggestions have also been made that certain passages in *Die Götterdammerung*, *Tristan*, and *Parsifal* were originally noted for the Buddhist opera.[42]

More important than an attempt to find Buddhist scenes in parts of the other operas will be the effort to identify a pervasive influence traceable to his conception of Buddhism. And one must be prepared to look for this musically as well as dramatically. Wagner the artist, not Wagner the scholar, encountered both Schopenhauer and Buddhism. He early decided what was the true Buddhism, and was plainly irritated when presented with "facts" about Buddhism which conflicted with his image. He wrote to Mathilde Wesendonck on October 5, 1858:

A while ago the Countess A. announced a "little figure" that would soon arrive for me. I didn't understand her, and meantime finished reading Köppen's History of the Religion of Buddha. An unedifying book: instead of sterling features from the oldest legends,

[40] *Richard Wagner's Prose Works*, trans. William Ashton Ellis (London: Kegan, Paul, Trench, Trübner & Co., Ltd., 1899), VIII, 385–86. The sketch is also reproduced in Ernest Newman, *The Life of Richard Wagner* (4 vols.; New York: Alfred A. Knopf, 1933–46), II, 486–87; and in Dorothea W. Dauer, "Richard Wagner's Art in its Relation to Buddhist Thought," *Scripta Humanistica Kentuckiensia* (*Supplement to the Kentucky Foreign Language Quarterly*, VII; Lexington, 1964), pp. 27–28. The latter article, interesting and important in its conception, is disappointing in execution.

[41] Schwab, pp. 459–66.

[42] Newman, II, 487–88. Also see Dauer, *passim*.

which I expected, for the most part a mere account of development in girth, which naturally turns out more and more repellant, the purer and sublimer is the core. After being so thoroughly disgusted by a detailed description of the ritual as last established, with its relics and preposterous simulacra of the Buddha, the "little figure" arrives, and proves to be a Chinese specimen of one of these sacred effigies. My abhorrence was great. . . . One has much trouble in this distortion-loving world to hold one's own against suchlike impressions, and keep unwarped the pure-beheld ideal. . . . Nevertheless, in spite of the Chinese caricature, I have succeeded in keeping pure to myself the son of Çakya, the Buddha.[43]

Köppen's book was not condemned unreservedly, for it occasioned a new insight on the subject of representing the Buddha in music-drama. "The difficulty here, was to adapt this entirely liberated mortal upraised above all passion, the Buddha himself, for dramatic, and *particularly for musical treatment* [my italics]." [44] Köppen's account of the Buddha's decision to admit women into the order stressed the Buddha's initial refusal and the role played by Ānanda in causing him to reverse that prohibition.[45] Wagner chose to see in this final decision the perfection of the Buddha himself—the redeemer redeemed —"one final advance to consummate perfection. Ānanda, standing nearer to life as yet, and directly affected by the young Tschandala maiden's impetuous love, becomes the medium of this last perfecting." [46]

Several scholars have shown that seeds of the love tragedy theme—of the profound, often perplexing, eros renunciation interplay—were present in Wagner's works long before he had read Schopenhauer, Burnouf, or Köppen.

[43] From Wagner's "Venice Diary" in *Richard Wagner to Mathilde Wesendonck*, trans. William Ashton Ellis (2nd ed.; London: H. Grevel & Co., 1905), p. 53.

[44] *Ibid.*, p. 54. See also Newman, II, 487–88.

[45] The unadorned account of the admission of women into the Buddha's Order (from the Pali Canon: Cullavagga, X.1) is conveniently available in translation: *Buddhism in Translations*, trans. and ed. Henry Clarke Warren, pp. 441–47.

[46] *Richard Wagner to Mathilde Wesendonck*, pp. 54–55.

Renunciation in one form or another runs through all Wagner's works from *The Flying Dutchman* to *Parsifal.* The Dutchman gains redemption, according to Wagner's explanation of the plot, "through *a woman* who shall sacrifice herself for the love of him. Thus it is the yearning for death that spurs him on to seek this woman." [47]

Albert Goldman and Evert Sprinchorn have characterized the Schopenhauerian will as "basically erotic in nature . . . ceaselessly and senselessly spawning and destroying life." [48] They also have highlighted an important distinction between Schopenhauer and Wagner concerning the tactics to be employed by men contending with the will. "Schopenhauer urged man not to cooperate with this force, but to withdraw from it or make it the object of intellectual contemplation." On the other hand, according to these scholars, Wagner's *Tristan* exhibits a profoundly un-Schopenhauerian tactic—as it were, a "tantric-Schopenhauerian" approach:

Where Schopenhauer advocates withdrawal and non-cooperation in order to impose one's own meaning on the essential meaninglessness of life, Wagner's lovers rush to embrace this will with such abandon and vigor that it is difficult to tell whether the force is overcoming the individuals or the individuals are momentarily mastering the force.[49]

On December 1, 1858, Wagner tried to describe what he had in mind:

It is a matter of demonstrating a path of salvation recognised by none of the philosophers, particularly not by Sch.,—the pathway to complete pacification of the Will through love, and that no abstract love of mankind, but the love which actually blossoms from the soil of sexual love. . . .[50]

Now it is clear—if, indeed, it has not been so all along—that the Buddha of *The Conquerors* is Schopenhauer and

[47] Elliott Zuckerman, *The First Hundred Years of Wagner's Tristan* (New York: Columbia University Press, 1964), p. 34.

[48] Goldman and Sprinchorn, p. 27.

[49] *Ibid.*, p. 28.

[50] *Richard Wagner to Mathilde Wesendonck*, p. 75.

Ānanda, Wagner. Prakriti could be taken as Mathilde, of course; but I suspect that the so-called affair with Mathilde was as much a creative projection of Wagner's imagination as Prakriti or Isolde. Perhaps, in fact, Mathilde is the least real of all. In any event, one despairs of analyzing all the crises and paradoxes in Wagnerian equations—equations not limited to such obvious ones as love equals death and orgasm equals oblivion.

Comments on Wagner the poet-dramatist-intellectual should not obscure Wagner the musician. It must be emphasized that Wagner viewed his subjects through music. The most significant influences from Schopenhauer, Buddhism, even the idea of nirvāṇa itself may, then, be found where they are least accessible, where they are the least susceptible to conceptual paraphrase—in the music he wrote.

It should not confuse us that Wagner composed first the poems and then the music for his operas. Zuckerman observes:

> Wagner always wrote and sometimes published his poems before he began to compose the music. But as early as 1844 . . . he had told a correspondent that when he sat down to write a verse or a plot he was "already intoxicated by the musical aroma" of his subject. There is little indication that he began the poems of the earlier operas with anything more than a general sense of what the music would be like. . . . But in the case of Tristan there is every sign that the music began to assert its chromatic will even before Wagner had drawn up a dramatic scenario.[51]

The particular importance of the music in *Tristan* is patent, allowing Zuckerman to declare, "Apart, perhaps, from the narratives and dialogues of the first act, Tristan is a vast symphonic poem. Moreover, it is not the sort of symphonic poem that illustrates a program."[52] *Tristan*, Wagner's "most thoroughly musical work,"[53] stands as the harbinger of a new era in music from its very first bar—the famous *Tristanak-*

[51] Zuckerman, p. 8.
[52] *Ibid.*, p. 9.
[53] *Ibid.*, p. 10.

kord. And *Tristan* was conceived during the period of Wagner's most intense encounters with—his appropriations from and reactions to—Schopenhauer and Buddhism.

Chromatic movement, modulation, and key transition—these, masterfully handled by Wagner, are the effective core of the musical statement in *Tristan.* " 'Music alone,' according to Rougement, 'could utter the unutterable, and music forced the final secret of Tristan.' It was Wagner's new power as a harmonist that enabled him to utter the unutterable." [54] The "final secret of Tristan" is unquestionably involved in Wagner's own conception of nirvāṇa and Schopenhauer's denial of the will to live. "If the unexpected movement into a remote key is, as Schopenhauer hyperbolically maintains, like death, then the second and third acts of Tristan represent (as they should) a continuous dying." [55]

More imaginative, though doubtless more hazardous, than searching through Schopenhauer's writings to find a theory for the music in *Tristan* would be to proceed from the following hypothesis: *Tristan* displays musically the impact of Buddhism—particularly the person of the Buddha, the idea of rebirth and remembrance of past lives, and the notion of nirvāṇa, that "land of being no longer"—on Wagner's creative genius. While no strict demonstration of its truth is possible, it is by no means preposterous to think of *Tristan* as a nirvāṇa symphony. There can be no doubt that *Tristan,* a work that "has influenced more works than any other score extant" (Zuckerman), is a product of the full flowering of Wagner's talent, an efflorescence which owed more than a little to impressions made by Buddhism and the Buddhist nirvāṇa.

Without the events of the 1850's, among which was Wagner's introduction to Buddhism, there would have been no *Tristan.* But this is not to say that it is a question of reducing Wagner's achievement to the sum total of impressions stamped on his talent from without. Here I accede willingly to Newman, who, while speaking of Schopenhauer's influence on

[54] *Ibid.*, p. 17.
[55] *Ibid.*, p. 19.

Wagner, might well have included Buddhism and, indeed, have extended his statement to encompass the question of Indian influences on Schopenhauer himself.

We talk too loosely of "influences" in an artist or thinker's inner life, naively conceiving him as a blank page on which this or that external "influence" writes itself. We forget that it is only because the page, and indeed the whole book, are what they already are that they lend themselves to the writing: as Pascal says of all similar phenomena of apparently sudden spiritual revelation and re-birth, "You would not have sought me unless you had already found me." Wagner did not take his philosophy from Schopenhauer: what happened was that *The World as Will and Idea* introduced into his mind the point of solid matter that was necessary to bring about the crystallization of a philosophy that was already latent in him: Schopenhauer merely reinforced his emotions and intuitions with reasons and arguments.[56]

It is not to be supposed that Schopenhauer or a Buddhist would be offended by that warning. Important here is the double truth that similarities and analogues are not identities and yet that the awakening of that which is latent is as much an influence as the direct introduction of something entirely new. This is, it seems to me, a good illustration of what Mircea Eliade suggests is the role of the history of religions: we may say that Wagner's encounter with Schopenhauer, Buddhism, and the Buddhist nirvāṇa functioned as a *maieutics*.

Just as Socrates, according to the Theaetetus (149a, 161e), acted on the mind obstetrically, bringing to birth thoughts it did not know it contained, so the history of religions could bring forth a new man, more authentic and more complete: for, through study of the religious traditions, modern man would not only rediscover a kind of archaic behaviour, he would also become conscious of the spiritual riches implied in such behaviour.[57]

In that light, perhaps Richard Wagner in the presence of the Buddhist nirvāṇa was just such a man. And in the quest for

[56] Newman, II, 431.

[57] Mircea Eliade, *Images and Symbols: Studies in Religious Symbolism*, trans. Philip Mairet (New York: Sheed and Ward, 1961), p. 35.

evidence of a reborn consciousness in Wagner's art, one should recall Zuckerman's comment about the music in *Tristan:* "Heard melodies are not always the sweetest." [58]

Friedrich Wilhelm Nietzsche—Buddha als Ubermensch?

Born in 1844, the year in which Burnouf's *Introduction* was published, Friedrich Nietzsche has been associated with themes of Iranian mythology far more often than with Indian, with classical Greece than with classical India. Closer scrutiny reveals significant influences and inspirations from India in his work, however; and to ignore or discount them would be to limit unnecessarily an appreciation of the totality of his philosophical attainments.[59]

Nietzsche's serious schooling began at Pforta, where he studied for six years. It was there that he met Paul Deussen, who was to be a lifelong friend and confidant. Deussen's contributions to the study of Indian philosophy are well known, and it is certain that this ardent student of Schopenhauer and the vedānta was responsible for much of what Nietzsche learned about Indian thought.[60] From Pforta, Nietzsche and Deussen proceeded in the early 1860's to the university in Bonn. Shortly thereafter, Nietzsche, who had become absorbed in the study of the Greek and Latin classics, followed

[58] Zuckerman, p. 175.

[59] Charles Philippe Théodore Andler devotes considerable attention to these factors in his important *Nietzsche: sa vie et sa pensée* (new ed.; Paris: Librairie Gallimard, 1958). Walter Kaufmann pares down the list of influences and does not mention Buddhism at all in that connection. See the latter's *Nietzsche: Philosopher, Psychologist, Antichrist* (New York: Meridian Books, 1956), p. 391, note 18.

[60] Andler, I, 349.

his tutor Friedrich Ritschl when the latter moved to Leipzig. Deussen did not accompany Nietzsche but moved to Tübingen.

At Leipzig, Nietzsche met Erwin Rohde, a contemporary who shared his enthusiasm for classical studies.[61] The two became fast friends—a friendship, however, not destined to endure as did that between Nietzsche and Deussen. Together, Nietzsche and Rohde retired for several days in 1865 to the Pleisse valley near Leipzig. In those idyllic surroundings, the two talked of Socrates and Plato and delivered themselves of their hopes and plans for the future. They carved a Greek maxim on a stone as a pledge and testament to their shared aspirations: "Become what you are." The name which they gave their retreat, however, had nothing to do with the Hellenism to which they were so devoted—they called the place "Nirvāṇa."

That mention of nirvāṇa in 1865 is Nietzsche's first reference to anything Buddhistic. Perhaps Deussen had introduced him to some aspects of Indian thought earlier, but that does not seem likely. The young Deussen was taken up with Schopenhauer, and one would suppose that the latter's work would have been suggested first to Nietzsche. Yet, apparently Nietzsche discovered Schopenhauer on his own, happening on a copy of *Die Welt* while browsing in a second-hand bookstore in Leipzig.

Nietzsche did learn some Sanskrit at Leipzig, and doubtless this took place under the instruction of Max Müller's first teacher, Herrmann Brockhaus (1806–77). He frequented Brockhaus' home, and it was probably there that he was introduced to many of the principal results of the Indological investigations of the period. Nietzsche was much more interested in the civilization of India than in its major classical language, and complained that Brockhaus was merely a philologist without any feeling for Indian philosophy. The criticism was excessive, as Andler remarks, and it is obvious

[61] Kaufmann, pp. 32–33.

that Brockhaus contributed significantly to Nietzsche's intellectual development.

> Herman Brockhauss [*sic*] . . . was without doubt a rigorous grammarian. But in neither his Indian nor his Iranian studies did he neglect the general problems of civilization; and without him perhaps Nietzsche would never have thought of a Zoroaster or the Laws of Manu.[62]

Brockhaus was important to Nietzsche not merely as a philologist and Indianist. He was, after all, Richard Wagner's brother-in-law. So it was that Nietzsche was exposed more or less simultaneously in the mid-1860's to Schopenhauer, Sanskrit, and Wagner. His first documented encounter with Buddhism—other than the reference to nirvāṇa in 1865—came after his move to Basel as professor of classical philology in 1869. On October 25, 1870, he signed out Köppen's two-volume *Die Religion des Buddha* from the university library.

> There was no religious belief that Nietzsche studied more passionately than Buddhism. Doubtless at the outset he only intended to strengthen himself at the very source of Schopenhauer's philosophy. Later, during his great inquiry into the various civilizations, Buddhism became for him the archetype of a perfect transvaluation.[63]

In 1881, following his retirement from Basel, Nietzsche carefully studied a new volume of Buddhist studies, one which to a great extent outdated all previous investigations of the subject: Hermann Oldenberg's *Buddha: Sein Leben, seine Lehre, seine Gemeinde*.[64] And throughout he closely followed the scholarship of his friend Deussen. In short, Nietzsche was by all odds the best read, most solidly grounded on Buddhism of the three figures under discussion in this chapter. And, though it is probable that he read most, perhaps all, source materials in translations, he knew some Sanskrit.

Among several aspects of Nietzsche's thought which could

[62] Andler, I, 322.

[63] *Ibid.*, p. 415.

[64] Hermann Oldenberg, *Buddha: Sein Leben, seine Lehre, seine Gemeinde* (Berlin: W. Hertz, 1881). And see Chapter VI, below.

be examined profitably in light of his Indian studies, the following three interrelated items may be singled out as most important: the notion of the eternal return and the accompanying idea of its creative potential as the two may relate to Indian theories of *saṃsāra;* Nietzsche's Zarathustra compared to the bodhisattva ideal in Buddhism; and, finally, his concept of transvaluation and its possible ties with his own understanding of the Buddhist nirvāṇa.

However much they differ from one another in matters of personal biography and achievements, Schopenhauer, Wagner, and Nietzsche stimulated their audiences to similar reactions. Those audiences neatly bifurcate: passionate supporters on the one hand, bitter detractors on the other. Extremists in their own distinctive ways, these three men have inspired equally extreme statements from admirers and critics.

Extreme evaluations, of course, need not be wrong. Their accuracy tends to be alloyed, however, and the emotive atmosphere of the statements in which they are expressed often obscures points at issue, limiting the effectiveness of the judgments tendered. Often—though by no means always—there is a counterbalancing merit to extremists' views: imaginative enthusiasts may be more helpful in illumining problems than lackluster pedants. They may foster new and correct insights by stimulating—or irritating—a response. Heat, sufficiently intense, may generate light. Barthélemy Saint-Hilaire's statements about the Buddhist nirvāṇa may be taken as an example.

In the case of Nietzsche's work, I have a pertinent illustration at hand. Charles Andler asserts, "Nietzsche founded a 'European Buddhism,' sprung from knowledge and energy and established for those conquering the world, not for ascetics who renounce life." [65] That provoking statement, inspired in part by Nietzsche's own words in *Wille zur Macht*,[66] is true in a very important regard; but it is only partly true. In fact, one may counter that Nietzsche was more profoundly Bud-

[65] Andler, I, 462.
[66] *Ibid.*

dhist—and not in some hybrid European transformation, but rather in an authentic sense—than either Schopenhauer or Wagner.

If that counter-assertion is to be made acceptable, it will be necessary first to explore Nietzsche's apparent divergence from Buddhist thought on some critical matters. If one grants that Nietzsche was captivated by Köppen's "Feuerbachian" presentation of the Buddha as an enlightened man reigning supreme over the gods, then, it is suggested, Nietzsche encountered a sort of archetypal *Ubermensch* who is freed from rebirth—that freedom being nirvāṇa. Such freedom—that nirvāṇa—involves a cessation of existence in course, according to such a portrayal, for the Buddha is free from the conditions of existence.

Andler insists that this is the precise point at which Nietzsche departs from Buddhism. He cites Nietzsche: "Not only man but the superman (*Ubermensch*) also eternally returns again."[67] Further, in what Walter Kaufmann calls Nietzsche's "apotheosis of creativity" it would seem that the *Ubermensch*, supremely creative and necessarily associated with the eternal recurrence, according to Nietzsche, would be the contrary of the Buddha in nirvāṇa. The question, it seems to me, is whether Nietzsche's Zarathustra or his *Ubermensch* could be the *Tathāgata*. Negative answers prevail. I disagree.

Certainly it cannot be maintained that the *Ubermensch* seeks annihilation or extinction except the specific extinction of weakness through the realization of full creative power. Kaufmann wisely points out, however, that the Buddha's refusal to be tempted into a show of magical powers (*siddhi*) can be interpreted as indicating a decision in favor of the acquisition of still mightier power.

> The issue here is not one between power and Nirvāṇa, but one between power and infinitely more power. What the ascetic wants is not power that is of this world, power over men, or power over

[67] Cited by Andler, I, 461–62.

many countries, but cosmic power, world-shaking power—power even over the gods.[68]

Indeed, Kaufmann is rather closer to understanding the dimensions of the Buddhist nirvāna than he realizes. Consider the following:

> The Buddhist masses, Nietzsche's advocate might proceed, conceive of happiness not as Nirvāṇa: they have their heavens and hells and their dreams of power, no less than do Yoga ascetics. And if Nietzsche were pressed to admit that at least there are some who do yearn for the absolute extinction of all consciousness and for the utter negation of life, will, and activity, he might retort either that this was indeed a rare exception, an abnormality, a disease—in one word: decadence—or he might say that Nirvāṇa was here conceived as the only chance to overpower life and suffering and that what is wanted here, too, is this ultimate and absolute triumph over the world. Just here—thus Nietzsche's defense might proceed to attack—power is wanted even at the price of consciousness; just here pleasure is not only incidental to ultimate happiness, but actually renounced altogether as incompatible with that highest power which man yearns for most.[69]

Throughout that suggestive and insightful passage, Kaufmann is tangled in one non-Buddhist, dictionary-bound acceptance of the meaning of nirvāṇa. He might well have paused to reflect on his own statement, going on to ask if the nirvāṇa-annihilation equation were not altogether too limiting. Had he done so, perhaps he would have reached my conclusion that nirvāṇa in its authentic Buddhist contexts may not be so conveniently replaced by such single-word equivalents as "extinction," "annihilation," or "nothingness."

Of course, I am not endeavoring to make the Buddha a Nietzschean. Nor am I declaring that Nietzsche was a Buddhist, strictly speaking. I *am* insisting that there is no basic conflict between Nietzsche and Buddhism on several important issues, and that there is sufficient evidence to indicate that Nietzsche's presentations do witness Buddhist influences.

According to Kaufmann, "Nietzsche himself might . . .

[68] Kaufmann, p. 240.
[69] *Ibid.*, p. 241.

declare that only the decadent require so radical a cure, while the truly powerful need not escape into any Nirvāṇa: they can win their triumph in this world and be creative."[70] This is question begging of the first order. No thought is given to the possibility that triumph and creativity in this world may in fact be components of the authentic Buddhist nirvāṇa. Here the paradoxes abounding in the later Mahāyāna and prajñāpāramitā are to be recalled. Identifications ("upaniṣads" in Edgerton's felicitous rendering as "equations") of *śūnyatā* and *saṃsāra* suggest that to some Buddhists at least the presence of the *muktī* in the cycle of *saṃsāra* is not a contradiction. In short, one may grant that, for early Buddhists, apparently Buddhahood and nirvāṇa involved a type of separation from the world, from rebirth, from eternal recurrence. Yet the bodhisattva ideal—implicit in Buddhism from its beginnings—suggests a theoretical and practical expansion and deepening of the conception of nirvāṇa and enlightenment.

The perceptive account of Buddhist salvation techniques advanced by Paul Masson-Oursel may be cited in this connection. "It was reserved for Buddhist insight," he declares, "to discern the servitude in good as in evil: to find egotism in traditional religion, in enjoyment, and in gain."[71] To unshackle men from this bondage, "oldest" Buddhism, according to Masson-Oursel, advocated the renunciation of all action.

> Liberation by a gradual exclusion of the residue that oppresses us—and this is the only liberation implied in the nirvāṇa of earliest times—gives moreover a purely negative solution. This solution shuns any positive statement concerning the essence—if it is one—that is thus liberated. Might it not be, as the term "emptiness" would seem to indicate, a pure nothingness?[72]

Masson-Oursel maintains that representatives of the Mahāyāna did not become ensnared by the absurdities implicit in

[70] *Ibid.*

[71] Paul Masson-Oursel, "Indian Techniques of Salvation," *Spirit and Nature: Papers from the Eranos Yearbooks*, ed. Joseph Campbell, p. 208.

[72] *Ibid.*, p. 209.

all attempts to distinguish between the liberation and enslavement of a pure nothingness.

Fundamentally, Buddhism excludes the substantiality of the spirit, not the spirit itself. It definitely does not negate life and its relativity; nor does it forbid the endeavor to work out a spiritual principle with the instruments provided by life—a principle that is spiritual because it is knowing and wise, but is nevertheless relative.[73]

In some cases this work is the very effort to create spirit. Such grand creative enterprises are started, however,

only after the nirvāṇa of the narrow way has been attained, they are provisional and inadequate because they are negative. Since they begin only after the entire store of karman is exhausted, since they originate in an activity free from egotism, and beyond good and evil, they do not give rise to any new, enslaving karman. And yet they are activities in the truest sense of the word: activities devoid of all passion because they are free from all bonds. Moreover, they may be said to be actions which engender and create freedom. We no longer have to do with liberation, but with a fecund autonomy.[74]

Masson-Oursel distinguishes so-called Hīnayāna Buddhists from Mahāyāna. I think it is striking how well his comments apply to the distinction between Schopenhauer and Nietzsche, for there also, in moving from the one to the other, "we no longer have to do with liberation, but with a fecund autonomy." It may be argued, on the other side, that Masson-Oursel tries to make Nietzscheans of his Buddhists. And, at the least, there is bitterly tragic irony in his concluding remark: "Let us not be dismayed; for even outside the sphere of sanctity, there are men who do not await their destiny, but create it." [75] It is hard to believe that that statement, uttered before a distinguished group of European scholars in 1937, escaped notice. Still, it should be impossible to fabricate an Adolf Hitler from an *Ubermensch* or a Bodhisattva.

Also Sprach Zarathustra—the title implies the reflex: *evaṃ*

[73] *Ibid.*

[74] *Ibid.*, p. 210.

[75] *Ibid.*, p. 212.

me sutaṃ, "so have I heard," familiar to all readers of the Pali Canon. And passages suggesting Buddhist parallels appear on every page. To take only a few:

"Transformed is Zarathustra; a child has Zarathustra become; wide awake is Zarathustra; what business have you among sleepers?" [76]

Zarathustra answered, "I love mankind." [77]

"What is the greatest thing you can experience? It is the hour of your great contempt. The hour in which even your happiness becomes loathsome to you and likewise your good sense and your virtue.

"The hour in which you say: 'What does my happiness matter? It is poverty and filth and wretched creature comfort. My happiness should be such that it justifies all existence." [78]

Zarathustra looked at the people and wondered. Then he said: "Man is a rope, stretched between beast and *Ubermensch*—a rope across an abyss.

"A dangerous crossing-over, a dangerous on-the-way, a dangerous looking-back, a dangerous shuddering and stopping." [79]

Schopenhauer, Wagner, and Nietzsche—together the three represent an intriguingly exact, microcosmic correspondence to the history of Buddhism in India, as it were, a curious rebirth of fifteen hundred years of Buddhism within a single century of European experience. In this "upaniṣad," Schopenhauer stands for the earliest Buddhist attitudes, and certainly those of the Theravāda. His emphasis, as theirs, was on deliverance—a notion first suggesting a from rather than a to. For Wagner, the idea of renunciation blended with various personal considerations, resulting in an attitude remarkably like that of the Tantrics. In both, enlightenment assures that participation in otherwise profane activities will bring salvation. Latent equations of the phenomenal and the noumenal, the profane and the sacred in Wagner's scheme become more

[76] Friedrich Nietzsche, *Thus Spoke Zarathustra*, trans. Marianne Cowan (Chicago: Henry Regnery Company, 1957), p. 2.

[77] *Ibid.*

[78] *Ibid.*, p. 5.

[79] *Ibid.*, p. 6.

or less explicit in Nietzsche's work—reminding one of the extreme conclusions in the prajñāparāmitā.[80]

Of course, one must be extremely cautious and delicate while conducting a full comparative investigation. In these few pages it has not been my intention to press superficial resemblances into identities or causal sequences; nor should the accomplishments of these three artist-intellectuals at any point be seen as exclusively or even principally dependent on their understanding of Buddhist thought. Their encounter with Buddhism is documented, and the presence of echoes of that encounter in their work will be conceded. That alone would confirm the importance of inquiries such as the one sketched in this chapter for an appreciation of the nirvāṇa controversies in Europe.

The benefits of this investigation will not be one-sided. A tolerably adequate understanding of the Buddhist speculations will aid in the study and explication of the work of this trio. And the benefits are reciprocal, for close study of the legacy of Schopenhauer, Wagner, and Nietzsche will better equip students to grapple successfully with the complexities in Buddhism. In great measure, our reactions to the work of these three men parallel our reactions to Buddhism. On our own terms and within our own traditions, three "alien" voices spoke out at the very time that we were being formally introduced to the history and institutions of Buddhism. As with Buddhism and the Buddhist nirvāṇa, so it is with Schopenhauer, Wagner, and Nietzsche: we have not yet determined what they mean.

[80] In order to accord with the historical sequence in India, it may be suggested that Wagner ought to have followed and not preceded Nietzsche. However, I am not at all sure that we can confidently assign the origins of Indian tantrism—in its many guises—to any specified century (let alone a particular date); and, in any case, whatever symbolic value there may be in this little equation would be utterly lost if it were to be subjected to such academic lint flicking.

[CHAPTER VI]

Hermann Oldenberg and the Silent Buddha

The first edition of Hermann Oldenberg's *Buddha: Sein Leben seine Lehre*, *seine Gemeinde* was published in 1881, when its author was still in his twenties. From that time until Oldenberg's death in 1920, *Buddha* was reissued in several revised editions and translated into English, French, and Russian.[1] This chapter is based on material drawn from more than one of those editions. By means of cross-references I shall try to dispel some of the uncertainties on the part of those

[1] Revised editions appeared in 1890, *ca.* 1894, 1906, 1914, and—just after Oldenberg's death—in 1921. The English version—*Buddha: His Life*, *His Doctrine*, *His Order*—was reprinted in 1888, 1904, 1925, and 1928 without revision. The French edition—*Le Bouddha: Sa vie*, *sa doctrine*, *sa communauté*, trad. A. Foucher (Paris: Felix Alcan, 1894)—was translated from the second German edition, and in 1903 revised according to the third German edition. (For much bibliographical assistance, I am indebted here and elsewhere to Shinsho Hanayama, *Bibliography on Buddhism*, pp. 545–46.) Hereafter in the notes I refer to the English translation of *Buddha* and the 1914 German edition, coding them, respectively, *Eng.* and *1914G.*

readers who have been able to consult only the English translation, a translation of the first German edition (1881).

In order to highlight the reasons that have led me to examine several editions of *Buddha*, I shall begin by outlining three accounts of Oldenberg's interpretation of nirvāṇa which rely—or purport to rely—on the same materials I have consulted. Following these quotations and summaries, I shall present my own evaluations. I find myself disagreeing with each at some important points.

First is E. J. Thomas' critique (I cite these in the order of publication). Following the quotation of two key passages from the Saṃyutta Nikāya, in which the Buddha refuses to answer questions concerning the destiny of the "perfected saint" and so on, Thomas asserts: "In spite of this repeated refusal to make any assertion one way or the other, Oldenberg came to the conclusion that it was a mere shirking of the question in order not to shock a weak-minded hearer." [2]

And, further, according to Thomas,

> Oldenberg's conclusion was, "through the shirking of the question as to the existence or non-existence of the ego, is heard the answer, to which the premises of the Buddhist teaching tended: the ego is not. Or, what is equivalent: The Nirvāṇa is annihilation." [3]

I have previously referred to Thomas' response to that alleged conclusion—namely, that annihilation is not the conclusion that the Buddhists themselves drew and, moreover, that it is beside the point to twaddle about conclusions which the Buddhists would have drawn had they been logical.[4] According to Thomas, then, Oldenberg exemplifies the attitudes of those scholars who try to "commit the Buddhists, in spite of all their efforts, to a one-sided dogmatism."

But Thomas is not content to level only one charge against Oldenberg. He fires another—an about-face. Eventually, Thomas insists, Oldenberg withdrew from the nihilistic in-

[2] Thomas, *History of Buddhist Thought*, p. 127.
[3] *Ibid.*
[4] *Ibid.*, pp. 128–29.

terpretation. "He pointed out that there is a change of standpoint from the view that the question *ought* not to be answered to the view that it *could* not be answered." Parenthetically Thomas ventures impatiently that "this merely means that different disciples discussed it in different ways."

Concluding his capsule summary of Oldenberg's supposed change of mind, Thomas writes:

Does the idea, says Oldenberg, which Buddhism had about that Beyond imply an absolutising of individual being as in later Samkhya, or had they floating in their minds a universal, absolute being in which the secret of achievement is realized? "From the way in which Buddhism treats this class of problems, or rather refuses to treat them, it follows that the ideas here in question can only be traced through a haze. But the traces that can be made out indicate rather that a universal being reaching far beyond the limits of the individual floated in their minds: an absolute, naturally not as *Weltgrund*, because in fact they had no impulse to ask about a *Weltgrund*, either openly or covertly, but an absolute as final highest goal." This is a withdrawal of the charge that if Buddha had drawn the last conclusion of his own principles, he would have arrived at annihilation.[5]

Shoson Miyamoto, the second of the critics under review here, has classified Oldenberg—together with Childers, Burnouf, and Joseph Dahlmann—under the rubric of the investigators characterized by "the rational grasping of the negative aspects of *Nirvāṇa*, *Nichts*, *Erlöschen*, *anéantissement*, annihilation—Buddhist nihilism."[6]

Finally, Heinrich Dumoulin, in his *History of Zen Buddhism*, echoes Thomas' explanation:

The chief exponents of the nihilist *nirvāṇa* interpretation are Childers, J. D. Alwis [*sic*], J. A. Ecklund, J. Dahlmann, and H. Oldenberg in the early edition of Oldenberg's work *Buddha*. Later Oldenberg came to the conclusion that nirvāṇa signifies something absolute, not in the sense of the cause of the universe but as an absolute final goal.[7]

[5] *Ibid.*, pp. 129–30.
[6] Miyamoto, *Studies on Nirvāṇa* I. *Is Nirvāṇa Nichts or Peace*, p. 8.
[7] Heinrich Dumoulin, *History of Zen Buddhism*, trans. Paul Peachey (New York: Pantheon Books, 1963), p. 292, note 21.

None of these statements fairly summarizes Oldenberg's conclusions about nirvāṇa—early or late. Before beginning my own reading of Oldenberg, it was my belief—partly on the basis of such secondary sources as those which I have just quoted and partly because of the number of revised editions of *Buddha* which appeared in the course of his career—that his interpretation of nirvāṇa probably underwent revision during the four decades separating the first edition from his death. Subsequent investigations lend no support to my earlier view.

The general content of Oldenberg's discussion in 1881 remains intact in the sixth German edition of 1914. The meaning—or, if you will, the intention—of these discussions is identical. Oldenberg does not dogmatically affirm in any of his writings that nirvāṇa is annihilation. There are no reversals. Conclusions about the meaning of nirvāṇa in later editions of Buddha in no way contradict the earlier statements.

A convenient place to begin is with two statements Oldenberg offers almost as methodological dicta. They deserve to be quoted in full because they provide clues to the professed spirit in which he conducted his Buddhist researches. Furthermore, they may be referred to later to check Oldenberg's consistent adherence to his own ground rules. First,

> Our speculations must not seek to discover what is the essence of a faith; we must permit the adherents of each faith themselves to determine this, and it is for historical inquiry to point out how they have defined it.[8]

(Do not overlook the fact that this was written more than half a century before E. J. Thomas' very similar-sounding statement on the same methodological point.)

The second of these general statements follows immediately on Oldenberg's account of Max Müller's refusal to believe that a religion could possibly be nihilistic and yet remain a religion. Oldenberg continues:

[8] *Buddha: Eng.*, p. 266; *1914G*, p. 307.

We cannot follow the famous inquirer when he attempts to trace the limits between the possible and the impossible in the development of religion. . . . Perhaps what is here [i.e., outside India] beyond comprehension may there be comprehensible, and if we reach a point which is to us a limit of the comprehensible, we shall permit much to pass and stand as incomprehensible, and await the future, which may bring us nearer the solution of the enigma.[9]

Here we are in the presence of a scholar singularly free from the distorting influences of a doctrinaire, tendentious spirit. It will be expected that Oldenberg will allow documents to confront readers through the medium of clear, straightforward translations which do not force those documents to declare doctrines which have been determined a priori by the investigator. Readers may expect this as a consequence of Oldenberg's methodological credo. No careful reader will be disappointed. Ready to be enlightened or confused by documents and doctrines, theories and practices, Oldenberg displays from the outset the attitudes of a true phenomenologist.

According to Oldenberg, this is the essential message of Buddhism: there is the world in which man lives, a world pervaded by the law of causality [10] and ipso facto a world of suffering. But there is a release from this suffering, from the law of cause and effect—in short, from this world. The state or condition of anyone thus released—that is to say, delivered—is the Buddhist nirvāṇa. Oldenberg begins his inquiry into the meaning of nirvāṇa modestly but exactly, saying, "We know this much only to begin with, that it is the domain over which the law of causality has no power." [11]

At this juncture we reach statements which are crucial for understanding Oldenberg's over-all evaluation. Nirvāṇa is "the domain over which the law of causality has no power." Yet it is apparent from the texts that nirvāṇa is not obtained

[9] *Ibid.: Eng.*, p. 268; *1914G*, p. 310.

[10] Pali: *paṭiccasammuppāda.* Oldenberg translates this technical expression as " 'Causal nexus of being.' " For his discussions on the subject, see *ibid: Eng.*, pp. 223–62; *1914G*, 251–302.

[11] *Ibid: Eng.*, p. 263; *1914G*, p. 303.

only after one is delivered entirely from the phenomenal world —that is, man can reach nirvāṇa before death. In opposition to Childers' view, Oldenberg declares emphatically:

> It is not an anticipation in parlance, but it is the absolutely exact expression of the dogmatic thought, when not merely the hereafter, which awaits the emancipated saint, but the perfection which he already attains in this life, is called the Nirvāṇa. What is to be extinguished has been extinguished, the fire of lust, hatred, bewilderment.[12]

On that account, the domain (*Reich*) which is nirvāṇa is not an ontic realm distinct from the phenomenal world. Rather, it is in Oldenberg's estimate the state of the man who is freed from domination by cause and effect. Nirvāṇa is a domain of the mind, a place in metaphor only. It is the status of the sanctified individual.

> If we are to indicate the precise point at which the goal is reached for the Buddhist, we must not look to the entry of the dying Perfect One into the range of the everlasting—be this either everlasting being or everlasting nothing—but to that moment of his earthly life, when he has attained the status of sinlessness and painlessness; this is the true Nirvāṇa.[13]

Oldenberg's meaning is clear: Metaphysical questions—is nirvāṇa annihilation? is it eternal being?—are wide of the mark. Nirvāṇa is sanctification in deliverance, deliverance in sanctification. Oldenberg declares simply:

> If the Buddhist faith really makes that saint's state of being disembody itself into nothingness . . . still entry into nothingness for nothingness' sake is not at all the object of aspiration. . . . *The goal to which he pressed was, we must constantly repeat this, solely deliverance from the sorrowful world of origination and decease.* Religious aspiration did not purposely and expressly demand that this deliverance should transport to nothingness, but when this was taught at all expression was merely given thereby to *the indifferent, accidental consequences of metaphysical reflections*, which prevent the assumption of an everlasting, immutable happy existence. In the religious life, in the tone which prevailed

[12] *Ibid: Eng.*, p. 264; *1914G*, p. 305.
[13] *Ibid: Eng.*, p. 265; *1914G*, p. 306.

in the ancient Buddhist order, the thought of annihilation has had no influence.[14] [My italics.]

Only through understanding the full implications of these early statements in Oldenberg's discussion, it seems to me, can anyone fully comprehend the sense of his conclusions about nirvāṇa. "If anyone describes Buddhism as a religion of annihilation," he warns, "and seeks to develop it therefrom as from its specific germ, he has, in fact, succeeded in wholly missing the main drift of Buddha and the ancient order of his disciples." [15] It is from this perspective that Oldenberg's subsequent arguments are to be approached. He insists that they prepare the ground for any consideration of whether or not nirvāṇa implies absolute annihilation at the conclusion of earthly existence.

Eternal bliss or everlasting nothing? There are three stages in Oldenberg's search for an answer. As these are not arranged with the clarity that is called for—witness the confusion of Thomas and others—I shall reorganize his presentation somewhat, while remaining faithful to his expression. The three stages are the following:

Oldenberg declares what he believes to be the answer which the Buddhist texts give to the question.

Comparing the Buddhist answer to the original question, Oldenberg decides that the question itself is misleading, that the texts affirm neither alternative.

Quite distinctly, Oldenberg hypothesizes about the reasons underlying the answer which the texts give. A desultory reading of this stage could suggest that Oldenberg believes that the declaration publicly given through the texts was the consequence of certain psychological and pragmatic considerations. That there is a great deal more to his conclusion I hope to illustrate in what follows.

Oldenberg prefaces his answer to the question of nirvāṇa's ultimate meaning according to the Buddhists with an account of his discovery.

[14] *Ibid.*

[15] *Ibid: Eng.*, p. 266; *1914G*, p. 307.

Before I undertook this task, it was my conviction that there is in the ancient Buddhist literature no passage which directly decides the alternative whether the Nirvāṇa is eternal felicity or annihilation. So much the greater therefore was my surprise, when in the course of these researches I lit not upon one passage but upon very numerous passages, which speak as expressly as possible upon the point, regarding which the controversy is waged, and determine it with a clearness which leaves nothing to be desired. And it was no less a cause of astonishment to me when I found that in that alternative which appeared to have been laid down with all possible cogency, *viz.* that the Nirvāṇa must have been understood in the ancient Order to be either the Nothing or a supreme felicity, there was finally neither on the one side nor the other perfect accuracy.[16]

In a single devastating paragraph, Oldenberg calls into question all the previous disputes in Europe over the meaning of nirvāṇa. The indictment is clear and inescapable: other investigators and debaters had not studied the texts carefully. If one scholar and one book could be said to have brought critical Buddhist studies to full maturity, without question they are Oldenberg and *Buddha.*

Oldenberg finds that all the knotty problems about the meaning of the Buddha's nirvāṇa are cut asunder by a single statement: "The official teaching of the Church represented that on the question, whether the ego is, whether the perfected saint lives after death or not, the exalted Buddha has taught nothing."[17] According to Oldenberg, V. Trenckner was the first investigator to point out "this disallowing of the question as to continuance in the hereafter."[18] The implications of the answer are unavoidable.

Our researches must accept this clear and decisive solution of the question, recurring often in the sacred texts, as it is given; it needs no interpretation, and admits of no strained construction. Orthodox teaching in the ancient order of Buddhists inculcated

[16] *Ibid: Eng.*, p. 269; *1914G*, pp. 310–11. These passages are not in complete accord.

[17] *Ibid: Eng.*, p. 274; *1914G*, p. 315.

[18] *Ibid.*, footnotes.

expressly on its converts to forego the knowledge of the being or non-being of the perfected saint.[19]

This is the historian's solution to the problem of nirvāṇa. But Oldenberg is not finished. The questions asked by European investigators as to the meaning of nirvāṇa are the very same questions asked and reasked in the texts themselves. It is clear that the question is consistently disallowed in the texts. This state of affairs prompts another question: Why is this repeated question disallowed? Oldenberg suggests that the texts offer two clues. First are certain nuances detectable in the dialogues, and second are the express statements of the Buddhist dogmatic with regard to the structure of the world.

The conclusion dictated by logic or dialectic alone, according to Oldenberg, would be that nirvāṇa is ultimately annihilation.

> A doctrine which contemplates a future of eternal perfection beyond transitory being, cannot possibly admit of the kingdom of the eternal first beginning only at the point where the world of the transient ends, cannot conjure it up immediately, as it were out of the Nothing. In the kingdom of the transient itself there must be contained, veiled perhaps like a latent germ, but still present, an element which bears in itself the pledge of everlasting being. . . .[20]

As "the finite world appears in the dogmatic of Buddhism to rest wholly upon itself," Oldenberg writes, everything in that world is considered to be conditioned and conditional. Hence, "if we follow the dialectical consequence solely, it is impossible on the basis of this theory of life to conceive how, where a series of conditions has run out, annihilating itself, anything else is to be recognized as remaining but a vacuum."[21]

Now, says Oldenberg, this is certainly a consequence. But he is careful to qualify the word "consequence." It is always a

[19] *Ibid: Eng.*, p. 276; *1914G*, p. 317.
[20] *Ibid: Eng.*, pp. 269–70; *1914G*, p. 311.
[21] *Ibid: Eng.*, pp. 270–71; *1914G*, pp. 311–12.

consequence viewed from the standpoint of a specific application of reasoning, not a factual consequence. It involves the "claims of strict dialectical sequence." It is a "dialectical consequence only." It answers "the demands of dialectic alone." The premises of the Buddhist teachings lead dialectically to this conclusion: "The ego is not. Or what is equivalent: the Nirvāṇa is annihilation." [22]

Apparently, Oldenberg observes, this conclusion of a strictly performed dialectic was obvious to many members of the ancient *saṃgha.* But if it had been introduced as a part of the dogmatics, he goes on, the "weak-minded" (*beschrankt*) individual would have been shocked and disturbed, perhaps to the point of abandoning the Buddha's path. It does not seem to me true that Oldenberg means to equate the logical consequence with the actuality of the Buddha's teachings or intentions. At no time will Oldenberg say that nirvāṇa is annihilation in fact. After all, how could he? Has he not already said with all possible emphasis that the nirvāṇa goal is sought after and can be attained completely in this life?

Given the official answer—or failure to answer—and some of the factors inspiring it, what of the practicing Buddhist? In the first place, the absence of a firm statement one way or another in the dogmatic provided opportunities for divergence of opinion.

> Could not that negative answer, which we have come to recognize as the true answer of close dialectic, be met by an affirmative also? Might not hearts, that quailed before the Nothing, that could not relinquish the hope of everlasting weal, gather from Buddha's silence above all this one response, that it was not forbidden to them to hope? [23]

Oldenberg insists, then, that a rather positive interpretation emerges from between the lines of several dialogues in the Pali Canon. After illustrating that attitude through quoting

[22] *Ibid: Eng.*, p. 273; *1914G*, p. 314. In *1914G*, the statement "Or what is equivalent: The Nirvāṇa is annihilation" has been deleted, but I cannot see any change in the effect of the argument.

[23] *Ibid: Eng.*, p. 277; *1914G*, p. 319.

the famous dialogue between Khemā Therī and King Pasenadi, Oldenberg comments:

> We shall scarcely be astray in supposing that we discover in this dialogue a marked departure from the sharply defined line to which the course of thought confines itself in the previously quoted conversation between Buddha and Malukya [i.e., Māluṅkyāputta or Mālukyaputta]. True, the question as to the eternal duration of the Perfect One is as little answered here as there, but why can it not be answered? The Perfect One's existence is unfathomably deep, like the ocean: it is of a depth which terrestrial human thought with the appliances at its command, cannot exhaust. The man who applies to the strictly unconditional predicates such as being and non-being, which are used properly enough of the finite, the conditional, resembles a person who attempts to count the sands of the Ganges or the drops of the ocean.[24]

Acknowledging such reasons as supporting the refusal to answer directly the questions about the ultimate destiny of the perfected, one answer appears.

> And is not this answer a Yes? No being in the ordinary sense but still assuredly not a non-being: a sublime positive, of which thought has no idea, for which language has no expression, which beams out to meet the cravings of the thirsty for immortality.[25]

In such dialogues, Oldenberg continues, viewpoints are visible which are not controlled by the negative conclusions of a rigorously applied dialectic.

> One who clearly and indefinitely renounced an everlasting future would speak in another strain; behind the veil of the mystery there flies the longing to escape from opposing reason, which declines to admit the conceivableness of everlasting existence, the hope for an existence, which is beyond reason and conception.[26]

The Pali Canon contains three attitudes toward nirvāṇa as an ultimate condition. First is the unquestioned official disavowal of both question and answer. Second is the implicit

[24] *Ibid: Eng.*, p. 280; *1914G*, pp. 321–22.
[25] *Ibid.*
[26] *Ibid: Eng.*, pp. 282–83; *1914G*, pp. 324–25.

conclusion drawn by certain text writers (for example, in the "Mālukyaputta Dialogue") that nirvāṇa is ultimately annihilation. Finally, there is an equally implicit, equally unofficial answer which reflects the vibrant religious consciousness: although nirvāṇa is eventually not being in any definable sense, it is definitely not the nothing.

Several scriptural passages describe the goal of the Buddhists as the uncreated. This calls to mind the speculations in the Upaniṣads. And, indeed, Oldenberg goes so far in later German editions of *Buddha* as to say "There is no doubt that the idea of nirvāṇa came from that of Brahman." [27] But in all editions the important conclusion is the same: whatever may be the kinship of the Brahmanic and Buddhist conceptions and expressions, an unbridgeable gap separates their respective intentionalities.

> To the Brahman the uncreated is so veritable a reality, that the reality of the created pales before it; the created derives its being and life solely from the uncreated. For the Buddhist the words "there is an uncreated" merely signify that the created can free himself from the curse of being created.[28]

Max Müller interpreted the words of Dhammapada 383—"If thou has learned the destruction of the Sankhara, thou knowest the uncreated"—to mean that the Buddha acknowledged the existence of an imperishable, an eternal something. Oldenberg objects:

> It appears to me that we can find in the expression another meaning, and if we consider it in connection with the Buddhist theory of the world, we must find another meaning: Let thine own aim be, to discover the cessation of impermanence. If thou knowest that, thou has the highest knowledge. . . . As for thee let the attainment of the uncreated consist in this, that thou reachest the cessation of the created.[29]

The state of sinlessness and painlessness, the status of deliverance through sanctification—that is the true nirvāṇa. And

[27] *Ibid: 1914G*, p. 326.
[28] *Ibid: Eng.*, p. 283; *1914G*, p. 327.
[29] *Ibid: Eng.*, pp. 283–84, footnote; *1914G*, p. 327, footnote.

that is Oldenberg's conclusion from the study of the Pali Canon. Sanctification is the goal of the Buddha's path.

> Does the path lead into a new existence? Does it lead into the Nothing? The Buddhist creed rests in delicate equipoise between the two. The longing of the heart that craves the eternal has not nothing, and yet the thought has not a something, which it might firmly grasp. Farther off the idea of the endless, the eternal could not withdraw itself from belief than it has done here, where like a gentle flutter on the point of merging in the Nothing it threatens to evade the gaze.[30]

In returning now to the scholars whose accounts of Oldenberg's interpretation of nirvāṇa began this chapter, it will not be difficult to note the injustices in their evaluations. E. J. Thomas accuses Oldenberg of drawing conclusions about nirvāṇa which the Buddhists themselves never drew. It seems unquestionable that Oldenberg did nothing of the kind. Reading the texts carefully, he notes two attitudes in addition to the overt, dogmatic position—one a rationalistic or dialectical attitude, the other religious, even mystical. Neither represents the official stand of Buddhism. That position, Oldenberg insists, was and is the only apt definition: the true nirvāṇa is a state of sanctification, of deliverance from the authority of the law of causality. This is the nirvāṇa that the Buddhists seek. This is their goal of goals.

Miyamoto's inclusion of Oldenberg in the category of those scholars who defined nirvāṇa as annihilation is justified in a limited sense only. Oldenberg ought at the very least to be included under his heading of those who, from "the standpoint of practical ethics," interpret nirvāṇa "as peace as opposed to nihilism." And, as the richness of Oldenberg's presentation defies compression within those categories, it would be better to create another division or not to mention him at all.

H. Dumoulin's statement reads like a summary of Thomas' judgment. It must be repeated that Oldenberg insists that nirvāṇa is an absolute, final goal. There is no reversal in his

[30] *Ibid: Eng.*, p. 284; *1914G*, pp. 327–28.

interpretation, no inconsistency, no ambiguity. In both Dumoulin's and Thomas's statements, the references to Oldenberg's other writings are not at all conclusive. They do not demonstrate that Oldenberg changed his mind about nirvāṇa.[31]

Of all the short accounts of Oldenberg's interpretation, that of Govind Chandra Pande in his *Studies in the Origins of Buddhism* is perhaps the most accurate.

Oldenberg seems to think that although logically the Nirvāṇa beyond death ought to have signified just Nothing and although the official position on the subject was to refuse to answer the question, there are some texts which would interpret the silence of Buddha to have been really due to the indescribable character of Nirvāṇa. Thus "Das Verlangen des nach Ewigem trachenden Herzens hat nicht Nichts, und doch hat das Denken kein Etwas, das es festzuhalten vermochte." [32]

Oldenberg does not suggest that the logical or rationalist interpretation is the key to understanding the Buddhist nirvāṇa. Buddhism is not a religion of annihilation; this is not its specific germ. Quarrels about Oldenberg's statements focus on only one aspect in the rich complexity of his total argument. It is for this reason, as I have stressed above, that the reader must thoroughly understand the first few pages of his discussion. It is there that Oldenberg announces just what sort of religious and philosophical institution he takes Buddhism to be. Those statements are the key to comprehending his evaluations.

Two limiting factors present for Oldenberg must also be taken into account. First is his complete reliance on the Pali texts. It is true that he sought the beliefs of the earliest Buddhist order, but it is not true that the Mahāyāna materials provide no assistance in this regard. The second factor is more

[31] Those references are to Oldenberg's *Die Lehre der Upanishaden und die Anfänge des Buddhismus* (Göttingen: Van den Hoeck & Ruprecht, 1915). Oldenberg does not "retract" any earlier statements about nirvāṇa, but rather concentrates on the somewhat dubious historical hypothesis that the source for the Buddhist idea of nirvāṇa is the Upaniṣadic Brahman.

[32] Govind Chandra Pande, *Studies in the Origins of Buddhism*, p. 454.

difficult to specify with precision. It has to do with the intellectual milieu of the late nineteenth and early twentieth centuries. Scholars were more and more attracted to the Pali tradition because it was relatively straightforward, they assumed, and free from the extravagances characteristic of the Mahāyāna. And, I am convinced, Europe's increasing dissatisfaction and disillusionment with metaphysical proposals of all kinds is manifest in the favoritism shown the Pali literature. In the study of the latter, the question of nirvāṇa in its metaphysical—if not its eschatological—aspects could be accommodated in a manner impossible in the confrontation with the Northern traditions.

Oldenberg spoke about Buddhism in terms congenial to the attitudes reigning in his Europe. Is nirvāṇa nothingness? "When this was taught at all expression was merely given thereby to the indifferent, accidental consequences of metaphysical reflections. . . ." There were not many well-educated Europeans in the late nineteenth and early twentieth centuries who had any higher regard for the conclusions of metaphysics generally.

Two Nirvāṇas?

Oldenberg stresses that nirvāṇa is a goal to be attained in this life. After arriving at a certain moral status, the Buddhist seeks no further. He has achieved the highest goal. He has arrived at the opposite shore. Insisting that

> it is not an anticipation in parlance, but it is the absolutely exact expression of the dogmatic thought, when not merely the hereafter, which awaits the emancipated saint, but the perfection which he already attains in this life, is called the Nirvāṇa

he challenges that interpretation of nirvāṇa advanced by Robert Childers. The latter maintained, as has been shown, that the term nirvāṇa was used to describe both the blissful existence of the arahat and his ultimate annihilation. Among the props that Childers provided for his contention, the following may be recalled:

Since Arhatship is necessarily followed after an insignificant interval by Nirvāṇa, to say that an Arhat has attained Nirvāṇa is merely to say that he has made sure of Nirvāṇa, that he has made Nirvāṇa his own, it is a figure of speech examples of which are to be found in the literatures of every religion.[33]

Childers sought to explain the apparent existence of two nirvāṇas in the Buddhist literature by saying that these were two descriptions of one and the same thing. His emphasis was directed to the so-called post-mortem condition, the absolute annihilation of the human phenomenon in all its parts. The state of perfection, Childers wrote, was called nirvāṇa in anticipation, for that would be the inevitable terminus of the purified condition. According to Childers (and Hardy and D'Alwis before him), the two nirvāṇas were distinguished as *savupādisesanibbānam* and *anupādisesanibbānam:* nirvāṇa, respectively, with and without remnants of *upādi.* And *upādi* in this view is merely a synonym for the aggregate of *skandha*-s (Pali: *khandha*), this aggregate being the phenomenal, psychosomatic complex which constitutes each particular sentient existence. Strictly speaking then, Childers interpreted the compound, *sa-upādi* (Sanskrit: *upadhi* [?])-*sesa*(Sanskrit: *śeṣa*), as a possessive *(bahuvrīhi, bahubbīhi)* whose members are in a descriptive (*karmadhāraya, kammadhāraya*) relationship: "(Nirvāṇa) accompanied by a remnant—namely *upādi.*"

That explanation did not satisfy Oldenberg. In the first edition of his *Buddha*, he devotes an intensive excursis to an examination of the term *upādisesa.* This particular technical question occurs in the discussions about nirvāṇa from the time

[33] Childers, *Dictionary*, p. 268a.

of Eugène Burnouf's *Introduction*, and several treatments of it may be examined here. Consideration of the manner in which scholars dealt with an important subtopic should afford additional insight into the various ways they conducted the enterprise of deciphering nirvāṇa.

Eugène Burnouf confessed that the designation *upadhiśeṣa* (the Sanskrit equivalent of the Pali *upādisesa*) was extremely difficult to understand. In the first place, he observed, there are orthographic differences in the representation of the term. Thus, beyond the fact that *nirupadhiśeṣa* and *anupadhiśeṣa* were often used interchangeably—certainly meaning absolutely the same thing (the same, privative sense in the prefixes *nir-* and *an-*)—the Pali Buddhists seem to have written *anupādisesa* and *anupadisesa* indifferently. With only the *Pañcakrama* gloss to assist him (and admitting that this work was definitely not representative of the earliest period of Buddhism [34]), Burnouf ventured a translation of the following stanza:

> *sopadhiśeṣam pañcaskandhamātra śunyam*
> *anupadhiśeṣaṃ sarvaśunyaṃ nirvāṇam//*

Sopadhiśeṣa, or that in which there remains some upadhi, is only void of the five skandhas; anupadhiśeṣa, or that in which nothing of upadhi remains, is void of everything, it is nirvāṇa.[35]

None of H. H. Wilson's three definitions of *upadhi*—fraud, wheel of a chariot, terror—seems to suit the sense of the Buddhist usage, according to Burnouf. Indeed, Wilson's account serves only to explain the basis for Clough's peculiar translation of *anupādisesa* as "not (*an*) producing (*upādi*) transmigration (*sesa*)." [36] Burnouf completely rejects this latter.

It tells us only one thing: the result of the nirvāṇa which puts an end to transmigration. Citing it here, I wish only to show that if

[34] Arthur Berriedale Keith in *A History of Sanskrit Literature* (Oxford: The University Press, 1920), p. 496, suggests *ca.* A.D. 850 for the compilation of the text.

[35] Burnouf, *Introduction*, p. 527.

[36] *Ibid.*, quoting Clough.

upadhi means "wheel" in the Buddhist expression, one would find in it the basis for the translation given by Clough.[37]

Tibetan texts, continues Burnouf, render the Sanskrit *upadhi* by the word *phuṅ-po:* "accumulation, heap, aggregation of material elements." *Phuṅ-po* is also the Tibetan designation for the collective assemblage of the five *skandha*-s. In support of his interpretation, Burnouf quotes Csoma's translation of the Tibetan equivalent of *anupadhiśeṣanirvāṇa:* "Entirely delivered from pain with respect to the five aggregates of the body." [38]

On the basis of these corroborations, Burnouf is satisfied that there need be no doubt as to the meaning of *upadhi* in the compound *anupadhiśeṣa.*

All these comparisons lead me to believe that the term upadhi designates the collective union of the five Skandhas, a union of the principal elements of human individuality. So I propose to give to this term a sense analogous to that of support, foundation, that is to say, to that which one supposes to be; so that upadhi designates individuality taken subjectively and objectively. Consequently, the expression anupadhiśeṣam nirvāṇam can be translated in this way: "Annihilation, that in which nothing remains of individuality." [39]

But Burnouf does not resolve all the problems to his satisfaction, for he is puzzled about what translation may be given *sopadhiśeṣa* so that the intention of the *Pañcakramam* would be preserved.

It is clear that this gloss distinguishes two voids: one in which upadhi remains—or the supported or supposed individuality, if I may so express myself; the other is the absolute or total void in which the Tibetan interpreters teach us to see the annihilation of individuality itself. Nevertheless it may be possible that the Pañcakrama understands by upadhi the person itself—or that which is called Pudgala elsewhere—in such a way that the void in which upadhi remains represents the human person or the pure spirit freed from all its attributes.[40]

[37] *Ibid.*
[38] *Ibid.*
[39] *Ibid.*, p. 528.
[40] *Ibid.*, p. 529.

Absence of further commentatorial assistance halts Burnouf at this point. He cannot resolve the problems, and retreats to his earlier comment that the *Pañcakramam* is a recent work which can be conveniently set aside when conducting investigations on manifestly ancient terms.[41] Despite the difficulties which follow on the citation from the *Pañcakramam*, Burnouf believes that he has an accurate definition of *upadhi:* it is an equivalent of the five *skandha*-s collectively and attains that technical signification by way of etymology—*upadhi* as "support."

Both Spence Hardy and James D'Alwis confirm this interpretation, though without referring to Burnouf's discussion.[42] Childers underscores this definition and makes it pivotal in his exposition of nirvāṇa. The confusion which plagues European scholarship about the true meaning of nirvāṇa, he declares, is caused by the fact that the Buddhist texts seem to describe nirvāṇa now as extinction, now as highest bliss. "Extinction," "total annihilation," he insists, is the primary meaning; and by extension and in anticipation, the status which qualifies a man for this extinction is also called nirvāṇa. "*Upādi* is a name for the five skandhas, and *savupādisesanibbānam* means annihilation of everything except the five skandhas, while *anupādisesanibbānam* means the extinction of Being."[43]

The word *upādi*, according to Childers' *Dictionary*, "is a masculine noun from the verb *upādā* as *upadhi* is formed from *upadhā* and is a name for the five Khandhas. . . ."[44] *Upādisesa*, the article continues, means "having the skandhas remaining." At this point a solution is offered to the problem which had annoyed Burnouf.

The North Buddhists, puzzled by the anomalous form *upādi*, concluded it must be a mistake for *upadhi*, and have turned *upādisesa* into *sopadhiśeṣa*. Hence we have the curious anomaly of the

[41] *Ibid.*
[42] See above, pp. 144–45.
[43] Childers, *Dictionary*, p. 526a.
[44] *Ibid.*

North Buddhists terming the Arhat *sopadhiśeṣa*, "having upadhi," while *nirupadhi*, "free from upadhi," is with the South Buddhists a distinctive epithet of the Arhat! [45]

The confusion worsens. Childers defines the Pali word *upadhi* as "a wheel; the body, a substratum of being." [46] When *nirupadhi* (in Pali) is used to describe the *arahat* it means "free from substratum." But Childers then turns round and accuses the Pali Buddhists of being imprecise. The substrata (*upadhi*) are listed as the *khandha*-s, *kāma*, *kilesa*, and *kamma;* and it is obvious, declares Childers, that the *arahat* is not yet free from the first of these. In Childers' less than elegant account, the Pali *nirupadhi* should be the equivalent of the Pali *savupādisesa* and the Buddhist Sanskrit *sopadhiśeṣa.*

Oldenberg was not convinced, and in 1881 (a few years after Childers' death) he contested the English scholar's solution to this complex problem. In later editions of *Buddha*, Oldenberg's excursis on the subject is not reprinted (presumably because of its technicalities and in the interest of reducing publication costs). But the author refers readers of those later editions to the earlier discussion—indicating to me that he remained satisfied with his treatment of the topic.

Oldenberg prefaces his excursis with a just summation of Childers' general position.

Childers has, as is known . . . propounded the theory that by Saupādisesanibbāna is meant the condition of the perfect saint, in whom the five Khandhas are still to the fore, but the desire which chains to being is extinct; Anupādisesanibbāna, on the other hand, is said to designate the cessation of all being, the condition or non-condition ensuing on the death of the saint.[47]

The first point of Oldenberg's own treatment is the classification of the "outwardly similar sounding expressions" used in reference to *nibbāna:*

[45] *Ibid.*
[46] *Ibid.*
[47] *Buddha: Eng.*, p. 427.

Upadhi;
Upādāna—connected with *upādā* and *upādāya;*
Anupādāna—connected with *anupada* and *anupādāya;*
Upādisesa, *saupādisesa*, and *anupādisesa.*

In Pali, *upadhi* and *upādāna* are almost synonymous, according to Oldenberg. "The attainment or non-attainment of Nirvāṇa, victory or defeat in the struggle against suffering is made dependent upon the presence or non-presence of Upādāna and quite as much so of Upadhi." [48] In a variant of the formula of the twelve *Nidāna*-s,[49] *upadhi* is said to proceed from *taṇhā* ("thirst," "desire," "craving"). And from *upadhi*, according to that account, come old age, suffering, and death. "In exactly the same way the well-known formula of the twelve Nidānas makes Upādāna come from Tanhā, and from Upādāna (through a few middle links) old age, death, suffering." [50]

Oldenberg believes that the distinction between *upadhi* and *upādāna* diminishes still more if the use of the term *upadhi* in Sanskrit is analyzed.

> Upa-dhā means "to lay one thing on another, to give it support," thus anything which would so to speak float in the air or fly about, to chain it to reality by a substratum, which is given it to localize it. This substratum is exactly Upadhi.[51]

And Oldenberg's definition of *upa-dā* and *upā*(= *upa* + *ā*)-*dā* is "the laying hold of or clinging to anything." *Upādāna*, then is "that laid hold of by a being, to which it clings, as well as the act of this catching. . . ." [52]

Concluding that the terms *upadhi* and *upādāna*—despite etymological differences—have almost the same meaning in the Buddhist technical vocabulary, Oldenberg encounters difficulty in treating the term *upādi*—a term which appears

[48] *Ibid.*, p. 433.

[49] *Ibid.*, p. 427 (passage from Saṃyuttaka Nikāya). Oldenberg did not believe, however, that the Nidāna formula was found in the earliest Order; *ibid.*, p. 224, footnote.

[50] *Ibid.*, p. 433.

[51] *Ibid.*

[52] *Ibid.*

only in the compound *upādisesa.* According to a passage in the *Itivuttaka* (which Oldenberg himself quotes) and also the argument of Childers, *upādi* would seem to be different in meaning from both *upadhi* and *upādāna.* Oldenberg is frankly puzzled by the disparity.

It must be in the highest degree astonishing that the limit between saupādisesa and anupādisesa is here removed to a wholly different place from the limit between saupādāna and anupādāna, or between the state of the nirupadhi and the burdened with upadhi. In the last two named cases we had to do with the ethical opposition of the internally bound and the internally free; in the case now before us, on the other hand, we could only have, according to the view of Childers and . . . the Itivuttaka, to do with the physical opposition of the internally free, whose external life still continues, and the internally free, whose external life has ceased. It is really very hard to believe that, of the three pairs of ideas which all belong to the Nirvāṇa doctrine, and which at first sight present an appearance of so close a parallelism, the third should actually have in view a point so thoroughly different from the first two. . . .[53]

Oldenberg's suspicions seem confirmed in several other texts. In them,[54] *upādisesa* "has not the physical meaning of a residuum of earthly existence, but the ethical meaning of a residuum of impurity, the same signification which we have found in Upādāna and Upadhi." [55] Moreover, in explaining a parable in which the term *anupādisesa* had been used, one of those texts substitutes the term *nirupadhi.*

Anupādisesa in Pali corresponds exactly with *anupadhiśeṣa* or *nirupadhiśeṣa* in the Buddhist Sanskrit; on this Oldenberg agrees with Burnouf. And Oldenberg declares that he has "no scruple in declaring the problematic upādi to be only a spelling of the word upadhi peculiar to the Pāli—probably we should rather say, peculiar to our modern Pāli manuscripts." [56]

[53] *Ibid.*, p. 435.

[54] Namely, the Satipaṭṭhānasutta (Majjhima Nikāya), the Vaṅgīsa Sutta (Sutta Nipāta), and the Sunakkhatta Suttānta (Majjhima Nikāya). See *ibid.*, pp. 435–37.

[55] *Ibid.*, p. 435.

[56] *Ibid.*, p. 437.

Problems in the *Itivuttaka* text, however, do not admit of easy resolution. Oldenberg encounters considerable difficulty. He states that the expression *anupādisesanibbānadhātu* is tautological, for absence of *upadhi* is implied in *nibbānadhātu*. All this is well and good, of course, only if one allows Oldenberg's equation of *upādi* and *upadhi*. But, though he stumbles about here and manipulates logic in a rather cavalier fashion, his suggested solution to the attitude in this text is reasonable enough. Psychologically, it is possible that the adjective *anupādisesa* was applied to *nibbānadhātu* in an overly enthusiastic attempt to underscore the meaning of the latter. Such a tautology in its turn might "easily suggest to a misinformed mind the opposition of a sa-upādisesa nibbānadhātu. . . ." If we follow Oldenberg this far, we may agree with him that in such conditions the *Itivuttaka* has made the best of a bad situation.

Although Oldenberg cannot completely convince either himself or his readers about his explanation of the *Itivuttaka* passage, he does present sufficient material to question the authority of Childers's interpretation of the terms *sopādi-* and *nirupādisesa*. And throughout his own examination of the terms *upādāna*, *upadhi*, and *upādi*, Oldenberg's estimate that the essence of nirvāṇa lies in its ethical and moral implications is reaffirmed. But it is not that Oldenberg was to be understood in his interpretation of nirvāṇa or followed in his explication of *upādisesa*.

In 1898, nearly two decades after the publication of Oldenberg's conclusions, Arthur Oncken Lovejoy presented an article on the subject to the *Journal of the American Oriental Society*. Discussing the technical terms *upādāna* and *upādisesa*, Lovejoy concludes that meanings are essentially the same, thus supporting Oldenberg's position. "Oldenberg's view seems, however, to have been pretty commonly ignored or rejected by subsequent expositors, who cling rather to the theory of Childers." [57]

[57] A. O. Lovejoy, "The Buddhistic Technical Terms *upādāna* and *upādisesa*," p. 133.

The ordinary translation of *upādāna* is "attachment" or "clinging to existence," according to Lovejoy. In Emile Senart's view, however, *upādāna* as a technical Buddhist expression is rather an abbreviation of the compound *upādānakkhandha* and signifies the collectivity of the *skandha*-s. Lovejoy rejects this latter notion totally. In fact, he continues,

> *upādāna* is specifically that result of desire which consists in the habitual identification of one's will and interests with the *skandhas*, i.e., with the conditions of ordinary sentient, and especially . . . of physical existence.[58]

Upādāna, then, would depend on the *skandha*-s and lead to a new combination of *skandha*-s in the next existence. "As distinguished from *taṇhā* [the eighth *nidāna*] *upādāna* seems to be the chronic condition of the will to which the particular cravings of desire lead. . . ." [59]

In the case of *upādisesa*, Lovejoy observes that the usual translation, following Childers, is "having the five skandhas remaining." Childers takes *upādi* to mean exactly what Senart thinks *upādāna* means. Indeed, Childers's etymological derivation of *upādi* makes it almost the same word as *upādāna*. But, Lovejoy crows proudly, "The latter is no more the skandhas than a hen is a hen's egg."

Lovejoy himself despairs of finding any assistance from etymology for disentangling the meanings of these terms. Not only is there "a confusing similarity between *upādi* and *upadhi*"; but one must also consider the technical term *upādhi* in the Nyāya and the Sāṃkhya. On the one hand, according to Lovejoy, some scholars—Joseph Dahlmann and E. Müller —derive the Pali *upādi* from this technical *upādhi*. And on the other hand are scholars—Böhtlingk, Childers, and T. W. Rhys Davids—who derive *upādi* from *upādā*, while maintaining that the Pali word *upadhi* is the equivalent of the technical Sanskrit term *upādhi*. It is perfectly obvious that etymology is not clarifying anything.

Lovejoy turns to three Pali texts in order to document the

[58] *Ibid.*, p. 129.
[59] *Ibid.*

truth of Oldenberg's position. The exegesis of one—Sutta Nipāta, verse 876—may be cited to illustrate something of his method as well as the similarity between his own understanding of nirvāṇa and Oldenberg's. After quoting and translating this text in which it is said that the truly wise seek to be *anupādisesa*, Lovejoy comments:

> No one familiar with Buddhist modes of thought could suppose that *anupādisesa* here means merely the extinction of the (present) skandhas, i.e., physical death. To the man who has once become freed from desire it is indifferent whether he lives or dies; to regard death, in itself, as the summum bonum would be the least Buddhistic of sentiments.[60]

On the contrary, Lovejoy asserts, the meaning of the term in this context is "freedom from attachment"—a moral not a physical condition.

With Oldenberg, Lovejoy concludes that the oldest and most numerous texts support the interpretation that *upādisesa* is the equivalent of *upādāna*. But he wisely refrains from dogmatism.

> Other passages might be cited in favor of the more usual view; so that the matter cannot be regarded as finally settled. The discrepancies in usage may, as I have suggested prove to be explicable as due to scribal errors resulting from the homophony of *upādi*, *upadhi* and the Sāṃkhyan *upādhi*.[61]

Thus, on the eve of the twentieth century, the opposing theories about the meaning of *upādisesa* were well articulated. Yet, neither view could account for every instance without recourse to such assertions as that the texts were in error. Further investigation into the Pali texts plus detailed study of the so-called Buddhist Hybrid Sanskrit have tended to reinforce Childers's conclusions. But it must be noted that Oldenberg and Lovejoy have not yet been refuted convincingly.

Oldenberg and Lovejoy not only share a common understanding of the meaning of *upādisesa;* in great measure they

[60] *Ibid.*, p. 135.
[61] *Ibid.*, p. 136.

agree about the meaning of nirvāṇa and the general character of Buddhism. In Lovejoy, to be sure, one reads the opinions of a scholar caught up in the pragmatic and psychologistic biases of the day. Still, it cannot be said that this standpoint is without benefits of its own, for there is an insight here which probes close to the heart of the Buddhist institutions. Consider Lovejoy's observation:

Buddhism—I speak throughout, of course, of the Buddhism of the Piṭakas and of the orthodox commentators,—is essentially a system of spiritual discipline based, not upon a metaphysic, but upon a psychology of sensation. It is this, of course, which sharply differentiates it from the other important Hindu philosophies, which are highly metaphysical. It seems difficult for European expounders of Buddhism to keep this distinction steadily in mind. There is a tendency to assimilate the doctrine to the type of the metaphysical systems.[62]

That tendency on the part of European investigators, Lovejoy argues, is completely antipathetic to Buddhism itself. For

Buddhism knows nothing of any ontological absolute, and it has a really morbid antipathy to the Unconditioned. The first nidāna simply asserts that salvation depends ultimately upon a certain theoretical insight; namely, an insight not into any ultimate truths about the prime substance and metaphysical essence either of the universe or of man, but into a certain simple psychological analysis of the nature and value of human sensation and volition.[63]

It is not so simple as all that. But there is an order of truth in the passage, and certainly the triumph of developing anti-metaphysical attitudes is written clearly there. The metaphysical aspect of the nirvāṇa controversy recedes as the ethical and psychological aspects are emphasized. It is the attitude of the investigator and the metaphysical poverty of much of the Pali literature that help bring about this modification in the course of Buddhist studies. Many students cease to be shocked about nirvāṇa, not because they find it obviously a positive goal, but because its moral implications are so modern.

[62] *Ibid.*, p. 131.
[63] *Ibid.*, p. 132.

In the next chapter, through a discussion of the theories of Thomas William and Caroline Augusta Foley Rhys Davids, the ethical and psychological bias of this phase will be seen in its maturity. And, as perfectly documented in the case of Mrs. Rhys Davids, the reader will also see the nature and scope of the reaction to this pervading psychologism.

[CHAPTER VII]

The Rhys Davidses

In the same Bulletin in which he reviewed the first edition of Hermann Oldenberg's *Buddha*, Auguste Barth devoted a paragraph to Thomas William Rhys Davids' *Hibbert Lectures*. "Actually, the views of the author," Barth observed, "do not differ essentially . . . from those of Oldenberg, and the limits of the subject there are almost the same." [1] That there should have been such a close correlation between the works is not necessarily surprising, for in the same year the first of a three-volume translation of the Vinaya (discipline) part of the Pali Buddhist Canon was published—a product of the cooperative efforts of Oldenberg and Rhys Davids.[2]

[1] "Bulletin de 1882," *Révue de l'Histoire des Religions*, V, 242 as reprinted in *Quarante ans d'indianisme: Oeuvres de Auguste Barth*, I, 345.

[2] *Vinaya Texts*, trans. T. W. Rhys Davids and Hermann Oldenberg (3 vols. as XIII, XVII, and XX of *Sacred Books of the East*, ed. F. Max Müller; Oxford: Clarendon Press, 1881–85). On the relationship between Oldenberg and Rhys Davids, the following is of inter-

Because of the undoubted similarities and correspondences in certain of these scholars' conclusions, it may seem somewhat strange—or wasteful of space—that I have chosen to examine their work in separate chapters. The rationale for this arrangement is twofold. First, the differences in interpretation (and they are more considerable than Barth's review might indicate) will be illumined better by means of separate treatments. And, too, this format will accord with the historical facts as we have them, because there is no trace of any "dialogue" between the two scholars on the subject of nirvāṇa.

Second, and more important, Rhys Davids and his wife Caroline Augusta Foley Rhys Davids represent far more than merely the "pioneer stage of Pali studies and of a scholarly interpretation of Pali Buddhism in England." [3] This husband-wife team, whose efforts span more than six decades and include such milestones as the practically complete publication of the Pali Buddhist texts, has provided what, is still, on the one hand, the standard interpretation of the Pali Buddhist tradition and, on the other, the grounding for a more sophisticated understanding of Pali Buddhism in the future. Even today, many non-specialists' ideas of Buddhism are scarcely more than paraphrases of the conclusions reached by Rhys Davids as early as 1877. And what was said shortly after the death of Mrs. Rhys Davids, in 1942, is still true in great measure: "It is not too much to say that the ideas of the educated layman about Pali Buddhism today [and here I should insert that this applies to Buddhists in South and Southeast Asia] are those first put forth by Mrs. Rhys Davids.

---

est: "His [Rhys Davids'] friendship with . . . Oldenberg began with an act of generosity. Professor Oldenberg came to consult him about an edition of the Dīpavaṃsa he was wishing to make, and Professor Rhys Davids at once handed over to him all the material he had himself amassed for the same purpose." (C. Mary Ridding, "Obituary: Professor T. W. Rhys Davids," *Bulletin of the School of Oriental Studies*, III [1923–25], 203.

[3] W. Stede, "Obituary: Mrs. C. A. F. Rhys Davids," JRAS, 1942, p. 267.

. . ." [4] Therefore, it will be an advantage to savor fully the attitudes and achievements of the Rhys Davidses in a single draught.

Thomas William Rhys Davids

T. W. Rhys Davids, born May 12, 1843, the son of a Congregationalist minister, attended Brighton and then studied Sanskrit with Stenzler at the University of Breslau. Entering the Ceylon Civil Service in 1864,[5] Rhys Davids embarked on a career that parallels with remarkable fidelity that of Robert Childers. Competent in Sanskrit, Tamil, and Sinhalese, he had his introduction to Pali as an official accident. "The production, as evidence in a trial, of a Pali sacred text that no one present could read led to the work of his life by making him resolve to master the unknown language." [6]

Forced to resign his post in the Ceylon Civil Service in 1877, Rhys Davids returned to England and read for the bar, though he was never to practice law. In 1881 he established the Pali Text Society, and from 1882 to 1904 he was—as Childers had been before him—professor of Pali in the University College, London. Appointed professor of comparative religion in the Victoria University, Manchester, in 1904, he served there until his retirement in 1915. He died in Chipstead, Surrey, a few months short of his eightieth birthday, December 27, 1922.[7]

[4] *Ibid.*, p. 268.

[5] According to another source, the date was 1866. See 'C.' [?] "Obituary: T. W. Rhys Davids," JRAS, 1923, p. 323.

[6] C. Mary Ridding, p. 201.

[7] Further biographical information will be found in the obituaries cited above.

Rhys Davids' tireless work in founding and guiding the Pali Text Society can only be alluded to here; [8] but, of course, it resulted in a singular accomplishment. Devoting unstingtingly of his time, talent, and perseverance, he introduced the project at a time when the very existence of the manuscripts was known to a mere handful of Europeans. At his death,

> The result shows that during 40 years 64 texts in 94 volumes, extending over 26,000 pages, were issued by the Society. True, the actual number of edited works that bear his name on the title-page is small, and some may wish that he could have edited more. But the extent of his work is to be estimated not only in figures, but also by the influence that he exercised on the other editors, for he supplied many of them with the necessary materials and advice.[9]

Before turning to the subject of this chapter, I shall note in passing that Rhys Davids may not rightfully be accused of ignoring the Sanskritic Buddhist tradition altogether. His spirit of inquiry is best illustrated perhaps in his comments in review of Sir William Hunter's *Life of Brian Houghton Hodgson.*

> The Sanskrit texts, for which Hodgson did so much, are acquiring new value precisely from the rapid publication of the Pāli texts, once considered their rivals. . . . The two sets of texts, the Pāli and the Sanskrit, represent different schools and come from different countries. But they deal with the same chapter in the history of human thought. A knowledge of both is needed for a proper solution of the problems that arise, and it is not easy—it is, indeed, scarcely possible—rightly to appreciate either of them without the other.[10]

Despite the eloquence and sincerity of his pleas for the

[8] For examples of his enthusiasm and promotion "techniques," see his *Lectures on the Origin and Growth of Religion as Illustrated by Some Points in the History of Indian Buddhism* (*Hibbert Lectures*), pp. 70–72, 232–35; and *Buddhism: Its History and Literature* (*American Lectures*), pp. 80–86.

[9] Pe Maung Tin, "T. W. Rhys Davids: The Scholar," *Bulletin of the School of Oriental Studies*, III (1923–25), 207.

[10] T. W. Rhys Davids, Review of William Hunter, *The Life of Brian Houghton Hodgson*, *JRAS*, 1897, p. 189.

publication and study of the Buddhist Sanskrit texts, Rhys Davids continued to believe that the Pali tradition presented the pure core of the Buddha's teachings. It is, in fact, with Rhys Davids that one encounters a new analogy for use in the presentation of Buddhism to Western audiences. Into the background dropped an earlier analogy which saw Buddhism as a phenomenon directly comparable with the phenomena produced by the Protestant Reformation—the Buddha reacting against a ritualistic Hindu "church" in a manner analogous to Luther and Calvin reacting against the Roman See. In place of that misleading comparativist utterance, Rhys Davids substituted an idea equally deceptive.

> When we remember how fundamentally opposed are the views of life set forth in the Pāli Piṭakas to those set forth in the New Testament, and how different are the characters, the ideas, the habits and customs, of some of the peoples among whom the two religions have been adopted, we can perceive how instructive is the fact—one of the most curious facts in the whole history of the world—that Buddhism and Christianity have both developed, in the course of fifteen hundred years, into sacerdotal and sacramental systems, each with its beads and rosaries and images and holy water; . . . services in dead languages . . . choirs and processions and creeds and incense, in which the laity are spectators only; . . . mystic rites and ceremonies . . . worship of virgins [!], saints and angels . . . reverence to the Virgin and the Child . . . confessions, fasts and purgatory . . . idols, relics, symbols and sacred pictures. . . .[11]

Rhys Davids does not depreciate the study of later—that is, Sanskrit, Tibetan, Chinese, Japanese, or, more simply, non-Pali—Buddhism. But he insists that all investigation concerning Buddhism must begin with the Pali institutions.

> It is impossible rightly to understand any one phase of later Buddhism in any country, without starting from the standpoint of the earlier Buddhism of the Pāli Piṭakas. No one can write the history of later Buddhism, say in Siam or in China, without being thoroughly acquainted with the Pali Suttas. The very interest of the later inquiries lies in the causes that have produced the manifold changes that they will disclose.[12]

[11] T. W. Rhys Davids, *Hibbert Lectures*, pp. 192–93.
[12] *Ibid.*, p. 195.

It should not be thought that Rhys Davids' attitude stems strictly from a desire to obtain support for the Pali Text Society. The cause is rather that he believed throughout his long career that earliest Buddhism is embodied in the Pali tradition, that the very words of the Buddha may be discerned there in many of the suttas. More emphatically than Oldenberg or Childers, Rhys Davids claims for Buddhist research arrival at the goal which so entranced scientific investigators in the latter part of the nineteenth century: the earliest stratum of an historical phenomenon—the origins.[13]

Six of Rhys Davids' works, representing more than forty years of scholarship and writing, are the sources from which I shall draw an outline of his understanding of the Buddhist nirvāṇa. They are: his article "On Nirvāṇa" in *The Contemporary Review* (January, 1877);[14] *Buddhism* (1877 etc.);[15] *Lectures on the Origin and Growth of Religion as Illustrated by Some Points in the History of Indian Buddhism* (*Hibbert Lectures*, 1881);[16] *Buddhism: Its History and Literature* (American Lectures on the History of Religions, 1894–95);[17] *Early Buddhism* (1908);[18] and *The Pali Text Society's Pali-English Dictionary* (1921–25).[19]

Previously, I have attempted to show that there was considerably less modification—or, if you will, growth—in

[13] Mrs. Rhys Davids went to absurd lengths after the death of her husband to show that earliest Buddhism was not at all what he had taken it to be. See below, pp. 240–47.

[14] "On Nirvāṇa, and on the Buddhist Doctrines of the 'Groups,' the Sanskāras, Karma and the 'Paths,'" 249–70.

[15] *Buddhism: Being a Sketch of the Life and Teachings of Gautama the Buddha.*

[16] See above, note 8.

[17] *Ibid.*

[18] *Early Buddhism.* "Rhys Davids himself was wont to maintain that his succinct volume on *Early Buddhism* . . . was intrinsically the best book he ever wrote." ("Obituary," JRAS, 1923, p. 324.)

[19] The *PTSD* developed from Rhys Davids' interleaved copy of Childers' *Dictionary*. Rhys Davids died having seen part of the *PTSD* in print and more than half the remainder corrected in proof. In those portions of the *Dictionary* that concern us here, I believe we can safely assume his imprimatur.

Hermann Oldenberg's understanding of Buddhism and the meaning of nirvāṇa than most of his critics have acknowledged. With regard to Rhys Davids' interpretation, there cannot be the slightest doubt: the evaluation of nirvāṇa which he presented early in 1877 is the same in all essential details as that definition given in *The Pali Text Society's Pali-English Dictionary*. Compare the following:

What is Nirvāṇa, which literally means simply "going out," "extinction?" It is the "going out," the disappearance, of that sinful, yearning, grasping condition of mind and heart which would otherwise, according to the great mystery of Karma, be the cause of renewed individual existence. That extinction is to be brought about by, and runs parallel to, the growth of the opposite condition of mind and heart; it is complete when that opposite condition is reached. Nirvāṇa is therefore a moral condition, a pure, calm, clear state of mind, and if translated at all, may best be rendered HOLINESS—holiness, that is, in the Buddhist sense—*perfect peace, goodness, and wisdom.*[20]

When in writing my manual of Buddhism, I was endeavouring to reconcile the apparently discrepant descriptions of Nirvāṇa which had led some scholars to the conclusion that it meant the annihilation of being or the annihilation of the soul, and others to the contrary conclusion that it meant the eternal existence of the soul in a state of bliss, and was gradually led to the startling conclusion that Gotama, in his description of Nirvāṇa, was expressing no opinion at all, either one way or the other, as to existence after death, but was proclaiming a salvation from the sorrows of life which was to be reached here on earth in a changed state of mind, I saw indeed that this explanation would remove all the previous difficulties in the passages then before me, but I little thought that further research in the Pāli Scriptures would disclose any passages in which the misunderstandings of European investigators would be clearly and authoritatively met. This has, however, been the case.[21]

To have acquired, as an habitual frame of mind, the eight positive characteristics laid down in the Noble Path, to have got rid of the ten failings specified in the list of the Fetters, constitutes

[20] "On Nirvāṇa," p. 263. Cf. *Buddhism*, 111–12.
[21] *Hibbert Lectures*, App. X, p. 253. Cf. Oldenburg above, p. 201.

Arahatship, the Buddhist ideal of life. . . . They had endless love names for it, each based on one of the phases of the many-sided whole. . . . One of the epithets is very familiar to us in the West; being indeed much more exclusively used by European, than by Buddhist writers, as a name for the Buddhist ideal. This epithet is Nirvāṇa, "the going out"; that is to say the going out, in the heart, of the three fires of lust, ill-will, and dulness.[22]

Nibbāna is purely and solely an *ethical* state, to be reached in this birth by ethical practices, contemplation and insight. It is therefore not transcendental. The first and most important way to reach N. is by means of the eightfold Path, and all expressions which deal with the realisation of emancipation from lust, hatred, and illusion apply to practical habits and not to speculative thought. N. is realised in one's heart; to measure it with a speculative measure is to apply the wrong standard.[23]

As early as 1877 (the year of Childers' death), Rhys Davids had arrived at what he was to consider for the rest of his life to be the only satisfactory explanation of the Buddhist nirvāṇa. Most of the elements of his account have already been encountered and discussed in connection with the views of other scholars. Rhys Davids himself considered that Max Müller and Robert Childers had provided the most assistance. Müller had insisted that many passages of the Dhammapada not only did not require a nihilistic interpretation of nirvāṇa but in fact demanded a positive reading. And Childers had maintained, along with Hardy and D'Alwis, that nirvāṇa is attained in this life. Childers and Müller shared the distinction of having drawn their conclusions following a study of at least some of the Pali materials.

Neither had been strictly correct, however. Müller, according to Rhys Davids, had not been aware of the dimensions of the *anatta* idea in Buddhism. Furthermore, the same mistake characterized the work of most European scholars. Clarification of this matter, Rhys Davids insists, could only come about after a thorough study of the Buddhist notion of the five *skandha*-s into which are divided and classified (not

[22] *American Lectures*, p. 151. Cf. *Early Buddhism*, pp. 72–73.
[23] *PTSD*, p. 326ab.

without some duplication and overlapping) "the constituent parts and powers of man."

These "Five Groups" include all the bodily and mental parts and powers of man, and neither any one group, nor any one division of any group is permanent; they are constantly changing, are never for two consecutive moments the same; their nature is to arise and pass away.[24]

Yet, Rhys Davids continues, all is not immediately well after the discovery that there is no soul, no abiding principle whatever, for the conclusion of analysis at this point encounters the human demand for a satisfactory explanation of the justice of the human situation. Why is it that justice is not apparently meted out in this life? Why are some children born lame? Blind? Why do so many scoundrels succeed in every venture, while many honest men suffer one personal tragedy after another? The transmigration theory, according to Rhys Davids, provided satisfactory answers to all such questions about the sufferings and inequities of the present life. Indeed, it could provide incontestable answers.

Now the doctrine of transmigration, in either the Brahmanical or Buddhist form, is not capable of disproof; while it affords an explanation quite complete, to those who can believe it, of the apparent anomalies and wrongs in the distribution, here, of happiness or woe. A child, for instance, is blind; this is owing to its eye vanity, lust of the eye, in a former birth; . . . The explanation can always be exact, for it is scarcely more than a repetition of the point to be explained; it may always fit the facts, for it is derived from them; and it cannot be disproved, for it lies in a sphere beyond the reach of human inquiry.[25]

A strong and uncritical admirer of Tylor,[26] Rhys Davids can muster little patience or imagination for a discussion of *saṃsāra*—that strange by-product of the animistically domi-

[24] "On Nirvāṇa," p. 253.

[25] *Ibid.*, p. 257.

[26] He refers to E. B. Tylor's *Primitive Culture* as "one of the most interesting books that our language contains," (*Hibbert Lectures*, p. 75); and on his rather uncritical acceptance of the term "animism," see *ibid.*, pp. 13–19.

…iousness, according to him. The Buddha's psy- … and existential analysis had been, if not unique … foundation for what could have been a "more decisive … ore lasting utterance, if it had not also borrowed a … in the curious doctrine of transmigration. . . ." [27] But … Buddha did borrow the belief, and that, according to Rhys Davids, would seem to lead to an untenable situation.

We have thus arrived at a deadlock: to save what it holds to be psychological truth Buddhism rejects the notion of a soul; to save what it holds to be the necessity of justice, it retains the belief in transmigration.[28]

The "bridge between one life and another" is found, Rhys Davids declares, in the Buddhist doctrine of *karman*. Here, he says, we encounter another of those confounding (almost certainly he was muttering "confounded") Buddhist mysteries, and the entire idea is surely wrong. According to this idea, at death the particular collocation of *skandha*-s dissolves and a man really and truly ceases to exist. But that is not the whole of it. The actions a man performed when alive—the good and evil he did—do not disappear, as it were, along with his constituent parts and powers. Rather a new existence—that is, a new person, a new collocation of *skandha*-s—comes forth which is, not merely the outcome of the "doings" of the previous individual but, so to speak, the previous individual all over again. In effect, this is Rhys Davids' explanation of the Buddhist scheme of the twelve *Nidānas* ("causes, sources") as it applies to the notion of transmigration. That which renders *karman*—the doing—effective for bringing about a new existence that is both *karmaphala* ("fruit, consequence, or result" of doing) and the *karman* itself is the habitual grasping state of mind (*upādāna*) of the previous doer.

It is this grasping state of mind (Upādāna) which causes the new being—not, of course, a soul, but a new set of "Groups"

[27] *Buddhism*, p. 89.
[28] "On Nirvāṇa," p. 257.

(Skandhas), a new body endowed with mental and moral tendencies and capabilities (Sanskāras).[29]

Upādāna—founded on thirst (*tṛṣṇā, taṇhā*)—arms *karman*, making it potent not only in this life but also in the next. Persevering in the Eightfold Path, one eradicates thirst and the ineluctable grasping which follows thirsting. Faithful adherence to the Path leads to the emasculation of *karman* and the transformation of the individual's mental state. "It is especially in the Noble Eightfold Path," says Rhys Davids, "that we shall find the original idea and motive force of the whole of Gautama's system." [30] The culmination of the Path is Arahatship (*arahatta*)—an ineffable state of human achievement in this world, one of the aspects of which is called nirvāṇa.

Now it can be noted that Rhys Davids' criticism of Childers' views would seem to be that the latter had emphasized the postmortem nirvāṇa as the fundamental notion in the Buddhist theory. Rhys Davids, on the contrary—and here he is in perfect tune with Oldenberg—believes that the nirvāṇa attainable in this life is the only real nirvāṇa. It is neither an anticipatory condition nor is it incidental to the postmortem state. It is the only goal—and even this must be qualified, for it is actually only one facet of the real goal, *arahatta.*

Rhys Davids' conclusions about nirvāṇa may be subsumed under the following four points.

1. Nirvāṇa is an ethical state achieved in this life: an unusual state in which *rāga* ("lust"), *dosa* ("malice"), and *moha* ("delusion, bewilderment, stupidity") are eradicated —extinct. Most succinctly:

> Nirvāṇa . . . the Buddhist *summum bonum*, which is a blissful, holy state, a modification of personal character; and we should allow the word to remind us, as it did the early Buddhists, both of the "Noble Path" which leads to the extinction of sin, and also of the break in the transfer of Karma, which the extinction of sin will bring about.[31]

[29] *Ibid.*, p. 258.
[30] *Ibid.*, pp. 260–61.
[31] *Ibid.*, p. 264.

2. In contrast to both Childers and Müller, Rhys Davids stresses the this-worldliness of nirvāṇa. The only extramundane significance which he gives the term is implied in his insistence that *arahatta* is a transcendent human condition, the state of men who are in the world but no longer of the world. Consequently—here, again, complete agreement with Oldenberg—Rhys Davids would not say with Childers that nirvāṇa refers strictly to the state following death.[32]

To Müller and all those who had previously taken sides on the question of whether nirvāṇa means eternal bliss or annihilation, Rhys Davids objects that for the Buddhists there is no abiding principle to be perpetuated or annihilated. Following a lengthy discussion of the *anatta* notion in his *Buddhism*, he asks rhetorically: "Would it be possible in a more complete and categorical manner to deny that there is any soul—any entity, of any kind, which continues to exist, in any manner, after death?" [33] Whereas Oldenberg emphasizes that the Buddhist texts expressly refuse to answer questions about the future life, Rhys Davids insists that the answers are patent. The questions, he avows, are absurd in the Buddhist context, for, on the one hand, there is nothing to be annihilated and, on the other, there is nothing which could be preserved.

3. Agreeing with Childers, Rhys Davids says that *arahatta* is also described in the texts as *sa-upādi-sesa-nibbāna:* "Nirvāṇa with the Skandhas remaining, upādi being a collective name for the five groups." [34] In *Buddhism* and the *Dictionary*, however, the definition of *upādi* shades somewhat closer to Oldenberg's interpretation. In the former, Rhys Davids writes: "A comprehensive name of all the five [*skandhas*] is upādi, a word derived (in allusion to the name of their cause, upādāna), from upādā, to grasp, either with the hand or with the mind." [35] In the *Dictionary*, *upādi* is also

[32] See Oldenberg's criticisms above, Chapter VI.
[33] *Buddhism*, p. 99.
[34] "On Nirvāṇa," p. 264, footnote.
[35] *Buddhism*, p. 113.

derived from *upādā* through *upādāna.* But there it is said further that the term "upādi is equivalent to upādāna, but in the more concrete meaning of 'stuff of life,' substratum of being, khandha. . . ."[36]

According to Rhys Davids, the condition of the *arahant* after death is described in the texts non-exclusively as *parinibbāna* or *nir-(an-)upādi-sesa nibbāna-dhātu.*[37] It is "complete extinction, death with no new life to follow."[38] In the *Dictionary*, however, a distinction between two types of *parinibbāna* is listed:

> *Parinibbāna* . . . "complete Nibbāna" in two meanings: 1. complete extinction of khandha-life; i.e., all possibility of such life & its rebirth, final release from (the misery of) rebirth and transmigration, death (after the last life-span of an Arahant). This is the so-called "an-upādi-sesa Parinibbāna," or "extinction with no rebirth-substratum left." 2. release from cravings & attachment to life, emancipation (in this life) with the assurance of final death; freedom of spirit, calm, perfect well-being or peace of soul. This is the so-called "sa-upādi-sesa-P." or "extinction (of passion) with some substratum left."[39]

Earlier, Rhys Davids had insisted that the distinction between nirvāṇa and parinirvāṇa is clear, that they are no more alike than "phrase" and "paraphrase."[40] But either he or Stede finally decides that *parinibbāna* refers also to a condition of the present life. That modification and expansion brings Rhys Davids' interpretation into closer agreement with Childers, who says that "*Parinibbāna* means merely Nirvāṇa, or the attainment of Nirvāṇa. . . ."[41]

4. Rhys Davids challenges even the accepted etymology of the word nirvāṇa. Since the time of Colebrooke, it had been customary to explain the term from the root *vā* ("blow").

[36] *PTSD*, p. 149b.

[37] *Ibid.*, p. 340ab; *dhātu* being taken in the sense of "set of conditions or state of being." Cf. "On Nirvāṇa," p. 264, footnote.

[38] *Ibid.*, p. 264.

[39] *PTSD*, p. 427b.

[40] "On Nirvāṇa," p. 264. Cf. *Buddhism*, pp. 115–17.

[41] Childers, Dictionary, p. 268a. *Pari-* thus being employed in a *perfective* rather than a *perfect* sense.

But in the *Dictionary*, Rhys Davids and Stede suggest rather that the Old Indic root *vṛ* be consulted.

Although *nir* + *vā* "to blow" . . . is already in use in the Vedic period . . . we do not find its distinctive application till later and more commonly in popular use, where *vā* is fused with *vṛ* in this sense, viz. in application to the extinguishing of fire, which is the prevailing *Buddhist* conception of the term. Only in the older texts do we find references to a simile of the *wind* and the flame; but by far the most common metaphor and that which governs the whole idea of *nibbāna* finds expression in the putting out of *fire* by *other* means of extinction than by blowing, which latter process rather tends to incite fire than to extinguish it. The going out of the fire may be due to covering it up, or to depriving it of further fuel, by not feeding it, or by withdrawing the cause of its production. Thus to the Pāli etymologist the main reference is to the root *vṛ* (to cover) and not to *vā* (to blow).[42]

Rhys Davids' emphasis, then, rests on the insistence that the metaphor is more perfect than previous scholars had believed. Nirvāṇa is not so generally a "going out" as it is specifically the "going out of fire"—the fire of passion, wrath, and ignorance. And "fire may be put out by water, or may go out of itself from lack of fuel. The ethical state called *Nibbāna* can only rise from within. It is therefore in the older texts compared to the fire going out, rather than to the fire being put out." [43]

Responses outside the Household

In the main, Rhys Davids' interpretation of nirvāṇa is so unambiguous and is maintained with such tedious consistency that it is easy to comprehend the attitudes of other scholars

[42] *PTSD*, p. 362a.
[43] *Ibid.*, p. 363a.

towards it. Two examples from the supporters will suffice to indicate the sort of acceptance his views received.

In an unsigned critical review of Joseph Dahlmann's *Nirvāṇa*[44] (JRAS, 1897—it is possible that Rhys Davids or his wife wrote the review), the Rhys Davids' interpretation is the accepted standard.

> The author [Dahlmann] starts with the proposition that the intellectual life of India is nowhere so clearly and originally shown as in the idea of Nirvāṇa; but that on the meaning of the Buddhist Nirvāṇa there reigns the greatest uncertainty. Is it annihilation, or is it everlasting bliss? He has not heard of the real answer (put forth as long ago as 1878 [1877] that it is neither, but an epithet of a state of mind to be reached and enjoyed only in the present life; and he seeks in vain to solve the riddle to his own satisfaction. Herein he is precisely in the position of a writer who should take for granted that "regeneration" in the Christian usage of the term, must mean either a physical rebirth, or a rebirth in heaven; and who should then seek (in vain) to reconcile, either with the one or the other of these hypotheses, the expressions used concerning it. The problem in either case is insoluble, because it is wrongly stated.[45]

E. J. Thomas, in his *The Life of Buddha as Legend and History*, gives Rhys Davids' position all possible support:

> It is unnecessary to discuss the view that Nirvāṇa means the extinction of the individual. No such view has ever been supported from the texts, and there is abundant evidence as to its

[44] Joseph Dahlmann, S.J., *Nirvāṇa: Eine Studie zur Vorgeschichte des Buddhismus* (Berlin: Felix L. Dames, 1896).

[45] *JRAS*, 1897, pp. 407–8. Father Dahlmann's little volume is not, as the title would have one believe, really concerned with Buddhism. Rather, it is an attempt to document his own thesis that the Mahābhārata contains a coherent philosophical system, an *Ur-Sāṃkhya.* As such, the book is of interest for this study principally as an example of the abandonment of the "Buddhist nirvāṇa problem" by some German scholars in favor of a more comprehensive scheme of interpretation in which efforts are made to collapse all major problems of Indian philosophy into an all-encompassing discussion of monism and dualism. As Stcherbatsky comments, Dahlmann assigns to nirvāṇa "the meaning of an extinction of all personal life in an impersonal absolute, [and] it then becomes 'a simple equivalent of brahman.'" (Review of *Nirvāṇa* by Louis de La Vallée Poussin, *Bulletin of the School of Oriental Studies*, IV [1926–28], 359, footnote.)

real meaning, the extinction of craving in this life, as Rhys Davids always insisted.[46]

Not all scholars were so completely comfortable with Rhys Davids' interpretation, however. Among those who raised objections to one or more aspects of his presentations was Henry Clarke Warren, one of his former students. Warren's candor, his sympathy toward Buddhism—demonstrated clearly throughout his classic *Buddhism in Translations*—is epitomized in the remarks which preface a series of translations of passages from the Pali Canon referring to nirvāṇa. Commenting on the number of investigations which had been made into the meaning of nirvāṇa as taught by the Buddha, Warren confesses:

> A large part of the pleasure that I have experienced in the study of Buddhism has arisen from the strangeness of what I may call the intellectual landscape. All the ideas, the modes of argument, even the postulates assumed and not argued about, have always seemed so strange, so different from anything to which I have been accustomed, that I feel all the time as though walking in fairyland. Much of the charm that the Oriental thoughts and ideas have for me appears to be because they so seldom fit into Western categories. Nirvāṇa is an illustration of this; and, therefore, all short and compendious definitions necessarily leave much to be desired. If it be said that Nirvāṇa is getting rid of the round of rebirth, that is perfectly correct; but then, we do not believe in repeated rebirth. Nor can we call it annihilation; for annihilation implies something to be annihilated whereas Nirvāṇa occurs when the elements that constitute the stream of any individual existence have their dependence undermined and cease to originate. If, again, it be said that it is a getting rid of the threefold fire of lust, hatred, and infatuation, that is also a correct definition; but it is rather an ethical than a philosophical one, and implies a pessimistic view of life of which we Occidentals have but little conception. But I hope that . . . I have been successful in giving the native point of view of what the religious problem really is of man's relation to the universe; for I conceive that Nirvāṇa can only be properly understood by a tolerably thorough comprehension of the philosophy of which it is the climax and cap-stone.[47]

[46] E. J. Thomas, *The Life of Buddha as Legend and History*, p. 187.
[47] H. C. Warren, *Buddhism in Translations*, pp. 283–84.

Over all, Rhys Davids doubtless would have been proud of his student's method and his service to critical Pali Buddhist studies. The suggestion that all the questions about nirvāṇa had not been answered—and could not be answered by "short and compendious definitions"—however, probably elicited a sigh. Certainly Rhys Davids was not distressed to read that his own definition of nirvāṇa was "ethical rather than philosophical," for, after all, nirvāṇa was purely an ethical state.[48]

Other and more explicit critical statements about Rhys Davids' interpretation are all of the same genre—that is to say, there are no declarations insisting that he is mistaken, but rather that his definition is too short, too inflexible, too narrow, too reductionistic. Another American, Edward Washburn Hopkins, displays a more definitely agnostic and pragmatic attitude apropos the meaning of nirvāṇa than Warren, but his critique of Rhys Davids' position is substantially the same. In his *Religions of India*, Hopkins declares that there are three separate meanings of the term nirvāṇa.

Eternal repose (such was the Nirvāṇa of the Jains and in part of Buddhism), extinction and absolute annihilation (such was the Nirvāṇa of some Buddhists), and the Nirvāṇa of Buddha

[48] The following paragraph from an unsigned review of Warren's anthology (*JRAS*, 1897, pp. 145–49) reaffirms the Rhys Davids position:

"A point of considerable importance is the constant rendering . . . of *parinibbāyati* by 'passes into Nirvāṇa.' It is sufficiently clear . . . that the author is quite aware of *the only meaning of Nirvāṇa*—that is to say, *a state of mind to be reached and enjoyed in this life* [my italics]. How, then, can he also use the term Nirvāṇa to designate a state beyond the grave? And yet what else can the English phrase that a man at death, 'passes into Nirvāṇa,' mean? The Pāli for that phrase would be *Nibbānam adhigacchati*—words that would only be used to express that a living man had reached the state of mind called Nirvāṇa. It is true that the version here objected to has been used in nearly all English books on Buddhism, being, in fact, an old Anglo-Indian blunder which arose in a time when Nirvāṇa was supposed to refer exclusively to the next life. But its use now only serves to perpetuate an error which will be hard enough to eradicate, however careful scholars may be to confine its use within strictly accurate limits." (Pp. 148–49.)

himself . . . namely, the extinction of lust, anger, and ignorance.[49]

Hopkins concludes that the Buddha did not speak any further on the subject and must, therefore, have believed that nirvāṇa was also ultimately absolute annihilation. Had the Buddha believed otherwise, Hopkins muses, surely he would have said so, for the postulation of some sort of final bliss would have aided in obtaining acceptance of his teaching among the people. Immediately following that inference, however, Hopkins retreats to more secure scholarly footing, emphasizing that

> one has no right to "go behind the returns" as these are given by Buddha. The later church says distinctly that Buddha himself did not teach whether he himself, his ego, was to live after death or not; or whether a permanent ego exists. It is useless, therefore, to inquire whether Buddha's Nirvāṇa be a completion, as Müller defines it, or annihilation. To one Buddhistic party it was the one; to the other the other; to Buddha himself, it was what may be inferred from his refusal to make any declaration in regard to it.[50]

From that statement, one can fairly well anticipate the objections which Hopkins sets forth when reviewing Rhys Davids' *American Lectures.* "It is not to be wondered," he writes,

> that, in the elucidation of Buddhist eschatology, Mr. Davids still holds the simple, if not altogether convincing, dogma that Nirvāṇa has nothing to do with the next life, but that it connotes merely the idea of earthly happiness attained by him who has extinguished lust and passion. For the author himself was the first to substitute this explanation for the older one, which held that Nirvāṇa meant either psychic extinction or the post-mortem bliss of eternal peace. It is only to be regretted that he presents it here as the only explanation, for in the early Buddhistic works there are many passages which will not admit this definition of Nirvāṇa. It is, indeed, evident to the historical scholar that Nirvāṇa had several meanings, and that it was variously interpreted.[51]

[49] Edward Washburn Hopkins, *The Religions of India*, p. 321.

[50] *Ibid.*, pp. 321–22.

[51] Edward Washburn Hopkins, Review of *Buddhism: Its History and Literature* by T. W. Rhys Davids, [*International Journal of*] *Ethics*, VII (October, 1896, January, April, and July, 1897), 123–24.

That there are passages in the Buddhist texts which will not support Rhys Davids' views is a pertinent and telling observation. That Hopkins does not cite even one is perhaps more telling still. Hermann Oldenberg, who does not directly contest Rhys Davids' conclusions, challenges them obliquely —lamenting in a review of the German translation of *Buddhism* the fact that a work nearly two decades old had not been substantially revised. The hard lines of Rhys Davids' interpretation of nirvāṇa, one may safely infer, did not satisfy Oldenberg, for he notes that Rhys Davids is dead wrong when he maintains that he has cited all texts in which nirvāṇa is mentioned.[52]

Rhys Davids devotes much attention to the point that the Buddha's nirvāṇa is unique among the ultimate goals in the various religions in that it is completely realizable in this life. Louis Finot objects. This feature is not unique to the Buddhists, he writes. The notion of the *jīvanmuktī*, "one delivered while alive," is prominent in Hindu thought. Furthermore, Finot insists, there is no indication of Buddhist influence in this, because the notion can be traced back to before the time of the Buddha.[53]

I do not have sufficient space to assess the total contribution which Rhys Davids made to Buddhist studies in Europe. With regard to his interpretation of nirvāṇa, however, this much must be stressed. Rhys Davids explained, and beyond doubt explained correctly, one aspect of nirvāṇa. His interpretation crystallized before the Pali texts were available for study in their entirety, and it would be foolish to berate him for leaving out of account the materials which were not accessible to him. What can be said with justification is that he did not continue to be sensitive to the nuances in many passages relating to nirvāṇa which came to light during the latter half of his life.

[52] Hermann Oldenberg, Review of *Buddhism* by T. W. Rhys Davids, *Deutsche Litteraturzeitung*, 20 Jahrgang, XLI, 1550.

[53] Louis Finot, Review of *Buddhism: Its History and Literature* by T. W. Rhys Davids, *Révue de l'Histoire des Religions*, XXXVII, 247–48.

"We work that others may do better than we," he said when praising Childers' *Dictionary*. He added that no one should bemoan the fact that it was superseded, "for it was the foundation of the subsequent work . . . which rendered it inadequate." [54] The statement is so characteristic of Rhys Davids' attitudes that I am convinced that he would have approved its being repeated with regard to his own efforts and accomplishments.

Caroline Augusta Foley Rhys Davids: The Wife's Turn

Throughout his career, T. W. Rhys Davids tended to view the Pali Canon as an organic whole, claiming that he could not find any indications of doctrinal development there except in the attitudes displayed toward the person of the Buddha. Thus, in 1877, he wrote in his *Buddhism* (and the statement is repeated exactly in all the many subsequent editions):

> It may be possible, hereafter, when the Pitakas shall have been published, to ascertain which parts of them are older than the rest, and whether they contain an older system hidden under a later one; at present it can only be said that of difference in age there is already sufficient evidence, but of growth or change in fundamental ideas none of any certainty.[55]

C. A. F. Rhys Davids began this next phase of Pali Buddhist studies: the attempt to ascertain a stratification of doctrines within the Pali Canon. The conclusions she drew—which is really to say, in most instances, the hypotheses she posed—were at considerable variance with her husband's.

The great bulk of Mrs. Rhys Davids' writings is such that

[54] C. Mary Ridding, p. 205.
[55] *Buddhism*, p. 87.

it would demand an entire monograph for elucidation and commentary. Fortunately, as she freely admits, she repeats herself at every opportunity with regard to a limited number of ideas which directly relate to this study. It is particularly important to concentrate on the theories which she expounded after the death of her husband (1922). Her position during the last twenty years of her life (she died, June 26, 1942, at the age of eighty-four) constituted an open challenge to the "accepted" interpretation of Buddhism and Buddhist thought. She begins a lecture to the Cambridge Theological Society in May, 1935:

> I have been invited to talk to you about the position I have taken up in my books for nearly a decade as to what was for me the truer notion of original Buddhism than that which either Buddhists now teach, or books about Buddhism tell you. . . . Little "books about Buddhism" by "verts and non-Buddhists" are easily and cheaply got. But I have come to conclusions, after many years of study, differing from those of the little books. Different not merely in particulars, but as to that which was vitally, essentially the message, the new word, in what we have lately come to call Buddhism.[56]

Throwing down the glove, which falls on, among other places, the grave of her husband, Mrs. Rhys Davids announces buoyantly that she "cheerfully" believes that "vera prevalebunt" (her "truth" of course),

> because these, my true things, are founded on evidence, because they will stand historical criticism better than the views now holding the field, and because they are founded on what is, I hold, a truer hypothesis of what must be there to make a world-religion.[57]

What are her "true things"? For our purposes I shall single out her principal hypothesis: the Pali Canon, insofar as it presents a coherent system, presents a monk-dominated, institutional Buddhism which is discrepant and degenerate from the original message of Sākyamuni. She contends that frag-

[56] "Wherein I Differ," *Wayfarer's Words*, Vol. II, p. 415.
[57] *Ibid.*, p. 416.

ments of the "original gospel" of the Buddha remain as left-ins in the Tipiṭaka. From those so-called remnants, she derives her view that original Buddhism (she refers to this reconstruction as *Sakya* to distinguish it from all varieties of institutional Buddhism) was neither world-negating nor atheistic. Further, she writes, the notion of *anatta* (Sanskrit: *anātman*, *nairātmya*)—"the frightful canker of the Not-man"—arose only in the monkish Buddhist "Church." Finally, the original goal of Buddhism-as-*Sakya* was not nirvāṇa.

About the original message of Gotama the Buddha, Mrs. Rhys Davids arrives at these conclusions:

That message was clearly from the first intended for the people, for him we call Everyman—alas! how much is that not forgotten! And that message took for granted that Everyman, in his religion, was bent on a quest: something that he needed, through which he could evolve into (India said "become") a More than he in his earth-life amounted to, a something that he sought to win. In a "folk-gospel" like that message, we should expect to find in its quest something which was (1) the man seeking to attain, and finally attaining, his welfare as man, not a welfare without the man; man must be in it; (2) a quest which is positive, not negative; (3) a quest which is not something as yet inconceivable by man, but is something which he can even now comprehend, or at least conceive.[58]

Now, according to Mrs. Rhys Davids, nirvāṇa fails that three-part test. It cannot have been the original goal of Buddhism-*Sakya*, its supreme good, because it satisfies none of the criteria.

Nirvāṇa is an end without the man in it. Nirvāṇa is an end in negative terms. Nirvāṇa is a word prejudging what is as yet inconceivable, let alone comprehensible. Hence I believe, without going further, that nirvāṇa cannot have been the quest and end set before man in the folk-gospel which Buddhism appears to have been.[59]

Mrs. Rhys Davids insists that the original goal of Buddhism was *attha* (Sanskrit: *artha*), rather than nirvāṇa. The

[58] "A Historical Aspect of Nirvāṇa," *Indian Culture*, Vol. II, No. 3 (1936), as reprinted in *Wayfarer's Words*, II, 643–44.

[59] *Ibid.*, p. 644.

textual support for this contention seems dubious indeed, but it would be well to give some indication of the material she calls on. From the Vinaya Piṭaka, among the rules pertaining to the personal articles permitted a member of the Saṃgha, she quotes a part of a narrative affixed to a rule concerning the wearing of lined sandals. The narrative itself, she writes, is "foolish" (what she means by this is not clear). One of the characters in the narrative is King Bimbisāra of Magadha, supposed to have been a contemporary of Gotama.

The king, after convening and addressing village headmen, dismisses them with these words: "You have been instructed by me in the aims, the objects of this life. Now go and wait upon the Blessed One; he will instruct you in the aims, the objects of the life hereafter."

The words "aims and objects" are in Pali the one word *attha* (*artha*). "Of this life" is the usual term *diṭṭhadhamme:* seen things; of the life hereafter is the less usual, but current Sutta term *samparāyike. Attha* as aim, object, quest could thus be applied to mean things worldly and otherworldly.[60]

Directly opposing the conclusions reached by such scholars as her husband and Hermann Oldenberg (and, by her admission, contrary to the opinions and beliefs of most Buddhists), Mrs. Rhys Davids insists that a practicing Buddhist "ought . . . to see his teaching as *samparāyika*, but he does not." [61] Presumably what she is trying to point up here is that an important contemporary of Gotama's did not associate nirvāṇa with the Buddha's teachings but rather a special kind of *artha.*[62]

In the famous "Sermon of Benares," Gotama is "quoted" as declaring that men should avoid two extremes, each described as *an-attha-saṃhita* ("not connected with *attha*, not bringing advantage, unprofitable"). Logically, or so Mrs. Rhys Davids decides, the other—the Middle—way must be *attha-saṃhita.* "But somehow attha-samhita has got left out. We find instead four other terms 'bargeing in' as it were, in discordance with

[60] *Ibid.*, p. 646.
[61] *Ibid.*, p. 647.
[62] *Ibid.*, p. 649.

the context."[63] The intruding terms are *sambodhi* ("enlightenment"), *abhiññā* ("knowledge"), *upasama* ("quiet"), and *nibbāna.*

But why those four terms? They too are part of the history of Buddhism. The *former* pair shows a preoccupation with the new Indian psychology, which men were calling *sānkhya*, Pali: *sānkha*, *sankhānam*, analysis namely of mind. The gradual growth of this is visible in the Upanishads, both in those preceding, and in those contemporaneous with, the birth of Buddhism. The *latter* pair betrays the growth of the monastic vogue. Thus the former pair give us intellectual superiority; the latter, religious or "mystic" attainment. All four show us what had been engrossing religious attention during the few centuries following the death of the first missioners. We shall never understand the history of early Buddhism, if we do not see how these two influences were the main currents which swept it along and down.[64]

Otherworldly and positive in the fullest sense—that, according to Mrs. Rhys Davids, was the goal the Buddha taught. And, conveniently enough, it is also the only goal which she can conceive that a religion and a truly religious man could have.

Man in religion is a seeker, essentially and before all else a seeker; that man, in this seeking, may word his quest not necessarily in a word which tries to convey something he cannot yet conceive, but as a Better which, for the time being, is for him a Best. And we now see how in *attha* we get those three features suitable for a folk-evangel, which we did not get in nirvāṇa. *Attha* is essentially a standpoint of the man, not of one who in gaining it ceases somehow to be a man. It is the man who is valuing: this is my aim. It becomes meaningless if, in winning it he wane out. . . . Second, the word is positive, not a negation. It is that which *is* sought for, *is* to be won. It is not something that is a *NOT*. Lastly it is not something which having won, a man judges to be so "void," that he cannot value. It is ever true as being that which man, in seeking, ever figures as the Best, the Most he can as yet conceive.[65]

[63] *Ibid.*, p. 650.
[64] *Ibid.*, p. 651.
[65] *Ibid.*, pp. 653–54.

How did this elastic goal, this *attha*, come to be dropped from developing Buddhism? Mrs. Rhys Davids' theory is that the history of Buddhism shows a steady negativist trend which culminated in the acceptance of nirvāṇa as the *summum bonum*. The first stage was an atheism which developed out of the Buddha's own cautious agnosticism. Because in the spiritual environment of his time the Brahman-Ātman identity was accepted, the Buddha had not emphasized either the transcendent or the immanent side. To have done so, Mrs. Rhys Davids insists, would have been to cater to men's proclivity toward relaxing and basking in the assurance that they were one with the Highest. The Buddha, rather, interpreted the Brahman-Ātman equation as an imperative than as a declarative. In the absence of emphasis, there emerged the belief that both Brahman and Ātman had been renounced. Mrs. Rhys Davids depicts the process with Spenglerian somberness:

The dropping out of attha is preceded by that tragic worsening in values: the dropping out of "the man," that is, "the self." We know that, in drifting apart from the mother-teacher, Brahmanism:—the immanence of God as in and of the man—early Buddhism first cut out Deity from the term *attā*, then cut out the reality of the *attā* himself, a decadent process covering centuries.

With *attā* and the *attha* dropped from its quest of the ideal, Buddhism built over these buried stones the rococo superstructure which the founders of the movement would have had pain and difficulty in recognizing, and of which they would certainly not have approved. The *attha* which they taught was *not nibbāna*, a vanishing Less in a vanishing *attā*. It was a persistent living on in that More which saw the quest as a man becoming more in the worlds. . . .[66]

Wherever the term "nirvāṇa" appears in Mrs. Rhys Davids' writings, the same sentiments are found. "Isn't *nirvāṇa* the summum bonum of Buddhism?"

I have spent myself in showing that this can be conceded only if we read our Buddhist scriptures like Fundamentalists, ignoring

[66] *Ibid.*, pp. 656–57.

the latent history lying under the scriptural palimpsest. To the critical reader it is fairly evident that in the First Utterance [the "Sermon of Benares"] the original *summum bonum* of the Aim (*attha*) has been thrust aside (as having become ambiguous with the years) and nirvāṇa with three partners made to replace it. Both *nibbāna* and *nirodha* were terms for cathartic training, before they were promoted to figure as Goal.[67]

More briefly, but no less revealingly, she declares: "To those who say that any world-gospel began with a teaching of the Negative such as this, history replies 'You lie!' "[68]

The present generation of Buddhist scholars—those in India and Japan as well as Europe and the United States—has learned much from Mrs. Rhys Davids. We no longer "read our Buddhist scriptures like Fundamentalists." Neat attempts to package the teachings of earliest Buddhism within the confines of a few terse pages are no longer considered possible. To the extent, then, that she focused attention on the history and change in the Pali Canon, to the extent that she has made sophisticated textual criticism—higher and lower—an indispensable aspect of Buddhist studies, she has indeed won her battle with the "little books on Buddhism."

It is also to be hoped that Buddhist scholars have learned another lesson from Mrs. Rhys Davids—that they, largely on account of her example, have become increasingly critical of the use to which they put their tools of historical investigation. From a reading of her work it is hard to conclude that her belief in what a religion ought to be did not in fact determine what she "discovered" earliest Buddhism to be. Of her own presuppositions, I have given sufficient illustration through the material quoted above. Numerous other examples could be cited.[69] They may have been the force which motivated her to ask what was the original message of the Buddha. Most

[67] "Nirvāṇa in the Negative," *The Aryan Path* (April, 1939), as reprinted in *Wayfarer's Words*, II, 662.

[68] *Ibid.*, p. 663.

[69] For example, *What Was the Original Gospel in 'Buddhism'?* (London: The Epworth Press, 1938). For a penetrating and generally excellent critique of Mrs. Rhys Davids' personal crusade, see T. R. V. Murti, *The Central Philosophy of Buddhism*, pp. 20–35.

certainly they provided the essential elements of the answer she gave. In so doing, they helped her subordinate the complex historical phenomenon which is Buddhism in its manifold traditions to a slenderly documented hypothesis.

The lasting contribution which Mrs. Rhys Davids' legacy provides is the stimulus to further research. Her most effective roles were as a questioner and a polemicist. Indeed, her book reviews alone present ample material from which to assess her standpoint in Buddhist studies. In the following chapter there will be occasion to reconsider her attitude—the principal spokesman for Pali Buddhist scholarship—in the light of the achievements of two great students of the non-Pali Buddhist traditions: Stcherbatsky and La Vallée Poussin.

[CHAPTER VIII]

La Vallée Poussin and Stcherbatsky

Dissatisfaction with T. W. Rhys Davids' pat and clear interpretation of nirvāṇa and with the always fluid and dense explanations proposed by Hermann Oldenberg in successive editions of *Buddha* became more pronounced by the turn of the century. Rhys Davids' view was considered inadequate. New text discoveries seemed to show that there was more to the meaning of nirvāṇa than he would allow. Oldenberg, expanding the notes to his own discussion of nirvāṇa in order to account for some at least of the new findings, remained an agnostic interpreter of a Socratically ironic Buddha. Something was missing from these evaluations—individually and in combination—something which would give full substance and reassuring completeness to the discussion on the meaning of nirvāṇa.

Schrader and Senart

In 1905, F. Otto Schrader attempted to use the achievements of Rhys Davids, Oldenberg, and others as a springboard to a more satisfactory interpretation. "The problem of Nirvāṇa has hitherto been only half solved," is his sigh-provoking announcement in the *Journal of the Pali Text Society*.

> Whereas there is no longer any dispute about the *saupādisesa-nibbānam*, opinions concerning *anupādisesanibbānam* are still as far from unanimity as they were when the question arose. The view is more and more gaining ground among Western scholars that the Buddha absolutely denied the *attā*, and therefore necessarily understood by his doctrine of *parinibbānam* the absolute annihilation of being, while the assertion to the contrary, first advanced by Professor Max Müller, seems almost to be at the point of becoming extinct.[1]

Schrader suggests that there are two other views concerning what the Buddha thought and taught. The first is that the Buddha himself did not know or pretend to know the destiny of the *atta*—Jacobi's view of the Buddha's silence: true agnosticism. The other view is that of Schrader and, although this is by no means certain, perhaps of the later Oldenberg as well.[2]

[1] F. Otto Schrader, "On the Problem of Nirvāṇa," p. 157.

[2] The difference is, of course, that Oldenberg barely intimated that the Buddha might have grounded his system in a belief in an absolute. But Schrader proceeds to direct statements about what this belief must have been. I think that we can affirm no more of Oldenberg's over-all position than that he would have agreed with Arthur Berriedale Keith: "Whatever the secret thoughts of the Buddha, it is abundantly clear that he promised something eternal to his disciples, something not born, not made, not conditioned. But it is also clear that the Buddha differed from the Brahmanical conception by regarding Nirvāṇa as the end of striving, and not as the foundation of existence" ("The Doctrine of the Buddha," p. 398).

My study of the Nikāyas has led me to the conviction that the incomparable security in which the Buddha is said to have met every one of his many opponents is a real historical feature: and is only explicable if we grant that the master, when a youth, had indeed, as he often said, very seriously studied all the systems attainable to him. The Buddha certainly does not belong to those who are silent because of their not knowing enough, but to those who do so because they know too much.[3]

Here, then, was the crux of the difficulty in deciphering the meaning of nirvāṇa. On the one hand, numerous passages from the texts could be cited to support a contention that Buddhism allows no permanence in the world—consequently that there is no abiding soul or self; consequently that, with the emasculation of *karman* and the destruction of the possibility of *karmaphalam*, the individual, as personality or entity of any sort, perishes utterly at death. On the other hand, texts could be cited showing that this conclusion was not overtly drawn, that questions concerning survival in nirvāṇa were "reserved" questions whose answers were not forthcoming. Rhys Davids emphasized the former texts and harmonized the latter with them by means of insisting that nirvāṇa really appertained only to the ethical and moral status of the individual in this life. Oldenberg—always taking the more comprehensive view—declared that, whatever logical conclusions might be drawn, the fact seemed indisputable that the Buddha himself had disallowed the validity of the questions about individual survival.

Schrader tries to secure something more concrete and comforting from the texts. He confesses that a priori he cannot believe that the Buddha's doctrine culminates in nihilism. But, he says, he will not repeat Max Müller's question—namely, would not a religion preaching annihilation cease to be a religion? Rather, Schrader has this question—and its answer—in mind:

"Is it possible that a thinker who had drunk out to the bottom the cup of knowledge—and we cannot help believing that the

[3] Schrader, p. 158.

Buddha was such a thinker—could attain to the conviction that there was absolutely nothing behind or above or besides this transitory world we conceive by our senses and supply by our fancy—this world of terrestrial and celestial things and beings?" I say no! We cannot by any means believe the Buddha, such as we know him from the Suttas, capable of such a *testimonium paupertatis*, as would place him far under all the great thinkers of all times.[4]

That declaration certainly brings Müller's attitude to mind, and, though Schrader does not intend to rely solely upon an a priori sentiment, it is a measure of the deep-rootedness of the scheme of ontic and moral values in Europe that an Orientalist was able to write in this vein as recently as half a century ago. This type of question begging destroys any possibility of a phenomenological inquiry from the outset. Even if alloyed with textual substantiations, it predisposes one against any conclusions which the author insists are based on the primary sources.

As a matter of fact, Schrader's investigations turn up material of a surprisingly seductive kind. His point of departure is clearly defined: He writes:

If it were certain that the Buddha declined the idea of a substance in every sense, the answer concerning the Parinibbānam would of course be that it was annihilation in every respect. But this is by no means certain.[5]

Schrader's thesis is that the *anatta* doctrine represents a concerted effort to disengage the absolute from the phenomenal world—to break completely with all theories of immanence in favor of an uncompromising notion of transcendence. According to Schrader, *anatta* as a doctrine refers merely to the fact that the *atta*, the absolute, does not reside in the *skandha*-s, the constituent elements of particular phenomena. The Buddha is pictured as the great champion in a revolt against pantheism and immanentism.

The first step in this direction had probably been made before Buddhism arose; but it was the Buddha, without any doubt, who

[4] *Ibid.*, p. 159.
[5] *Ibid.*

banished out of the world the last glitter of immutability, and liberated, on the other hand, from the last terrestrial feature it still possessed, *viz.* consciousness, the notion of the Absolute; it was the Buddha who, for the first time saw clearly that only ignorance can devise any relation at all between nature and the Supernatural One, and that a true ethic must therefore necessarily be atheistic; it was the Buddha and no one else who made the doctrine of *anattā* a moral principle, and that not by denying the Absolute One, but presupposing it as the true self, the only reality.[6]

To Schrader's credit, it must be noted that he was no mere spokesman for a gross and naïve form of personal immortality, for he just as vigorously denies that there is any trace of individuality in nirvāṇa as he denies that nirvāṇa is annihilation. "It is beyond doubt that in Buddha's opinion there rests of the *parinibbuto* not the slightest shade of an individuality."[7] As E. J. Thomas observes, however, with such premises as these which Schrader adopts, one could prove almost anything about nirvāṇa.[8]

Schrader is inclined to raise the Buddha and Buddhist thought out of the Indian milieu and point to them as examples of world historical tendencies and the universal evolution, so called, of religious forms. Indeed, he presents them not merely as examples but as the ultimate stage of such history cum evolution. He concludes rhetorically:

If the word of Spencer is true—that the history of religion is the history of the dispersonification of God, then Buddhism is the natural end of this process. For this is the only religion which acknowledges so absolutely the total difference between Nature and the Supernatural that it forbids its followers even to speak of the latter, without, however, denying its existence.[9]

To the French Indologist Emile Senart there was no need to prune Buddhism from the Indian tradition in order to show that nirvāṇa did not signify annihilation. On the contrary, Senart spent a good deal of time trying to document

[6] *Ibid.*, pp. 162–63.
[7] *Ibid.*, p. 165.
[8] Thomas, *A History of Buddhist Thought*, pp. 130–31.
[9] Schrader, p. 170.

the fateful thesis that Buddhism was actually "a sect detached from the ancient and powerful tradition of Vaiṣṇava yoga,"[10] and consequently that Buddhism was inextricably involved in the discrete history of Indian thought. Nirvāṇa, so Senart believed, was to be understood in the Buddhist context by seeing it in relation to the meanings which it held in other Indian situations. At bottom, *nirvāti* means extinction —the extinction of fire or a shining light.[11] Now, Senart continues, nirvāṇa very naturally could acquire the significance of "destruction"; but, in fact, the figurative extensions of "refreshment," "coolness," and "well-being" predominate.

> The transition is all the more natural when religious language continually likens suffering to a consuming fire. As all passion is fire and suffering, the idea of "repose, separation" is immediately identified with this notion of "bliss."[12]

Citing examples from the Mahābhārata (following Father Dahlmann), Senart emphasizes that nirvāṇa definitely means both "peace" and "bliss" in Hindu thought.

> Each school of Hindu mysticism analyzes *mokṣa* into two moments: *jīvanmukti* and *apavarga*, *arhattva* and *parinirvāṇa.* Nirvāṇa, expressing at the very same time both the "peace" subsequent to the agitations of desire and the "bliss" of escape from the miseries of saṃsāra, was used more than any other term by all schools to embrace both meanings.[13]

According to Senart, then, nirvāṇa really acquires the sense of deliverance in all its aspects independently of Buddhism.

Nirvāṇa, as it appears in the Buddhist texts, would seem to have peculiar significance, however, for "Buddhist speculation denies the existence of the soul, of the personality." And, Senart notes, nirvāṇa is almost always interpreted by Europeans as meaning "annihilation" when found in Buddhist contexts.

[10] Emile Senart, "Nirvāṇa," *Album-Kern: Opstellen Geschreven ter eere van Dr. H. Kern*, p. 104.
[11] *Ibid.*, p. 101.
[12] *Ibid.*
[13] *Ibid.*, p. 102.

Nevertheless, even a priori such an interpretation could not have appeared so obvious. If the compound *nirvā* was on occasion naturally enough extended by way of comparison to the idea of suppression, disappearance, that usage does not seem to have been regular. Let me put it thusly: I know of no instance of *nirvāṇa* employed in the absolute sense of "destruction." [14]

And, Senart remarks craftily—thinking of the "reserved" questions:

When one observes to what extremes Buddhism went to avoid all categorical statements concerning its ideal of the beyond, how is it possible to believe that it was so eager to coin a word designed to express crudely the very nihilistic consequences that it tried to avoid? [15]

For Senart, the use of the term nirvāṇa in Buddhism cannot be separated from its use in Brahmanism. It occurs in the sense of each of the "two aspects of deliverance," and it is even associated with the same synonyms. The only problem is to determine the common source for the Brahmanic and Buddhist usages. Annihilation, Senart assures us, was not the common point of departure. And, as the history of the word in Brahmanic—that is to say, epic—texts seems transparent to him, Senart declares that nirvāṇa in all its significations was borrowed or appropriated from Brahmanism by the Buddhists. Will someone suggest that the Buddhists, while they may have borrowed the term, could easily have given it a specific technical sense?

It is quite natural that Buddhism, despite its doctrinal divergences, had perpetuated some traditional terms whose very general meaning favoured covering certain distinct viewpoints which agreed at least in so far as all of them aspired to the objective common to every sect: the happy deliverance from the passions and transmigration. At the very moment when Burnouf interprets *nirvāṇa* as "annihilation," he . . . is forced to declare that the Tibetans understand it as "exemption from sorrow." [16]

[14] *Ibid.*
[15] *Ibid.*
[16] *Ibid.*, pp. 102–3.

Should someone counter that a text like Sutta Nipāta (verse 235) compares nirvāṇa to a lamp which has been extinguished and that strict annihilation is the intent of the metaphor? Senart replies that the identical image is found in Mahābhārata XIV, 642.[17]

Thus, two positive reactions to the negative interpretation of nirvāṇa appeared early in the first decade of this century. On the one hand, the continuity between Buddhism and Brahmanism was stressed (Senart), and, on the other, a new, even culminatory plateau was said to characterize the achievement of the Buddha's religious transcendentalism (Schrader). Neither view seemed to harmonize with those opinions expressed by Oldenberg and Rhys Davids, among others. It was obvious that Rhys Davids' hope that he had found a definition to end all further attempts to define had been futile.

Neither Senart nor Schrader, however, but another Continental scholar was to pursue intensively a satisfactory answer to the nirvāṇa question. He was the Belgian Louis de La Vallée Poussin. From the publication of his *Bouddhisme: Etudes et matériaux* in 1898 until his last article, "Buddhica," published posthumously in 1938, he devoted more time and manuscripts to the meaning of the Buddhist nirvāṇa than had any European previously (in all likelihood, more by far than any scholar will again). In many important regards, what he says about nirvāṇa represents the state of the question today. Now I shall examine the salient points of his Buddhist investigations in chronological order. And at the appropriate historical moment I shall introduce the Russian Buddhologist Th. Stcherbatsky and describe the great decade-long debate between the two.

[17] *Ibid.*, p. 103. Also see Keith, "The Doctrine of the Buddha," pp. 396–98; and Louis Renou and Jean Filliozat, *L'Inde classique*, Vol. II, pp. 547–48 (§ 2296). The consensus is that, according to Indian thought, the dying flame is not annihilated but returns to an invisible, unmanifest (*avyakta*) mode of being.

Louis de La Vallée Poussin

Born in Liège in 1869, Louis de La Vallée Poussin attended the State University of Liège from 1881 to 1888, studying philology and philosophy. It was there that he was introduced to Sanskrit and Pali by Charles de Harlez and Philippe Colinet. The decisive influences on his career came after leaving Liège to spend two years at Paris. There the twenty-two-year-old La Vallée Poussin sat at the feet of some of the world's most eminent Indologists: Sylvain Lévi, Emile Senart, and Auguste Barth. In the academic year 1893–94, he was appointed professor of comparative grammar of Greek and Latin at Ghent. He died February 18, 1938.[18]

With his first important publication on Buddhism—*Etudes et matériaux* (1898)—La Vallée Poussin twisted several heads among the students of Buddhism in Europe. Cherished notions and hypotheses were calmly riddled by the young Belgian, who took himself to be the legitimate heir to Eugène Burnouf's program—halted for almost fifty years. The first pious hypothesis which fell under La Vallée Poussin's ax was that concerning the importance of Pali Buddhism. In brief, he flatly declares that the Buddhism of that tradition is by no means *all* of Buddhism. The Pali-ists, as he calls them, have said that we know the original Buddhism through the Sinhalese traditions and, further, that the materials found in North India, Nepal, and Tibet represent later and degenerate forms. To those assertions La Vallée Poussin responds:

> Far from giving us the key to the origins of Buddhism and reliable information about its historical evolution, the examination of the Pali Canon and chronicles merely informs us about

[18] For biographical details, I have relied on Paul Masson-Oursel, "Necrologie: Louis de La Vallée Poussin 1869–1938," *Journal asiatique*, CCXXX (April–June, 1938), 287–90.

one sect in the Southern Church. Moreover, this information has absolute value only for a relatively recent period in the history of this church. To describe the destinies of the community, the constitution of the Saṃgha, the formation of the scriptures, and the life of the Master on the authority of some documents which date from the first or fourth century of our era is an illusory enterprise.[19]

From the beginnings, Buddhism, the young La Vallée Poussin insists, is richer and more complex than the Pali-ists will acknowledge. The Pali Canon witnesses the fairly coherent viewpoint of only one among many Buddhist sects.

Reduced to the history of a Sinhalese sect that was established about the first century of our era, the history of the Buddha, his doctrine, and his Church—even if it were possible—would be singularly mutilated.[20]

It is necessary, La Vallée Poussin declares, to study *all* the sources—Sanskrit, Tibetan, Pali, and so on—in order to understand the Buddhism which underlies the various Buddhisms. "Il faut, en un mot, continuer l'*Introduction*. . . ."[21]

Rhys Davids and Oldenberg are singled out both for praise and reprimand by La Vallée Poussin. The principal point of criticism is that neither of them reached the Buddhist origins about which both pretended to talk. This explicit demand that the Ur-Buddhism be sought in all texts fell on many deaf ears, though it seems apparent that Mrs. Rhys Davids was greatly influenced (and, through her, a number of Pali scholars from India and Japan who are carrying out research today).

Representative of contemporary opinion concerning La Vallée Poussin's attitude toward the Pali Canon are the comments by E. J. Rapson. "Sufficiently startling," he observes with archetypically cool English reserve. In fact, Rapson's long review of *Etudes* seems to miss the point entirely, for he busies about defending the Pali texts against attacks which they do not receive from La Vallée Poussin. His statement

[19] La Vallée Poussin, *Bouddhisme: Études et matériaux.*
[20] *Ibid.*, p. 5.
[21] *Ibid.*, p. 6.

that the Belgian scholar "protests against the view very generally accepted that the Pāli scriptures are the best extant representatives of Buddhism in an early form, and contends that the Northern scriptures preserve traces of a far older state of things" [22] needs to be taken at its face value. La Vallée Poussin does not, as Rapson would have it, say that there is no ancient material in the Pali Canon. He contends, rather, that the materials are systematized there according to a later school and ought not to be taken as structurally representative of the oldest stratum of Buddhism.

In this regard, it is also interesting to refer to La Vallée Poussin's rejoinder to Rapson, printed in JRAS the following year (1899):

> The initial divergence bears on a definition of terms. Mr. Rapson calls Buddhism that doctrine preached by Śakyamuni. I call Buddhism the general state of belief that has condensed around the name of the Buddha. Both are beyond our immediate reach.[23]

History or—to be more exact—the quest for origins seems to be less interesting for La Vallée Poussin than for many of his contemporaries. But he does not ignore the historical problems, far less prove himself a poor historian. Rather, he shows a philosophical-theological concern, and he works (with the possible exception of his *Nirvāṇa*, which I discuss below) always as a cautious critical historian, not as a "constructive" historian. Paul Masson-Oursel attributes much of La Vallée Poussin's attitude toward history to the influence of Auguste Barth. And, though it appears to me that his intense involvement in the Roman Catholic Church must be kept in mind also, the following observation is pertinent.

> Barth's influence convinced the Belgian scholar from the outset of the impossibility of studying as an historian a civilization whose archaic elements are lost and in which the modern elements have archaic antecedents. So the collaborator of Cavaignac gave

[22] E. J. Rapson, Review of *Etudes*, *JRAS*, 1898, p. 909.
[23] *JRAS*, 1899, p. 141.

him, not history books properly speaking, but collections of problems with respect to history. . . .[24]

To return to *Etudes*, I should call attention to the fact that La Vallée Poussin develops there a perspective in regard to the relation between Buddhism and Brahmanism which persists throughout his career. He declares, for example:

> Buddhism is one of the forms of Hinduism, at every point comparable to the popular or learned religions organized under the aegis of the Brahmins and the patronage of the Veda.
>
> Buddhism and Brahmanism have produced certain theories of intellectual life and practice that are absolutely analogous.[25]

Almost forty years later:

> Buddhism is not wholly original; it appears during centuries, as a "buddhification" of institutions, ideas, or feelings, which were simply Indian . . . In short, Buddhism is only the "buddhized" aspect of contemporaneous Hinduism.
>
> It cannot be said that the most notable features of the Buddhist speculation . . . are specifically Buddhist.[26]

Those statements reveal an almost identical understanding of Buddhism's relation to the complex Indian civilization—or, as La Vallée Poussin would have preferred to say, the Indian civilizations. And they allow the reader to anticipate with

[24] Masson-Oursel, p. 288. For a brief critical sketch of La Vallée Poussin's accomplishments as an historian, see A. L. Basham, "Modern Historians of Ancient India," *Historians of India, Pakistan and Ceylon*, ed. C. H. Philips (London: Oxford University Press, 1961), pp. 274–80. "It was as an authority on Buddhism that he was known among indologists until he wrote his three volumes in the well-known *Histoire du Monde* series. The first of the three, *Indo-Européens et Indo-Iraniens*, appeared in 1924 (second edition 1936), the second, *L'Inde aux Temps des Mauryas*, in 1930, and the third, *Dynasties et Histoire de l'Inde*, in 1935. Together they form a complete political history of Ancient India down to the coming of the Muslims, and of all the comprehensive studies of the subject hitherto produced in Europe they are the most up-to-date and scholarly, and the most useful to the present-day student." (Pp. 274–75.)

[25] *Etudes*, p. 7.

[26] Louis de La Vallée Poussin, "Buddhism," *The Legacy of India*, ed. G. T. Garratt, pp. 162–63.

considerable accuracy his position regarding the Buddhist idea of nirvāṇa. Here may be mentioned another line of continuity extending from *Etudes* to his last works and developing his basic attitudes toward not only Buddhism but the history of religions in general. There are two types of Buddhist nirvāṇa, according to him, in the same way as there are two basic types of Buddhism. The types may be called "dogmatic" and "philosophical," and in each there may be further subdivisions. The labels themselves are not used consistently by La Vallée Poussin, however; and care must be taken not to apply them as such in checking his regularity of expression. There is an accepted nirvāṇa—one may say, the dogma about nirvāṇa—and it is variously interpreted and explicated in philosophies (or doctrines or systems) of nirvāṇa. Thus:

> At the very heart of the most orthodox church, the dogma of nirvāṇa is interpreted in several ways, and the passionate discussion that divides European scholars is but a weak reflection of the discussion among Sinhalese faithful. The nihilistic doctrine definitely prevails, but who can set forth an opinion documented by the numerous sects of the small vehicle and establish in time and space the successive phases of an evolution which may be of a secular order? . . .
>
> The thesis which we are combatting—namely, the historical priority of an atheistic and philosophic Buddhism—became manifest some twenty years ago.[27]

Old wine in new bottles, the reader may respond immediately, for it would seem that we have heard and read this before, time after time. But something new is being generated. The contrast here is between the religious and the philosophic (occasionally, the philosophumenic[28]) aspects of nirvāṇa.

[27] *Etudes*, p. 7.

[28] "Philosophumène" was a favorite expression of La Vallée Poussin's, reminiscent—as Masson-Oursel observed—of Auguste Barth's term, "philosophème." I am not convinced that this is used in a pejorative sense, as Masson-Oursel and many others seem to believe. It is to be observed that La Vallée Poussin uses the term with reference to specialists in ecstatic techniques who were not, strictly speaking, philosophers and did not pretend to be.

The doctrine(s) of nirvāṇa—the philosophic and speculative interpretations and systematizations of dogma—seem to be prevailingly negative, according to La Vallée Poussin. At least that is his position in 1898. Later, he was less inclined to believe that a thoroughly negative view dominates even in the philosophy. His own view of nirvāṇa remains constant: religiously, insofar as Buddhism is and continues to be a religious form, nirvāṇa does not mean annihilation.

> The philosophical schools of the small vehicle have elaborated very subtle doctrines not only about the Buddha but also about all the problems relating to the religious life, and by that very fact those doctrines are certainly in disaccord with popular belief.[29]

A little further on, La Vallée Poussin affirms that at bottom nirvāṇa for the religious Buddhist is really synonymous with heaven, the type of heaven to which all those who are religiously inclined aspire. Notice the opposition posed between the "Hīnayānist" and the "Buddhist" (Bauddha).

> What is the goal pursued by the faithful? The Hīnayānist, who denies the reality of the pudgala, hopes to attain nirvāṇa (cittavṛttinirodha) through the suppression of desire and karman. The Bauddha, who—though not making an issue of it—keeps the traditional and popular view of the human personality and of good and evil, hopes to attain to the svargas or to nirvāṇa conceived as an eternal svarga through the practice of good works (śuklāni karmāṇi) by the grace of the Master (Buddhadhiṣṭhānena).[30]

What most scholars at the end of the nineteenth century were taking as the degeneration of pure Buddhism in the Mahāyāna (or Bauddha) attitude La Vallée Poussin takes as representative of the earliest phase of Buddhism—a phase earlier than the systematized Pali Canon. The principal assumptions here are three:

> That it is natural for the human personality to aspire to personal immortality, relief of suffering, and eternal bliss—consequently, that nirvāṇa could not have meant annihilation as it was

[29] *Etudes*, p. 44.
[30] *Ibid.*, p. 45.

first introduced, except as annihilation of passions, sins, and so on.

That the argument above is supported by tradition, for Buddhism has not developed any particularly distinctive notions apart from the Indian–Brahmanic matrix.

That there is in the growth of any religious institution an inexorable tendency for that institution to systematize and doctrinalize its fundamental dogmas, to become case-hardened and artificial. In brief, that Buddhism was a religion, a faith before becoming a philosophy.

Some readers may think that the La Vallée Poussin dichotomy of dogma and doctrine, dogma and system, faith and philosophy almost dies on the vine in his huge two-part essay "Dogmatique bouddhique," which appeared in the *Journal asiatique* in 1902 and 1903.[31] There he examines one of the cardinal tenets (or dogmas) of Buddhism: *nairātmya* (*anatta*). The *nairātmya* notion is seen at various levels—from a basic position in dogma to elaboration in the sophistication of the systems. In this way, the author preserves the distinction between dogma and doctrine.

In the first installment of "Dogmatique," La Vallée Poussin begins to criticize in detail the work of Hermann Oldenberg. In *Etudes*, he had been content to say that Oldenberg's *Buddha*, although a fine effort, was mistitled. It should have been called, he jibed, *Buddha: His Life, His Doctrine, His Order—According to the Pali Sources and the Principles of the Ceylonese Church.* In "Dogmatique," he insists that both Oldenberg and Rhys Davids have misunderstood the doctrines of *anatta* and *kammaphalam* in the Ceylonese Church.

Rhys Davids, it will be recalled, had consistently held that the Buddhists and the Buddha himself ran into a blind alley by holding two incompatible notions: momentariness, the composite nature of entities and the consequence that nothing survives (or abides); and the felt necessity, in the interest of

[31] La Vallée Poussin, "Dogmatique bouddhique. La négation de l'âme et la doctrine de l'acte." And "Dogmatique bouddhique II. Nouvelles recherches sur la doctrine de l'acte. Grand Véhicule. Système mâdhyamika. Les deux vérités. Prajna, karuna, bhakti."

preserving some order of human justice, of holding the notion of the retribution of acts. Doctrines of *karman* and *karmaphalam* bridged these incompatible notions, according to Rhys Davids, who added that the whole idea of *karman* was merely a word game. *Karman* carried over from one life to the next. The person born blind in this life is reaping the evil fruit of the actions performed by the previously existing person of whom he is the immediate karmic descendent. Oldenberg had maintained that, by virtue of the so-called reserved questions and a certain positive tone in a few dialogues, there might be something persisting even unto nirvāṇa after death. Or at least, he said, it seems that a segment of the Buddhist community interpreted the Buddha's silence in that way.

La Vallée Poussin's "Dogmatique I" (1902) clearly shows that Rhys Davids had missed an important ramification of the *anatta* doctrine and that Oldenberg had failed to see the consistency of doctrinal presentations in the Pali Canon itself. The focal point of these discussions is the theory of *vijñānasaṃtāna*, "the continuity of 'mind.' "

The *vijñānasaṃtāna* theory, according to La Vallée Poussin, provides a substitute for the *ātman*—that is, a dynamic process which serves all the purposes and answers all the requirements for an abiding individual personality. Mrs. C. A. F. Rhys Davids, reviewing "Dogmatique I" in JRAS (1903), catches the full significance of the Belgian's elucidations. She is atypically succinct:

> This notion, he holds, gives us a continuous "I"; responsible yet susceptible of interruptions. . . . He concludes that since in place of Soul the Buddhists substituted a protagonist who played the part of soul so uncommonly well, we must put into the background all of their reiterated rejection of the Atta.[32]

This substitute soul is merely the replacement of a dynamic conception of mind for a static, entity concept. Rhys Davids' interpretation had been foggy, and it seemed, according to

[32] C. A. F. Rhys Davids, "The Soul Theory in Buddhism," *JRAS*, 1903, p. 588.

his analysis, that retribution was not effected in the Buddhist doctrine. The blind person of the present would seem to be more the object than the subject of the previous evil action. With La Vallée Poussin's explanation of the dynamic vijñāna continuity theory, death's supposed disruptive power vaporizes. Rhys Davids had not penetrated and understood the full implications of "momentariness" (*anitya*, *anicca*), had not seen that the mind process or personality process suffers the same sort of breaks in continuity within the same life as he imagined would obtain only between two distinct, if successive, *skandha* aggregates. And La Vallée Poussin's explication brought with it the additional benefit of reminding some Europeans of yet another aspect of modernity in Buddhist thought. Mrs. Rhys Davids is again spokesman:

> Now I venture to think that in breaking up the notion of an abstract vijnana-entity into a series of intellectual processes or force-moments, Professor Poussin shows true insight into Buddhist thought. Dimly and crudely, without scientific language or instrument the early Buddhists were groping, under the crust of words, after that view of phenomena which we are tending to make fundamental in our science today. They were feeling out after a dynamic conception of things—after a world-order of becoming, movement, process, sequence, force.[33]

With this illumination in hand, La Vallée Poussin turns to Oldenberg's ideas on the subject of the survival of the Tathāgata after death. The official dogma on this, Oldenberg had said, was that the Buddha has remained silent. La Vallée Poussin insists, however, that Oldenberg was wrong when he said that the question of what the ancient community believed about nirvāṇa had been incorrectly stated by previous inquirers. It is not true, the German scholar had written, that the early community believed that nirvāṇa was either annihilation or bliss unending. The official dogma was, rather, that the Buddha has taught nothing on the subject and refused to answer or even acknowledge the validity of questions so framed.

[33] *Ibid.*

La Vallée Poussin counters Oldenberg's correction of the classic question about alternatives with another objection about the formulation of the issue.

> It does not seem to me that the problem is well posed. If by "ancient community" the primitive community is meant, we are very poorly informed about its doctrine. And an examination of the Piṭakas reveals several systems, only one of which can pretend to be official: the annihilationist system.[34]

Both Oldenberg and La Vallée Poussin believe that the Buddha had been silent on some matters and that the texts preserved at least the historical fact of that refusal to answer certain questions. The divergence of their positions comes at the point of interpreting what the redactors of the texts —the systematizers—made of that silence: what they thought it meant. Oldenberg sees here a confirmation of his idea that the Buddha's silence inspired some positive—though veiled —responses. La Vallée Poussin insists, on the contrary, that the responses—the dialogues where the Buddha's silence is featured, as it were—are all in accord with the prevalent system of the Piṭakas. On the subject of the survival of the Tathāgata, he goes on, it is true that the Tathāgata is not destroyed in nirvāṇa. And this is because he never existed at all. Not only is that idea consistently rendered in the texts, according to La Vallée Poussin; it shows also the seeds of later Mādhyamika and Mahāyāna dialectic.

One thing more needs to be said about La Vallée Poussin's idea that the dialogues of silence reveal both the early faith position in Buddhism and its metamorphosis into acceptable illustrations for the annihilation system in the canon. Consider again the question of the Tathāgata's existence in nirvāṇa:

> Here we have a precious survival of the ancient belief: "It is false that the Tathāgata will perish." The compiler of the *Saṃyutta* has interpreted this venerable proposition in his own way, conformably to that spirit which reigns in the *Piṭakas:*

[34] "Dogmatique I," p. 245, note.

"Anyone who affirms the destruction of the Tathāgata is anathema: in order to perish, he has to have existed!" [35]

The system of the Piṭakas is perfectly consistent. But it is not in accord with original Buddhism, for no philosophical handmaiden could be. "According to the Piṭakas, the saint actually dies completely. This dogma [in the sense of a postulate of the system] is not contradicted." [36] All of which goes to prove something quite different.

The religious life cannot accommodate itself to a dogmatic that isolates every being and makes of him a suffering automaton. This dogmatic forms a single whole: either one sought to find faults in it, or else he knew nothing about it. In a similar way, Protestant Christianity remains rich in works and hope, although Calvin had taught predestination and Luther, faith without works.[37]

In short, "Let us say that the logical edifice that was acknowledged and official—in a word: *darśana*—is only one of the important elements in the religious organism." [38]

In 1908, La Vallée Poussin delivered a series of lectures at the Catholic Institute of Paris. Given the opportunity to speak his mind in congenial surroundings, he tried his hand at debunking some of the mystique of Buddhist studies. (In this connection, reference to Barthélemy Saint-Hilaire would seem unavoidable.) A few sentences from the introduction suffice to illustrate the attitude.

It may seem surprising that Buddhism encounters marked sympathy, even indiscreet zeal, to some extent everywhere, notably in America, England, and Germany; while the other Indian religions leave the curious indifferent. Actually, anyone who knows the Indian literatures does not doubt that Vedism, with its great mythological and divine figures, Brahmanism, with its profound theories and rational disciplines, and Hinduism, with its humble and fervent devotional practices, in many respects surpass Buddhism, where everything is second-hand so to speak: mythology,

[35] *Ibid.*, p. 245.
[36] *Ibid.*, p. 244.
[37] "Dogmatique II," p. 446.
[38] *Ibid.*, footnote.

doctrine, and piety. But one finds some strange ideas about Buddhism. Many writers assert that by a privilege unique in the history of religions it possesses a purely rationalist philosophy, an ideal compatible with modern science, and a morality without god and without soul. It is added that Buddhism, organized several centuries before the Christian era, was propogated (or insinuated) into the West as far as the Mediterranean. That is enough to make it a success; but it is to pay it too much honor. Certainly Buddhism merits our close attention, but not for those reasons. Rather is it deserving because of its legends and by virtue of its very particular view of humanity and friendship. It is especially noteworthy when viewed with the other Indian religions because of its historical character: its founder, its organization, its canons and sects, its inconography (dependent on Greek art), the force of its propaganda, and its conquest of the Far East. To some extent Buddhism has been in certain regards for Asia what Christianity has been for Europe.[39]

By that statement one should not merely be reminded of the crusade against Buddhism conducted by Barthélemy Saint-Hilaire. Nor should one be put off by the nature of the audience which La Vallée Poussin addressed. This is the announcement of a new and critical period of Buddhist studies. Modesty and an uncompromisingly scrupulous avoidance of speculation are central to this approach.

One cannot gainsay the fact that Buddhism challenged the Belgian scholar severely. We may say that Masson-Oursel's observation about his studies and attitudes toward Buddhism is apt but incomplete. Masson-Oursel writes:

It seems to us that this scholar found solutions of vital importance in his Christian faith, and that those which Asia proposed engaged his curiosity but not his sympathy. He did not study the frenzy of mysticism, but rather the scholasticism in India, that aspect which it has in common with medieval Christianity. Perhaps he even felt some ironic pleasure in denouncing or in supposing certain aberrations of pagan subtilty in its metaphysics.[40]

Whatever may be the drawbacks stemming from La Vallée Poussin's personal commitments, he was at all events singu-

[39] Louis de La Vallée Poussin, *Bouddhisme: Opinions sur L'histoire de la dogmatique*, pp. 1–2.

[40] Masson-Oursel, "Necrologie," p. 289.

larly free from enthusiasm in his elucidations of Buddhist thought. And the dogmatics of enthusiasm, as Yves Simon has wisely pointed out, constitute the greatest pitfall to clear thinking.

The most important weakness in a severely critical investigation would seem to be that absence of sympathy of which Masson-Oursel speaks. Without a certain tolerance and sympathetic receptivity, many crucial aspects in any historical phenomenon may be completely lost sight of. Inordinate hostility may transmogrify the critical approach—changing it into a polemic and apologetic discourse. Against the latter possibility La Vallée Poussin was careful to guard himself, and not without taking the opportunity to throw a little cold water on historians of religions.

> There can be no doubt that the study of Buddhism, thus conceived [as the analysis of texts], could not furnish legitimate assumptions in favor of the transcendance of Christianity and, at the same time, the fruitlessness of objections to it. But this is not our affair, and we remain foreign to such a preoccupation as legitimate as it may be. Apologetics is the concern of theologians, and requires clear and certain conclusions to shore up its arguments; but prudent Indianists refuse to consider the results of their inquiry as such. They work in their own province without ulterior motives and without involving themselves in that which does not concern them. If they unravel Buddhism, that will surely be a notable gain for universal history, and we shall gain thereby some interesting and, as the English say, suggestive insights concerning the genesis, the economy, and the developments of religious and philosophical institutions. But were it necessary that Buddhism be elucidated because of that and if it were, this chimerical discipline called the history of religions would still be a long way from existing in fact. And that is not a personal impression. The time is passed when, following the presumptuous formula of the Hibbert Lectures, learned individuals explain "the origin and spread of religion" in light of the religions of India or of Assyria. Philologists have learned to be modest, and they abandon to anthropologists and sociologists the unguarded speculations.[41]

[41] *Opinions*, pp. 9–10. Various aspects and significations of the concern for "origins" that characterized so much of late nineteenth-

Cold water, moreover, on the nineteenth-century dreams of uncovering the origins.

Two substantive discussions in *Opinions* now claim our attention: the question of nirvāṇa, and the doctrine of the Mādhyamika school. La Vallée Poussin stresses the middle-way standpoint of Buddhism—its path between all extremes. Applied to the idea of nirvāṇa, he observes:

> The canonical literature presents three responses among which we would have to choose: the ego is not a person but merely an aggregate of psychological phenomena, and nirvāṇa is nothing more than the end of existence; a person does exist, and there is an immutable abode called nirvāṇa; finally, the third response: the two points of view above—nihilist and eternalist—are equally false, equally incompatible with the religious life and the road to nirvāṇa: the Good Law is "the middle way" and the two types of error are held off.[42]

What have Europeans thought? We have devoted a great deal of space to finding out; but let La Vallée Poussin present his own summary, and notice the place of honor accorded to Oldenberg.

> Some—Max Müller and Foucaux in the first rank among them—refused to believe that the Buddha had been able to preach annihilation as the supreme goal of the religious life. Not knowing or ignoring more solid arguments, they clung to considerations which were necessarily contestable a priori. How does one actually determine where the exigencies for Indian thinkers of the sixth or fifth century before our era with regard to metaphysics, morality, and eschatology conclude? In fact, even our own contemporaries surprise us! Other scholars have thought that nirvāṇa is the nothing. This latter interpretation appears justified because of direct witnesses. In fact, it rests on a deduction the logic of which seems to be a touch too rigid. Because nothing exists other than thought and the transitory elements of the ego, it would seem that nirvāṇa is non-existence. That was the state of affairs when Oldenberg had the good fortune and the great merit to

---

century historical research are discussed most imaginatively by Mircea Eliade, "The Quest for the 'Origins' of Religion," *History of Religions*, Vol. 4, No. 1 (Summer, 1964), pp. 154–69.

[42] *Opinions*, pp. 78–79.

discover the solution to the problem. We dare to call it the solution because it lacks none of the clarity of the texts which proclaim it and no document contradicts it in proper terms.[43]

La Vallée Poussin's thinking has adjusted somewhat. He sees the Buddhism of the Piṭakas—the doctrines—here in closer relation to the original intentions of the founder. The solution to the problem of nirvāṇa turns on the role of the Buddha and the nature of the path to nirvāṇa: "The Buddha is a doctor, the Good Law therapy." [44] The so-called reserved questions carry an answer, namely: "Not to believe in the ego, or rather not to be preoccupied with it: that is the road to renunciation and salvation." [45] Philosophy as an assistant to religion may tend to carry its conclusions to extremes. In Buddhist thought, the philosophy is not competent for the specific job it is called upon to perform. It is, in La Vallée Poussin's estimate in *Opinions*, a meditational and disciplinary aid, not an end in itself.

Obviously, speculation is only an accessory here, a relief from hypnotic exercises, from the meditations on impurity which focus on aspects of a putrefying corpse, from those devoted to benevolence in which one affirms his affection for all beings, from those on empty space. In a word, notions of a rational order are only part of Buddhism. Moreover, these very notions are not lucid Hellenic or Latin concepts, but rather elements of Hindu theosophy, ambiguous, mysterious, susceptible of being interpreted in widely differing senses at the very same time, and which in order to be understood (obliquely or not at all) must necessarily retain their religious value.[46]

The importance of Buddhist speculation and philosophical doctrine is diminished to the point of disappearing. The essence of Buddhism is in the idea of deliverance. "Such is the leading idea of most of India's theosophies: the idea of deliverance or nirvāṇa. It is common to Buddhism and to Brahmanism." [47]

[43] *Ibid.*, pp. 90–91.
[44] *Ibid.*, p. 99.
[45] *Ibid.*, p. 96.
[46] *Ibid.*, p. 106.
[47] *Ibid.*, p. 107.

La Vallée Poussin's estimate of Buddhism was not to change materially for the rest of his life, except for his evaluation of the Mādhyamikas. In *Opinions*, he characterizes them as "pure nihilists."

Were appearances other than a sort of magic, they would be indestructible. The theory of the Elders—the hypothesis of a series composed of real members—could not satisfy the orthodox Buddhist, because it supposed the annihilation, the regular disappearance . . . of the final member of the series and, consequently, of the last thought to precede nirvāṇa. This notion was hardly philosophical and was formally condemned by the Buddha. Happily, however, appearance is only an illusion, and, from a critical standpoint, one cannot speak of the origin, continuation, or termination of the illusion. It is absolutely void, and resembles the daughter of a sterile woman. Because of this, nirvāṇa is actually, eternally realized in the absolute nothing. . . .[48]

Later, as we shall have occasion to note, La Vallée Poussin changes his mind about the fundamental principles of this philosophical school of Buddhism.

The themes in *Opinions* distill to this: The primary phase of Buddhism is faith in the Buddha and the Buddha's way to deliverance, the road to nirvāṇa. Buddhism is seen in its Hindu matrix with nirvāṇa thus corresponding in every detail to the *mokṣa* of Hinduism. As a system, Buddhism is a discipline for attaining deliverance, and all philosophy, so called, is developed to aid—and is always subservient to—the disciplinary practices.

In February, March, and April, 1916, few Europeans were devoting their full attention to Buddhist studies. But La Vallée Poussin was continuing his own research and publication uninterrupted by the great war. During those months he was at Manchester College, Oxford, delivering—the Hibbert Lectures. The following year, these lectures, *The Way to Nirvāṇa: Six Lectures on Ancient Buddhism as a Discipline*

48 *Ibid.*, pp. 199–200. And see Vincente Fatone, *El Budismo "Nihilista,"* (*Biblioteca Humanidades*, Vol. XXVIII; La Plata, Argentina: 1941), pp. 154–55 and footnotes.

of Salvation, were published,[49] and also an article signed by La Vallée Poussin appeared in James Hastings' *Encyclopedia of Religion and Ethics*.[50] Both may be considered as a single source, and I shall offer cross-references where appropriate.

At the beginning, one might possibly expect that La Vallée Poussin, having abandoned his ban on the Hibbert Lectures as an institution, has changed his mind about the meaning of nirvāṇa. Certainly this does not seem to be the case. Rather, he is mainly concerned in structuring the complex of meanings of nirvāṇa into a more intelligible presentational framework. He reiterates the importance of the work of defining the term, insisting that nirvāṇa is the essence of Buddhism. "Deliverance or Nirvāṇa," he says in *The Way*, "is the central idea of the teaching of Sakyamuni and the *raison d'être* of the religious life." [51] (In the *Encyclopedia of Religion and Ethics*, nirvāṇa is more pointedly called the "*raison d'être* of Buddhism." [52])

What is nirvāṇa? La Vallée Poussin, master of irony, answers the question with startling calm and more than a trace of that disdain for Indian thought which has made him such a notorious figure in many Indological coffee breaks.

> As a matter of fact, we know what Nirvāṇa is as well as the Buddhists themselves, and it is not our fault if we are not able to give an unambiguous statement. The Buddhists were satisfied with descriptions which do not satisfy us.
>
> On the one hand, whereas we have been for centuries trained to make our ideas clear, this was not the case with Indians. The historian has not to deal with Latin notions worked out by sober and clear-sighted thinkers, but with Indian "philosophumena" concocted by ascetics . . . men exhausted by a severe diet and often stupified by the practice of ecstacy. Indians do not make a clear distinction between facts and ideas, between ideas

[49] La Vallée Poussin, *The Way to Nirvāṇa: Six Lectures on Ancient Buddhism as a Discipline of Salvation.*

[50] Louis de La Vallée Poussin, "Nirvāṇa," *Encyclopedia of Religion and Ethics*, ed. James Hastings, IX (1917), 376a–79b.

[51] *The Way*, p. 110.

[52] *ERE*, p. 376a.

and words; they have never clearly recognized the principle of contradiction.

Moreover, we look at the Buddhist doctrines from the outside. Whereas Nirvāṇa is for us a mere object of archaeological interest, it is for Buddhists of paramount practical importance. Our task is to study what Nirvāṇa may be; the task of a Buddhist is to reach Nirvāṇa.[53]

Barthélemy Saint-Hilaire is again brought to mind. And if there is a serious flaw in La Vallée Poussin's analyses, it is here in his refusal openly to acknowledge that the Indians ever had one clear philosophical insight. As Stcherbatsky remarked with regard to the meaning that the Indian thinkers have attributed to the word "yoga," "a complaint, if any, can be only about the detailed and subtle precision with which this notion is analysed, not about its vagueness." [54] This was the type of comment which was totally lost on La Vallée Poussin—lost at least in public but perhaps not in private, for one has the feeling that the Belgian took the philosophical enterprise in Buddhism far more seriously than he was able to let on.

In *The Way*, La Vallée Poussin explains that he is dealing with the Buddhism of "the Older Books" and characterizes it as almost exclusively a discipline of salvation. Using "discipline" in a specific technical sense, he says that " 'Buddhism as a discipline of salvation' is to be contrasted with 'Buddhism as a religion.' " [55] In India, according to him, a number of disciplines arose in the seventh century B.C. They were "bodies of doctrines and practices, together with a rule of life, aiming at a practical end. . . ." [56] Thus, "they are something more than philosophies, theories, or scholasticisms." Yet, on the other hand, "in contrast with religions, the disciplines are made for ascetics, for ascetics only. Another feature . . . is

[53] *The Way*, pp. 110–12. Cf. *ERE*, p. 376ab.

[54] Th. Stcherbatsky, *The Conception of Buddhist Nirvāṇa*, p. 7. Cited hereafter as *CBN*.

[55] *The Way*, p. 1.

[56] *Ibid.*, p. 4.

that they are not concerned with mundane ends at all."[57]

The questions raised in *The Way* involve understanding what nirvāṇa meant to the Buddhist both as devotee and as *yogī* (follower of the discipline). To begin answering those questions, La Vallée Poussin gives a précis of the original meaning of nirvāṇa. Initially it was twofold—that is to say, its non-technical meanings were (and here Senart's influence will be obvious[58]) "cooling" and "extinction."

> Hence two directions in the evolution of the religious or philosophical meaning of the word. Cooling, refreshment, the refreshment of a man who is suffering, the cooling of a man who is hot with desire, comfort, peace, serenity, bliss. Also extinction, detachment or extinction of the fire of the passions, negative bliss or extinction of suffering, annihilation or extinction of individual existence.[59]

"Cooling" is the metaphor that refers to the condition called *arhattvam* (*arahatta*), which La Vallée Poussin translates as "sanctity" and about which Childers, Oldenberg, and Rhys Davids discoursed at length. And "extinction" refers primarily to the postmortem condition. But La Vallée Poussin is at special pains to stress that the metaphors are applicable to each situation indifferently. For the balance of his discussion in *The Way* he employs nirvāṇa only in reference to the postmortem condition, calling the condition in the present life which corresponds to it "Sanctity".

The next problem encountered is that there may be three separate interpretations of nirvāṇa sanctioned by the texts.

> It can be maintained either (1) that the dead saint is annihilated, cut off, does not exist any longer; or (2) that he has reached an immortal state; or (3) that we can only assert, without being able to state positively what deliverance is, that he is delivered from transmigration.[60]

We may subdivide the remainder of this discussion under the headings of these three options, which La Vallée Poussin

[57] *Ibid.*, p. 5.
[58] See above.
[59] *The Way*, p. 113.
[60] *Ibid.*, p. 115. Cf. *ERE*, p. 377a.

calls doctrinal possibilities. His intention is, acknowledging that each option had adherents in Buddhism, "to realize the relative importance of these conflicting views, and to state which is the prevailing teaching of the Scriptures and the ruling idea of the Buddhist religious life." [61]

1. "That Nirvāṇa is annihilation results—at least for us—both from the general principles of Buddhist philosophy and from clear statements." [62] "We have here in view the whole fabric of the speculative texts which force upon us the identification of deliverance with annihilation, because they do not leave room for doubt." [63] The consequences of the doctrine of *anatta* were realized by the compilers of the texts, and, from a philosophic standpoint, annihilation is strictly maintained in them all. Here, two other points must be noted. In the first place,

> Does that imply that Buddhists aim at annihilation? Not exactly so. Scholars who have maintained that Nirvāṇa was chiefly looked upon as annihilation do not say that a monk leads the religious life in order to be annihilated at death, but that he leads the religious life in order to become a Saint. Sanctity is the goal. Sanctity is the *summum bonum*, deliverance, Nirvāṇa.[64]

The difficulty with this proposition—that of Rhys Davids in particular and perhaps the central point for Oldenberg as well—is that "Buddhism would thus be only a discipline of happy life here below." And La Vallée Poussin observes that sanctity is not actually nirvāṇa but rather the possession of nirvāṇa.[65]

In the second place, La Vallée Poussin notices in this connection that nirvāṇa = annihilation does not constitute the primary orientation of the texts. It is, rather, an inescapable, secondary consequence in certain instances. He writes:

[61] *The Way*, p. 115.
[62] *Ibid.*, p. 116.
[63] *ERE*, p. 377a.
[64] *The Way*, p. 118.
[65] The transcendent aspects of nirvāṇa for the Buddhists, completely overlooked or discounted by Rhys Davids in his late nineteenth-century "common sense" approach, were thus brought into focus by La Vallée Poussin.

We must confess that this identification, "nirvāṇa = annihilation" is not one of the "primordial" doctrines of Buddhism. The doctrine of annihilation was not an original "purpose"; it was a result. That is to say, Sakyamuni (or the Church) did not start with such an idea of deliverance; this idea has been forced upon him (or upon them) because he has been rash enough to deny the existence of a soul.[66]

2. The opinion that nirvāṇa is some sort of blissful, though inconceivable, existence will not find support in the texts, according to La Vallée Poussin. Here he adduces arguments which he had previously raised against Oldenberg's interpretation of the reserved questions. Doctrinally, he says, nirvāṇa as immortality is a chimera. But, again, it must be underscored that La Vallée Poussin agrees with Oldenberg that the Buddha did actually refuse to answer questions about man's ultimate condition. The dispute with Oldenberg centers on La Vallée Poussin's belief that the dialogues which record the Buddha's silence are viable historical records only so far as they report the Buddha's reticence. Doctrinally, the content of the dialogues harmonizes with an annihilation motif. The Buddha's silence was truly inscrutable, and the textual redactors have been truly consistent in reading a tacit negation into each instance of that silence.

Doctrinally, there is no indication of the nirvāṇa = immortality equation. However, La Vallée Poussin insists that, from the perspective of the practicing Buddhist, nirvāṇa was often considered to be a blissful paradise. And the joyous anticipation of nirvāṇa, as illustrated in many texts, is no less real for its lack of doctrinal substance.

It may be said that such feelings draw their strength and their import from mysticism and religious exaltation; and we must agree that there is little doctrinal speculation in them. Nevertheless the fact remains that Buddhists spoke of nirvāṇa as a firm believer in happiness after death would speak of paradise; and this fact is an important point in the description of what the Buddhist thought of nirvāṇa.[67]

[66] *ERE*, p. 377a. Cf. *The Way*, p. 124.
[67] *ERE*, p. 377a.

3. According to La Vallée Poussin, "The commonest attitude concerning nirvāṇa" is discerned in the so-called agnostic texts in which the Buddha's silence is emphasized. Admittedly, the ideal of nirvāṇa among Buddhists is a negative one for the most part. Still, the important point is that it is specifically negative—deliverance from a certain condition and not unto a specific other condition.

> We believe that the most exact and the most authoritative definition of Nirvāṇa is not annihilation, but "unqualified deliverance," a deliverance of which we have no right to predicate anything.[68]

That is the attitude of the monk, the yogin, the follower of Buddhism, as a salvation technique; and this "man does not want to be happy; he only wants to be delivered from the miseries of this life." [69] Pessimistic certainly, says La Vallée Poussin, but not nihilistic.

> Not absolute nihilism, nihilism boldly looked at in the face. It is a negative attitude, which does not appeal to the most innate needs of our mind; but it is also to some extent an expectant attitude, which leaves some food to the needs of the human heart. The monk strives for unqualified deliverance; he does not inquire whether deliverance is destruction or a mysterious kind of existence; but he knows that Sakyamuni is omniscient and compassionate, and such a "caravan-leader" is the great man upon whom it is safe to rely.[70]

The key to deciphering the dominant interpretation of nirvāṇa is to be found in the attitude of those Buddhists who are yogins, "disciplined." And faith, the primordial stance of the Buddha's followers, is a major factor in this. As for the whole of Buddhism, neither annihilation nor immortality can claim real importance. Certainly not annihilation, for "everything supports our surmise that 'annihilation' is the result of the philosophic inquiry, a mere scholastic corollary." [71] La

[68] *The Way*, p. 131.
[69] *Ibid.*, p. 132. Cf. Nietzsche's comments on happiness.
[70] *Ibid.* Cf. *ERE*, p. 376b.
[71] *The Way*, p. 133.

Vallée Poussin also wants it clearly understood that, as all three attitudes are represented in Buddhism and the Buddhist texts, "the ancient Buddhist tradition was not clear on the nature of Nirvāṇa." Of this latter point, he comments:

> This conclusion does not please those scholars who are prepared to turn primitive Buddhism into an orthodoxy. While we believe that the scriptural contradictions—Nirvāṇa annihilation, Nirvāṇa immortality, Nirvāṇa a prohibited problem—are to be accepted as they are; while we believe that the true Buddhist state of mind is a happy syncretism, scholars of a more orthodox or less catholic temperament make a choice among the conflicting views; they deny, expressly or tacitly, the authenticity or the authority of the texts which support the view they have rejected.[72]

It is with this idea of Buddhist thought in his mind that La Vallée Poussin suggests that one may discount the importance of nirvāṇa per se for the Buddhist. What he initially calls the *raison d'être* of Buddhism is seen at a critical turn to be of secondary importance for the Buddhist.

> Buddhism ends in an act of faith. Sakyamuni will lead us to salvation provided we close our eyes and follow blindly his ordinances. The important thing in Buddhism is not dogma, but practice, not the goal, the mysterious and unascertainable Nirvāṇa, but the Path, Sanctity.[73]

Despite some terminological inconsistencies, La Vallée Poussin might well have been satisfied with those analytical discussions, remembering Aristotle's comment: "Our discussion will be adequate if it has as much clearness as the subject-matter admits of, for precision is not to be sought for alike in all discussions. . . ." [74] Yet, having attempted to show that the Buddhist nirvāṇa is an absolute of an indescribable, eschatological order—as distinguished from the ontological and cosmological absolute of the Brāhmaṇas—he was unhappy.

[72] *Ibid.*, pp. 134–35.
[73] *Ibid.*, p. 138.
[74] Aristotle, *The Nicomachean Ethics*, trans. W. D. Ross, *The Basic Works of Aristotle*, ed. Richard McKeon (New York: Random House, 1941), p. 936, lines 12–14.

Neither was my conviction resolute nor my ideas precise. I should certainly be afraid to reread the pretentious statements that I have dedicated to nirvāṇa in many articles. And the more recent among them are not less bad.[75]

That declaration appears in the Foreword to his *Nirvāṇa* (1925), his classic effort to solve the nirvāṇa problem.

La Vallée Poussin is still convinced, in 1925, that "To look at things from a certain point of view—and in theory at least—two Buddhisms can be distinguished: a popular, devotional form, and a clerical, mystical form." [76] But, he goes on,

When one studies monastic Buddhism as a theologian, one can construct the pure theorem and exclude from it all devotional considerations as also any active morality. But history faces other exigencies: *it prohibits the separation of that which is strictly connected*—Buddhism the religion and Buddhism the discipline of nirvāṇa.[77] (My italics.)

From an analytical inquiry he shifts to a more specifically historical inquiry, trying to clarify the meaning of nirvāṇa in part by means of the perspective afforded by "historical probabilities." He explains the change of focus:

I have applied myself to composing a nirvāṇa with complicated blending procedures: a bit of nihilism, a bit of optimism, a bit of agnosticism, and a great deal of mystery. But the historian will be lead to believe that the old community—and Buddhism altogether—has had a clear belief concerning the final end and, if not a system, at least a doctrine, a dogma, a faith. The goal of the present memoir is to ascertain if such a doctrine did actually exist and, if it did, what it was.[78]

In the main, La Vallée Poussin still adheres to that view of the Pali Canon which he enunciated in *Etudes* (1898). That is, these texts present a system (or set of not always harmonious systems) which is at the same time sophisticated, obscure, contradictory, and—above all—recent. How is the puzzle of the canon to be solved? Fortunately,

[75] La Vallée Poussin, *Nirvāṇa*, p. xvii.
[76] *Ibid.*, p. 1.
[77] *Ibid.*, p. 8.
[78] *Ibid.*, p. 9.

The study of nirvāṇa does not depend on its solution. Without taking part in the controversy which this problem raises, we can easily construct a reasonable idea of the probable history of nirvāṇa. One cannot see that the canonical texts should be susceptible to two interpretations by those who are well read. And one can see quite clearly why they have been interpreted in an arbitrary manner as much by certain Buddhists as by the Indianists. In addition, we have some illumination—almost enough to try to assign a place for these texts in the religious literature and the mystical doctrines of India.[79]

Stressing the importance of Buddhism's Indian backgrounds, La Vallée Poussin suggests that the meaning of nirvāṇa must be sought within a history, not of Buddhist thought alone, but of Indian thought. Attention is directed to what nirvāṇa originally meant. Has La Vallée Poussin taken up again that nineteenth-century quest for the Samarkand called "origins" which he dismissed earlier? Not exactly. But

As for the origins, the idea we have of them depends on the conception we have of the history of ancient India. That is to say that if we try to describe the origins, it is especially because many questions of detail that we believe to be resolved remain too obscure if they are not disposed of in an integrated scheme.[80]

The point of departure for La Vallée Poussin's attempt to show the history of Buddhism and the meaning of nirvāṇa in an integrated "schéma d'ensemble" is the assertion: "Buddhism is a branch of yoga or 'asceticism.' "[81] Essentially—and La Vallée Poussin uses the word advisedly—yoga has at all times been the same:

An ensemble of practices held in esteem since the most ancient times of Aryan or autochthonous India; practices of sorcerers and thaumaturges of which the dominant motif appears to be an inquiry into hypnotic states. . . . In itself it is a technique foreign to all morality as to any religious or philosophical view. But . . .

[79] *Ibid.*, p. 10.

[80] *Ibid.*, p. xx. And it should not be forgotten that *Nirvāṇa* was composed during a period of intensive research and writing on Indian history.

[81] *Ibid.*, p. 11.

to this technique morality, theology, devotion, and—as is said—theosophy could be added.[82]

The specifically Buddhist character of this branch of yoga comes, he says, from the person, legend, and cult of the founder. One thing is certain above all.

Earliest Buddhism was eminently plastic, an image of contemporary India. This was not an era of doctrinal orthodoxies or even of disciplinary orthodoxies. All Yogins pursued the same goal by parallel roads. But they willingly changed sect and master.[83]

Although philosophical problems were posed, only quasi- (or, as La Vallée Poussin himself would have said, *pseudo-*) philosophical answers were forthcoming. Ecstasy and its accompanying intuitions were considered the highest—the only true—knowledge. The Vinaya (disciplinary text) parts of the Pali Canon are obviously the earliest in his estimation. Accordingly, they witness the truth of the assertion that Buddhism did not begin as a closely reasoned philosophical movement but rather as a way of life. "From an incoherent jumble of practices collected all together in the tradition of the yoga have emerged the Vinayas and the customs of the different schools." [84]

Finally, from yoga, according to La Vallée Poussin, came four basic ideas: *saṃsāra* (transmigration, wandering, the cycle of existences, birth and rebirth), *karmaphalam* (retribution, the realization of the consequences of all actions), *mokṣa* (deliverance from *karmaphalam* and *saṃsāra*, release, nirvāṇa), and *yāna* (vehicle, method, specifically a method for realizing deliverance).

Simple and solid, these ideas were nonetheless still fluid and supple, liable to many modifications and accommodations. Buddhism—along with all the congregations and schools—inherited these ideas. It has given them a Buddhist turn without altering their first signification.[85]

[82] *Ibid.*, p. 12.
[83] *Ibid.*, p. 14.
[84] *Ibid.*, p. 19.
[85] *Ibid.*, p. 26.

Happily, La Vallée Poussin presents the essence of his view of the probable origins of Buddhism in a single paragraph. From it, the reader—having come thus far in the preceding sketch—may easily predict his conclusions with regard to the Buddhist conception of nirvāṇa. Correctly seen, La Vallée Poussin declares,

> The earliest Buddhism had no metaphysics at all, no learned or strictly reasoned theory concerning the totality and nature of things. Relying on the word of the Buddha, it believed that man consumes the fruit of his acts from existence to existence until the day when, delivered through illumination, he obtains supreme happiness in nirvāṇa. To this faith will be added—later or perhaps immediately; perhaps successively, perhaps simultaneously—certain conceptions which are properly speaking philosophical. Some of them—for example, the negation of the free soul, which negation is a contradiction in terms in the belief in responsibility for and the remuneration of actions—are destructive of the faith. But with a few exceptions that faith remains immutable, the systems in some way being external to it.[86]

As for the historical development of the idea of nirvāṇa in Buddhism, La Vallée Poussin is convinced that the earliest Buddhist statements about it come from the period following the Brāhmaṇas and preceding the impact of Upaniṣadic thought.

> Considering the progress of ideas (and of course all chronology, properly speaking, escapes us), the origins of Buddhism seem to take place at that period when the problem of immortality was posed, at a moment or in a milieu in which that problem had not received a metaphysical solution.[87]

And a few sentences later, he announces a definite statement of nirvāṇa's meaning—a restatement in historical perspective.

> The yoga from which Buddhism arose was then, we believe, without definite speculative tendencies and without exclusive or particular devotional practices.
>
> In short, that is what Buddhism of the Lesser Vehicle—from the Mahavagga to Buddhaghosa—continues to be: namely, yoga

[86] *Ibid.*, pp. 26–27.
[87] *Ibid.*, p. 52.

almost unalloyed. The immortal—declared to be ineffable—is the goal of the saint because it is deliverance from birth and death. No philosophical or ontological relation can be established between that immortal and the world of transmigrating beings. The immortal is called "nirvāṇa." . . .[88]

And, finally, he smashes forever the Buddhism:Brahmanism::Protestantism:Roman Catholicism analogy, particularly in regard to the nirvāṇa theory. It would be impossible, he writes, to imagine that the Buddhist nirvāṇa is a protestant conception somehow thrust in the face of Brahmanic and Upaniṣadic eternalism.

Above all, nothing will permit the declaration that the Buddhist nirvāṇa was conceived in opposition to any Brahmanic theory. Nirvāṇa—the immortal or deliverance—seems to us to be a basic given, free from all metaphysical speculation (involved rather in myth than in metaphysics). Nirvāṇa is an invisible abode into which the saint—often amid flames and in a sort of apotheosis—disappears.[89]

La Vallée Poussin freely admitted that he would be considered heterodox for those opinions; but it is doubtful that he was prepared for the vigorous criticism which they were to receive immediately following publication. In fact, five years later he observed with restrained bitterness: "My *Nirvāṇa* . . . has been judged very harshly [sans grand besoin ou extreme bienveillance] by Th. Stcherbatsky . . . and by DasGupta. . . ."[90] Surendranath Dasgupta's judgment seems to be based exclusively on Stcherbatsky's review, strongly suggesting that the great Indian scholar had not even skimmed La Vallée Poussin's book.[91] Small wonder that the Belgian was distressed by the criticism that his *Nirvāṇa* received.

[88] *Ibid.*, p. 53.
[89] *Ibid.*, p. 57.
[90] La Vallée Poussin, *Le dogme et la philosophie du bouddhisme*, p. 180.
[91] Surendranath Dasgupta, "Some Aspects of Buddhist Philosophy," *The Modern Review: A Monthly Review and Miscellany*, Vol. XLIV, No. 1, pp. 62–71.

Th. Stcherbatsky—Was the Buddha a Philosopher or an Ecstatic?

Stcherbatsky, one of the only Buddhist scholars whose reputation matches that of La Vallée Poussin, could not be accused of having dismissed *Nirvāṇa* casually. His criticisms are to be found both in a BSOS review and his study *The Conception of Buddhist Nirvāṇa*. The conflicting evaluations of Buddhist and Indian thought which had divided Europe into two opinions from the first are epitomized in modern attire in the controversy between La Vallée Poussin and Stcherbatsky. I shall try to review the major points at issue between the two.

Since Stcherbatsky's name is not as familiar to Western European audiences as are many of the figures thus far discussed, a few biographical details will not be out of place. Stcherbatsky [Fedor Ippolitovich Ścherbatskoi], born September 19, 1866, in Keltse, Poland, was the son of a government administrator and grew up in comfortable surroundings on an agricultural estate near St. Petersburg. From the gymnasium of Tsars Koye Selo, Stcherbatsky entered St. Petersburg University in 1884. Studying Indo-European linguistics there, he read on various Indian subjects under Professors Minayeff and S. Oldenberg. In 1888, he moved on to Vienna, where he studied Sanskrit poetics with Bühler.

The years from 1893 to 1900 were spent on the family estate, but Stcherbatsky's attention to Sanskrit and Indian thought did not diminish. In 1899, he attended the International Congress of Orientalists in Rome. Shortly after the conference, Stcherbatsky went to Bonn for extensive study of Indian philosophy with Jacobi. It was while doing field work in Mongolia that he conceived the idea that the Buddhist philosopher Dharmakīrti was the Indian Kant. From that idea and his further researches came Stcherbatsky's first important volume: *Theory of Knowledge and Logic in the Doctrine of the Later Buddhism* (1903, in Russian).[92] Eventually translated into German and French,[93] this work became the basis for Stcherbatsky's magnum opus: the two-volume *Buddhist Logic*.[94] His death was announced in 1942.[95]

Stcherbatsky has been described as a good-natured giant. Well over six feet tall, he was by all standards a physical giant. And his mental capacities seem to have been proportional. Master of half a dozen European languages—to the point that he wrote and conversed in each with complete ease—he attained such fluency in Sanskrit that he earned the highest praise and honors from European scholars and traditional Indian paṇḍitas alike. And, too, he was probably as competent a Tibetanist as Europe has produced. But the mighty impression which Stcherbatsky has made on Buddhist studies stems from his abilities in logic and philosophy as much as from his language skills. It is this combination of talents which helps to explain his singular achievements in the elucidation of the most abstruse Buddhist texts.

As for Stcherbatsky's good humor, that is perhaps more difficult to see in his writings than is his giant intellect. Shortly after the publication of La Vallée Poussin's *Nirvāṇa* (presumably still in 1925), Denison Ross, director of the London School of Oriental Studies, invited Stcherbatsky to submit a review of the work to the school's *Bulletin*. The latter took up the assignment with a vengeance, producing both a critical

[92] Th. Stcherbatsky, *Teorija poznija i logika po uceniju posdnejsich buddhistov* (St. Petersburg, 1903–9).

[93] Th. Stcherbatsky, *Erkenntnistheorie und Logik, nach der Lehre der späteren Buddhisten*, übers. Otto Straus (München, 1924); and *La théorie de la connaissance et la logique chez les bouddhistes tardifs*, trad. Mme. I. de Manziarly et Paul Masson-Oursel (Paris: Librairie Orientaliste Paul Geuthner, 1926).

[94] See above, "Introduction," p. 10, note 14.

[95] D. Hosie, "Obituary: Th. Stcherbatsky," *JRAS*, 1943, pp. 118–19.

review [96] and *The Conception of Buddhist Nirvāṇa*,[97] neither of which betrays the least trace of good humor. La Vallée Poussin's book has put Stcherbatsky in a very dark humor, in fact, and he quickly indicates his irritation. Stcherbatsky begins his review:

In his newest contribution M. de la Vallée Poussin makes an attempt to prove that *nirvāṇa* is not Nirvāṇa. Since the term has passed into almost all our modern languages with the definite meaning of an annihilation comparable to the extinction of fire when the fuel is exhausted, we shall all have to drop the habit of this expression if the author is right, i.e., if nirvāṇa really means supreme bliss without any afterthought of annihilation. The Oxford English Dictionary, which contains what, in my opinion, is the exact truth, will be obliged to drop the word or change its explanation.[98]

(In point of fact, the OED refers to nirvāṇa as a Buddhist doctrine meaning extinction *and* absorption into the supreme —which is hardly what Stcherbatsky had in mind. Moreover, what the term has come to mean in English—its history in an alien language—is irrelevant to the discussion at hand.)

Stcherbatsky accuses La Vallée Poussin of transforming the Buddha into a mere magician and nirvāṇa into a simple, gross faith object signifying the soul's immortal bliss in paradise. Further, he insists that the Belgian scholar has equated a thousand years of Hīnayāna Buddhism with "a literature of spiritual exercises in hypnotism." In short, Stcherbatsky declares that La Vallée Poussin's *Nirvāṇa*, punctuated with contradictions, is the product of an "original blunder,"

an attempt to dethrone Nirvāṇa from the place it occupies in full right on the basis of the works of our best scholars who were unanimous in assigning to this term of Buddhist philosophy the meaning of life's annihilation.[99]

[96] Th. Stcherbatsky, Review of *Nirvāṇa* by Louis de La Vallée Poussin, *Bulletin of the School of Oriental Studies*, IV (1926–28), 357–60.

[97] See above, note 54. Written later, this work appeared before the critical review, and the revised review refers to it.

[98] Stcherbatsky, Review of *Nirvāṇa*, p. 357.

[99] *Ibid.*

La Vallée Poussin was the first important scholar to question intensively the rather complacent assumption fostered by the late nineteenth-century Pali scholars—notably Rhys Davids and Childers—that original, genuine Buddhism is found only in the Pali texts. For some time, La Vallée Poussin had been content to explicate as much of the Buddhist materials as possible, eschewing any attempt to discover the pristine state of Buddhism. It was not, according to him, that other scholars were obsessed with valid historical questions as that, in their search for origins and reasonable assertions about the Buddhist doctrines, they displayed poor historical sense. Complaining of the inadequacy of various interpretations given nirvāṇa and other Buddhist doctrines by his contemporaries and precursors, La Vallée Poussin remarks:

> These estimates, which are understandably disconcerting, are explained by the state of our philology in which such structuring factors as chronology are lacking and by the intellectual predispositions of the investigators, who are too often linguists lacking historical training. The interpretations have their beginning in an initial error. Buddhism is an ascetic, religious, Hindu institution. Indianists in general consider it a system of pure ideas, a scientific theory. In coordinating and elucidating it, they transpose a part of the pratityasamutpada formula into such European terms as "production on account of causation"—they rationalize and abbreviate the entire tradition—and they order us to see in this occidental redaction of the mutilated scholastic the very image of Buddhism.[100]

Stcherbatsky, in his turn witnessing the efforts of La Vallée Poussin (and the derivative excursuses of Arthur Berriedale Keith and Mrs. Rhys Davids), is dismayed about the ramifications of the "new historical quest."

> As for the genuine Buddhism of the Buddha himself, there seems to be a strong tendency to surmise that it must have been something utterly different from what is recorded in the Pali Canon, our best source. Some scholars pick up out of the whole canon, the Canon containing a wealth of Scholasticism, the single utterance from the Mahavagga (vi. 31), "Make good actions,

[100] La Vallée Poussin, *Nirvāṇa*, pp. xii–xiii.

do not make bad actions," and contend that this alone is the genuine Buddhism of the Buddha himself. All the remainder is "church-made." Others, like Professor B. Keith, think that Buddha was nothing of a philosopher, since we cannot possibly admit "reason to prevail in a barbarous age," but he "believed" in nothing less than "the non-existence of a substantial soul." At last M. de la V. P. comes with the assertion that Buddha, although resorting to magic and thaumaturgy, had just the contrary belief, he believed in an existing soul. Is it not clear from the comparison of these opinions that the results represent much more what their authors desire Buddhism to be than what it really was? [101]

Stcherbatsky's own idea of the history of Buddhism derives from the Tibetan Buddhist historian Buston. "The history of Buddhism in India may be divided, and is divided by the Buddhists themselves, into three periods which they call the three 'Swingings of the Wheel of the Law.' " [102]

Each of them has its central conception; they are respectively Pluralism, Monism, and Idealism. The Sanskrit terms designating them are *pudgala-śūnyatā*, *sarva-dharma-śūnyatā*, and *bāhya-artha-śūnyatā*. These are negative definitions meaning: (1) Unreality of the Ego, (2) Unreality of all Elements of Existence, (3) Unreality of the External World. Their implied positive meaning is respectively, (1) Plurality of interrelated and ultimate Elements of the Personality, (2) Relativity and consequent Unreality of all these Elements, and the unique Reality of the Immutable Whole, (3) Ideality of these Elements and of all cognizable things.[103]

The common feature of these three Buddhisms is contained in the original theme of "elementariness":

Disregarding the pluralism, relativity, and ideality of the elements of existence, there are these elements themselves, the "elementariness" of Existence, the denial of a permanent substantial Ego, and the splitting of it into separate elements—that is the central conception out of which all the subsequent diversity of doctrine developed.[104]

[101] Stcherbatsky, Review of *Nirvāṇa*, pp. 359–60.

[102] Stcherbatsky, *Buddhist Logic*, I, 3. Cf. *La théorie de la connaissance*, p. vii: "The history of Buddhism, like that of its philosophy, is divided into two quite distinct parts."

[103] Stcherbatsky, "The Doctrine of the Buddha," p. 871.

[104] *Ibid.*

Stcherbatsky lists ten features common to all three aspects of Buddhism—features which include: the denial of an abiding soul or self-principle; the analysis of existence into discrete, evanescent elements or energy moments; salvation conceived as quiescence of the functionally interdependent elements, the attainment of nirvāṇa, the annihilation of existence totally.

> Is there any other, fourth, kind of Buddhism? Is there any simple Buddhism without this complication of soul-denial and without a system of energies, scientifically constructed, interrelated and steering towards final quiescence? No, there is no such form!—except in the imagination of some European scholars.[105]

It seems likely that Stcherbatsky believed that La Vallée Poussin's *Nirvāṇa* was an attack on his 1923 monograph *The Central Conception of Buddhism and the Meaning of the Word "Dharma,"* [106] in which the Russian scholar had discussed what he considered the central idea of the first phase of Buddhism—and of all three Buddhisms in turn. He insists there:

> The conception of a *dharma* is the central point of the Buddhist doctrine. In the light of this conception Buddhism discloses itself as a metaphysical theory developed out of one fundamental principle, viz. the idea that existence is an interplay of a plurality of subtle, ultimate, not further analysable elements of Matter, Mind, and Forces. These elements are technically called *dharmas*, a meaning which this word has in this system alone. Buddhism, accordingly, can be characterized as a system of Radical Pluralism (*saṅghata-vāda*): the elements alone are realities, every combination of them is a mere name covering a plurality of separate elements. The moral teaching of a path towards Final Deliverance is not something extraneous to this ontological doctrine, it is most intimately connected with it and, in fact, identical with it.[107]

In Stcherbatsky's view, it seems to me, the moral teachings in Buddhism are hardly worthy of the name. The aim of Buddhism as a method of salvation is conceived to be the sup-

[105] *Ibid.*, p. 872.
[106] Th. Stcherbatsky, *The Central Conception of Buddhism and the Meaning of the Word "Dharma."* Cited hereafter as *CCB*.
[107] *Ibid.*, p. 62.

pression of the world process, a process of successive *dharma* moments. The famous Buddhist equation, existence equals sorrow (*duḥkha*), which had seemed dubiously synthetic to most Western interpreters, becomes at best a tautology in Stcherbatsky's treatment, since he translates *duḥkha* not as "sorrow" but as "unrest."

The Buddhist conception of *dharma* (or *dharmas*) is then, according to Stcherbatsky, the fundamental conception or principle out of which the particular doctrines are logically developed. In Hīnayāna Buddhism—Stcherbatsky's phase one —the *dharmas* are ultimates.

> Although the conception of an element of existence has given rise to an imposing superstructure in the shape of a consistent system of philosophy, its inmost nature remains a riddle. What is *dharma?* It is inconceivable! It is subtle! No one will ever be able to tell what its real nature (*dharmasvabhāva*) is! It is transcendental! [108]

In the second period of Buddhism—that period in which the Mādhyamaka sage Nāgārjuna is chief spokesman—the *dharmas* are stripped of their ultimacy, seen to be relative, and void of reality in themselves. This is the theory of *śūnyatā*, according to Stcherbatsky, and it is as uncompromisingly monistic a vision as the Hīnayāna was pluralistic.[109]

From the time of Burnouf through the most famous writings of Louis de La Vallée Poussin, Europeans had been generally agreed that, whatever nirvāṇa might signify, there could be no doubt that the *śūnyatā* (so-called voidness) theory of the Mādhyamika stamped that school as completely nihilistic. Stcherbatsky was almost alone in insisting that the Mādhyamika's denial of the reality of the *dharma* moments was not nihilism. *Śūnyatā* meant "relativity," he declared, the voidness of the interdependent moments in themselves. This essential voidness is certainly a tenet of the Mādhyamika, but it does not mean that they do not recognize an absolute. Rather, *śūnyatā* designates the reality of the one and of the many

108 *Ibid.*, p. 63.

109 Stcherbatsky, *Buddhist Logic*, I, 7–11. And see *CBN*, pp. 40–43.

sub specie aeternis. And this, after all, said Stcherbatsky in *CBN* and *Buddhist Logic*, allows for the reality of the eternal, cosmic Buddha in the Mādhyamika scheme.[110]

La Vallée Poussin, as has been shown, believed that the seeds of doctrinal nihilism and the Mādhyamika doctrines were apparent in some of the earliest strata of Buddhist writings. In the 1930's, however, after further study and under the impact of Stcherbatsky's arguments, he was less inclined to believe that the Madhyamakas were nihilists. Stcherbatsky, meanwhile, influenced in his turn by La Vallée Poussin's discussions, withdrew from his earlier view, saying that while the Mādhyamika school was not true nihilism it evidently affirmed no reality other than the statement of universal relativity—the *śūnyatā* theory itself.[111]

To return to Stcherbatsky on nirvāṇa—the question of the sources which he used for his information about early Buddhism must be faced. A. Berriedale Keith insists in his article "The Doctrine of the Buddha" that, considering the "extraordinary diversity of doctrine which has developed from the teaching in the sixth century B.C. of the Buddha, it is perhaps the most natural conclusion that it is really impracticable to discover with any precision the doctrine which in fact he expounded."[112] There are two problems, Keith continues:

> What assurance have we that the Pali Canon, on which Professor Stcherbatsky relies for his conception of the views of the Buddha, really presents these views with any approach at accuracy? . . . In the second place, even when we accept the Pali Canon as authoritative, it is not only possible, but probable, that it suggests a very different doctrine of the evolution of the Buddhist doctrine,

[110] *Ibid.*, pp. 44–48.

[111] See, for example, Stcherbatsky (ed. and trans.), *Madhyāntavibhaṅga: Discourse on Discrimination between Middle and Extremes ascribed to Maitreya and commented by Vasubandhu and Sthiramati*, Vol. XXX: *Bibliotheca Buddhica* (Moscow-Leningrad: 1936), p. vii: "True [it] is however that the Mādhyamikas have a *paramārtha-satya* ['Supreme' or 'Absolute *Truth*'], and that this *paramārtha-satya* consists in the negation of every *paramārtha-sat* ['Absolute' or 'Absolutely existing *Thing*']."

[112] Keith, "The Doctrine of the Buddha," p. 393.

and justifies us in ascribing to the Buddha views more simple, more in accord with the trend of opinion in his day, and more calculated to secure the adherence of a large circle of followers.[113]

"But," Stcherbatsky argues in return, "nevertheless, the Pali Canon remains our main source for establishing the early form of Buddhism." [114] Has he himself used the Pali Canon as the primary source for his writings? Stcherbatsky must answer no. His excuse:

Accuracy, indeed, is not to be found at all in the Pali Canon. Accuracy is not its aim. It is misleading to seek accuracy there. Accuracy is found in later works, in works belonging to the *śāstra* class. All Buddhist literature is divided into a *sūtra* class and a *śāstra* class. The first is popular, the second is scientific. The first is propaganda, the second is precision.[115]

A śāstric source, according to Stcherbatsky, is a systematic, laconic, comprehensive treatment of a sūtra source. And the Russian scholar cheerfully admits that he relies upon the *śāstra*-s, not the *sūtra*-s. In *CCB* he writes:

Our chief source will be, not the Pali Canon, but a later work, the *Abhidharmakośa* of Vasubandhu. Although late, it is professedly only a systematized exposition of a much earlier work—the *Abhidharma-vibhāṣa-śāstra*, which, in its turn, is but a commentary on the abhidharma of the Sarvastivadin school. This school is one of the earliest, if not the earliest, of Buddhist sects. . . . It must be left to later investigation to determine the points where Vasubandhu's exposition may be at variance with the primitive doctrine; but, generally speaking, he seems to have rendered the original doctrine very faithfully. Since his age is about the same as that of the Pali commentaries, the difference between him and the Pali sources is not so much one of time as of school.[116]

The final point is crucial: Vasubandhu is a "scholastic." Stcherbatsky cannot avoid that, and of scholasticism he has commented: "It is either (1) philosophy in the service of

[113] *Ibid.*, pp. 394–95.
[114] Stcherbatsky, "The Doctrine of the Buddha," p. 868.
[115] *Ibid.*
[116] *CCB*, pp. 1–2.

religion or (2) excessive subtlety and artificiality in philosophical constructions."[117]

Mrs. Rhys Davids, in her review of *CCB*, declares that Stcherbatsky ought to have kept his original title for the work: *Vasubandhu on the Fundamental Principles of the Sarvastivada School of Buddhism and the Meaning of the Word Dharma.*[118] He has pretended to illumine a basic Buddhist doctrine solely by means of the work of a fifth-century A.D. Sanskrit Buddhist schoolman. As expected, such an undertaking is a red flag to Mrs. Rhys Davids.

> Dharma may well have come to be all, for his early medieval school, that Vasubandhu said it was. But for anyone, who has spent much time groping after *the true historical perspective* [my italics] in the teaching of the Pali Pitakas, to see in dhammā, as "metaphysically conceived elements" a "central conception" is impossible.[119]

Stcherbatsky himself maintains that the Pali Canon is our best source, and then turns round to say that it is an inaccurate *sūtra* which can only be understood through a school *śāstra*. Mrs. Rhys Davids, more in accord with La Vallée Poussin and by all odds more direct than either he or Stcherbatsky, insists that the Pali Canon is a monk-oriented compilation and "one of the greatest pieces of literary botchwork in the world."[120]

"The true historical perspective"—that is certainly the only vantage point from which to evaluate the meaning of Buddhism and its nirvāṇa. Without attaining it or, at the least, struggling after it, Buddhist thought is little more than a saffron-robed mirror of our prejudices, presuppositions, and scholarly inadequacies. On the one hand, Stcherbatsky postpones critical historical investigation and argues that the origin of Buddhism is to be found in a philosophical vision.

[117] *CBN*, pp. 2–3.

[118] C. A. F. Rhys Davids, Review of *CCB*, *Bulletin of the School of Oriental Studies*, III (1923–25), 346.

[119] *Ibid.*

[120] *Ibid.*, p. 350.

> Between the Materialists who denied retribution and the Eternalists who imagined a return to a pure spiritual condition, Buddha took a middle course. . . . It seems that he was deeply impressed by the contradiction of assuming an eternal, pure, spiritual principle which, for incomprehensible reasons, must have been polluted by all the filth of mundane existence. . . . He was thus led to a denial of every permanent principle. Matter and Mind appeared to him as split in an infinite process of evanescent elements (dharmas), the only ultimate realities, beside Space and Annihilation. . . . He established a system of the most radical pluralism. That the essence and the starting point of Buddhism were speculative appears very early.[121]

Mrs. Rhys Davids, on the other hand, cannot find her Buddha there.

> He was a gentleman admittedly of no philosophical education, very earnest to help his fellow-men by substituting, as the best way to heal sorrow, the good life, the being one's "best" (*sammā*) for decadent, moribund cults, cults so moribund that in his addresses they are a negligible quantity, and not they, but the carnal life and the ascetic life are the only alternatives to the good life of the middle way he takes into account. But his church became overwhelmingly monkish, developing the ascetic outlook and spiration. . . .[122]

La Vallée Poussin, historian, analyzes the records of Indian history, and he follows neither of the above alternatives in his mature evaluation of Buddhism and nirvāṇa. According to his interpretation, his careful consideration of the "vraisemblances historiques," Buddhism has emerged from a non-upaniṣadic, yogic milieu. His estimate of the original meaning of nirvāṇa in Buddhism derives from this understanding of its non-nihilistic, non-philosophical matrices.[123] He has consulted a wide range of Buddhist materials and finds an equally wide range of doctrines deployed through the turnings of the wheel of the law.

[121] *CBN*, pp. 2–3.
[122] C. A. F. Rhys Davids, Review of *CCB*, p. 346.
[123] See Louis de La Vallée Poussin, *La Morale bouddhique*, pp. 17–21.

What to conclude? What the philosophers say is not very important. What they want to say is the important thing, and what they want to say is that which all the ascetics have always thought: Deliverance from desire is impossible as long as one treasures the idea of an "I." The conquest of nirvāṇa is impossible as long as one sees in it some form of existence; for one ought to desire nirvāṇa in order to obtain it and all desire for existence imprisons the covetous in the circle of transmigrations. The way to nirvāṇa is meditation without content.

Buddhism, then, after so many centuries of speculation, . . . appears to us as yoga—the old discipline of ascetics plunged in unconscious meditations. Yoga involved itself in philosophy, because India, land of ascetics and thaumaturges, Sakyamuni and Maudgalyayana, is also a country of dialecticians. . . . It is also a country of ritual and disciplinary traditions: Upāli, legendary and sagacious compiler of the monastic rules which have been the strength and endurance of Buddhism, is, after Sakyamuni, the founder of this great institution.[124]

[124] La Vallée Poussin, *Le dogme*, pp. 209–10. In his foreword to Nalinaksha Dutt, *Aspects of Mahāyāna Buddhism and its Relation to Hīnayāna*, pp. v–viii, reaffirms that nirvāṇa "is a problem full of difficulties because it is not easy for unmystical minds to understand a thing which can only be 'realized' in trance. . . . For early Buddhists, the Nirvāṇa was, of course, an immortal state beyond existence and non-existence. The thirst for non-existence is very bad, the aspiration to Nirvāṇa is the very root of salvation and happiness." (P. viii.)

Dutt's own examination of the nirvāṇa question is thorough and dispassionate; see *Aspects*, pp. 129–204. He strongly opposes Stcherbatsky's "negative" interpretation (pp. 154–57). His sympathy with Arthur Berriedale Keith's estimate (pp. 157–58) seems well-founded; and this suggests in turn that the summary dismissal of Keith's scholarship by several eminent Indianists and Buddhologists—as being, for example, merely "supercilious" (Conze) or "mundane" (Robinson)—ought to be reviewed. For more on Keith's interpretation of nirvāṇa, see his *Buddhist Philosophy in India and Ceylon*, especially pp. 61–68.

Mircea Eliade's classic *Yoga: Immortality and Freedom* (Bollingen Series, LVI; New York: Pantheon Books, 1958), contributes significantly to the literature on nirvāṇa. Especially in its consideration of the Yoga-Buddhism relationship and the mystic, ecstatic nature of nirvāṇa for early Buddhists, it witnesses the strong influence of La Vallée Poussin, pp. 162–99, 395–96.

Conclusion

We cannot speak adequately of the "object of religion" without simultaneously removing its character as an object. That which is ultimate gives itself only to the attitude of ultimate concern. It is the correlate of an unconditional concern but not a "highest thing" called "the absolute" or "the unconditioned." . . .[1]

Conclusions to studies such as this are commonly expected to consist of a summary plus the advancement of the author's own personal view. These final pages may be something of a

[1] Paul Tillich, *Systematic Theology*, Vol. I (Chicago: University of Chicago Press, 1951), p. 12. Robert H. Lawson Slater, from whose *Paradox and Nirvana* I have profited greatly, comments: "Nibbāna is the religious ultimate of Buddhism, and, just as men have failed to express all that God IS, so they have failed to express all that Nibbāna is. Like all such terms which reflect, however dimly, the 'reality of realities' it eludes philosophy while it inspires life." (P. 68.)

It should be observed that there is perhaps a bit more "theological coloration" in Slater's otherwise valuable study than is desirable.

disappointment in that case, for, though I shall commit myself concerning the "meaning" of the Buddhist nirvāṇa, I shall not offer a brief or convenient gloss. By now it should be obvious that to essay the latter would be to say a great deal more about oneself than about the Buddhists' ultimate concern.

Reviewing the many estimates discussed in the preceding chapters should serve to underscore one significant point: none of those interpretations is to be rejected categorically. Granted that many are more impressionistic than scholarly. And most are based on an imperfect acquaintance with primary source materials. ("The study of Buddhism has always suffered from the fact that its most characteristic technical terms were discussed before the texts were known. . . ." [2]) Still, many of the insights are valuable to the present-day student.

The legacy is impressive, and the implicit warning is no less so. It is the exclusivity and shortsightedness of many of the interpretations and the tendentious presentation of most that are to be cautioned against. No longer studying nirvāṇa through the prism of any one of the particular *Weltanschauungen* displayed on the foregoing pages, we may be prejudiced as fatefully by our own *Zeitgeist.*

"We wish experience to make us, not shrewder (for next time), but wiser (forever)," said Jacob Burckhardt.[3] Before us is a very small but representative sample of our experience with an alien concept. Perhaps this experience can be organized to make us wiser. In its turn, that knowledge may even make us methodologically shrewder. In any event, we may be made more humble through knowledge. And, after all, humility is a quality worth cultivating in the face of that which the Buddhists declare to be their ultimate concern: nirvāṇa.

[2] E. J. Thomas, "Nirvāṇa and Parinirvāṇa," p. 294.

[3] Jacob Burckhardt, *Force and Freedom*, ed. James Hastings Nichols (New York: Meridian Books, 1955), p. 294.

Evam mayā śrutam ekasmin samaye

Even in such texts as the *Nikāya*-s the Buddhist nirvāṇa appears as a complex term, itself part of a still more involved complex of expressions concerning a religious ultimate. There is no way to isolate a simple, primordial meaning of nirvāṇa in the Buddhist usage. Clearly, no claim that nirvāṇa ever signified merely annihilation or bliss—in our tradition's acceptance of such terms—could be substantiated. I incline to the view of Louis de La Vallée Poussin (and further reinforced by Mircea Eliade) that, in earliest Buddhism, nirvāṇa—if the term was used at all (and, of course, it is most unlikely that a Sanskrit rather than a Prakrit form would have been employed)—probably signified "un séjour inébranlable." [4]

Conze repeatedly reminds us that "the custom of trying to ascertain the meaning of Nirvāṇa by collecting and examining many disconnected quotations cannot yield good results." [5] To a degree, the warning is pertinent, for, as Nalinaksha Dutt among others has emphasized, even the *Nikāya*-s do not represent a coherent system or even a consistent "school attitude." [6] And the texts have a way of being *kāmadhenu*-s or *kṛtakalpataru*-s, yielding the fruits we desire and withholding those which do not suit us. But we should not despair of using the texts.

The Buddha was not a philosopher. Still, this should dismay the student no more than the patent truth that Plato was not an Aristotelian. Obviously, the Buddha was a genius as a soteriological tactician. Depending on the context and in par-

[4] Etienne Lamotte, *L'Histoire du Bouddhisme indien des origines à l'ère Śaka*, p. 676. And see above, Chapter VIII.

[5] Edward Conze, *Buddhist Thought in India*, p. 77. Cf. Conze, "Buddhist Philosophy and Its European Parallels," p. 12.

[6] Nalinaksha Dutt, *Aspects of Mahāyāna Buddhism*, pp. 145–47.

ticular the needs of the individual(s) to whom he spoke, his emphasis varied. To those full of self, his message was expressed negatively. To those full of fear, the message expressed confidence. To those full of suffering, the message expressed hope.

The "critique of authenticity" has been of lively concern to Buddhists from the beginning. *Evam mayā śrutam ekasmin samaye* ("so have I heard on one occasion") is one formulaic device used to introduce "authentic" statements of the Buddha.[7] We must not be put off by the "context sensitivity" of the Buddha's statements about nirvāṇa any more than the Buddhists themselves are. His grand strategy, we may assume, will be visible through his tactical encounters. Hermeneutics is charged with the task of discovering that intentional infrastructure.

To impose our own categories on the data provided by the Buddhist source materials is to run the risk of violating their intentionality and, consequently, to vitiate the entire interpretive enterprise. The problem is not lost on many contemporary scholars, and Richard H. Robinson's comments are representative.

> Earlier European comparative studies began with a meta-system set up to handle European philosophy, religion, language, etc. and nothing else. Not realizing how parochial it was, they applied their particular meta-system naively and often unconsciously to systems that it was inadequate to describe, with consequent distortion, omission and misrepresentation. . . . Indian religion was described within the Christian scheme for contrasting Christianity with its rivals in the Roman empire. Often such studies have translated a non-Western system into a Western one and have misrepresented this destructured, untextured changeling as a description or explanation of the original. Th. Stcherbatsky's Kantian and Hegelian paraphrases of Indian Buddhism are the most brilliant and flagrant instance of this type.[8]

[7] Etienne Lamotte, "La critique d'authenticité dans le Bouddhisme," *India Antiqua*, p. 215.

[8] Richard H. Robinson, "Comments on 'Non-Western Studies: The Religious Approach' by Wilfred Cantwell Smith," *A Report on An Invitational Conference on the Study of Religion in the State*

Understanding and insight, however, as Robinson observes, take "precedence over the problem of meta-systems and explanatory schemes. . . ." [9]

Why is it so important to be able to see Hinduism through Hindu eyes, to see the tradition from the inside? For one thing, doing so is a prophylactic against superimposing alien and inappropriate conceptualizations. But more profoundly, this empathetic identification is prerequisite to seeing meaning in the objects of study.[10]

Buddhism's nirvāṇa and *nairātmya* ideas are classic stumbling blocks. They have challenged the willingness to know in generations of students. Indeed, many scholars, declaring that those terms irreconcilably oppose the values which they themselves cherish, have decided that nirvāṇa and *nairātmya* are meaningless. Rather than decry the fact that neither term has been consistently treated as a religious expression, it need only be pointed out that our encounters with many aspects of Buddhism document the fragile and inadequate nature of our understanding of what religion itself may be.

After reading an earlier draft of this study, M. G. S. Hodgson commented that he found it significant that Buddhism has almost always been defined in terms of the teachings of Gautama himself without allowing any possibility of a different sort of validity in a cumulative tradition. This, he suggested, presupposes at least three identifiable attitudes on the part of the investigators: first, a resolutely humanistic approach to the Buddha as a teacher and a thinker; second, an originistic bias—the conviction that the first form is best or at least the most genuine; and, third, a self-conscious systematism which insists that a religion is a doctrine, a system of which all else is the logical consequence. But, Hodgson remarked aptly, a religion may be defined, for example, as an event and dialectic sequences of responses thereto.[11]

University (New Haven: The Society for Religion in Higher Education, nd. [Conference held October 23–25, 1964]), p. 63.

[9] *Ibid.*, p. 64.

[10] *Ibid.*

[11] M. G. S. Hodgson in a private conversation with the author, late summer, 1963.

It need be neither cowardice nor ignorance that forces us to say finally that nirvāṇa's "meanings" are many and include both annihilation and bliss, negation and affirmation, nonexistence and existence. That we accept the fact that this is not (and, as an expression of the Buddhists' ultimate concern, could not be) a philosophical conception about which we may calmly converse in sovereign detachment will indicate that we are at the gateway to an understanding of it. That we accept and not attempt to correct the statements of every Buddhist who regards nirvāṇa as his ultimate concern will assure us that we are proceeding correctly.

Vinaya: Discipline, Freedom, and Creativity

In his article "L'Absolu dans le Bouddhisme," André Bareau observes that the four *āryasatya*-s of Buddhism offer "a good example of ascending dialectic." [12] The first truth declares that all is suffering in "daily experience." The second:

> The origin of suffering is thirst, the thirst for rebirth and to know new existences in which one undergoes suffering again. Here we find an investigation into the cause of the given, a given that would have been able to serve as an absolute if Buddhism had been a purely contemplative and objective doctrine and not an active doctrine seeking the salvation of beings.[13]

The Buddhist absolute does not appear in the second, but rather in the third truth: *duḥkhanirodha*, "the suppression

[12] André Bareau, "L'Absolu dans le Bouddhisme," *Entretiens 1955*, p. 37.

[13] *Ibid*., p. 38. I have learned much from Bareau's recently published study on Indian Buddhism. See André Bareau, "Der indische Buddhismus," *Die Keligionen indiens: III Buddhismus—Jinismus—Primitivvölker*, pp. 3–215. (Of particular interest is his capsule account of the history of scholarly research on Buddhism, pp. 198–204.) Bareau's estimate of the meaning of nirvāṇa according to primitive Buddhism is not novel, but deserves mention here: "It is the contrary of our phenomenal world. . . . It is the 'wholly other,' the Absolute changeable world. We can give it no positive definition, because all

(restraint, destruction) of suffering." The fourth truth declares the way to the realization of the absolute.

Buddhists at all times have held the truths—all of them—to be the standard against which any purportedly authentic statement or doctrine must be measured.[14] And it is vitally important that the student of Buddhism at no time lose sight of two facts in this connection. First, the third and fourth truths are affirmations, though the third is expressed negatively. They are positive: there *is* an absolute, and there *is* a way to realize it. Second, the culmination of this dialectic rests not in the declaration of the absolute but rather in the presentation of the method for attaining it.

It seems scarcely possible that one could overestimate the significance of discipline (*vinaya*)—specifically incorporating meditation practices—in Buddhism. If it leads nowhere, if it accomplishes nothing, this discipline is only an elaborate, monumentally cruel hoax. That has been as clear to Buddhists as it ever has been to European scholars. In the Pali anthology the *Udāna*, the Buddha addresses himself to this very point:

> There is, O monks, a not born, a not come into existence, a not made, a thing not composite; because, if there were not something which is not born, has not come into existence, has not been made, and is not composite, there would not be any deliverance for that which is born, has come into existence, is made, and is composite.[15]

Paul Masson-Oursel has compared the titans of art with the Bodhisattvas. Correctly, it seems to me, he emphasizes

---

about which we have no conception; for every idea pertains to the the words at our disposal relate to a phenomenal and relative universe. One also cannot say that nirvāṇa, which is the non-existence of this universe, is only a nothingness as Western scholars have often maintained. (P. 54.)

[14] Of course, it is irrelevant to object that absolute authenticity cannot be asserted of any of the Buddha's statements. The words themselves were less important than the ideas conveyed. See Lamotte, "La critique," *passim*.

[15] André Bareau, "L'Absolu," p. 38. Cf. Paul Oltramare, *L'Histoire des idées théosophiques dans l'Inde: La théosophie bouddhique*, p. 455; T. R. V. Murti, p. 271; E. Lamotte, *L'Histoire . . .*, p. 45. For *asaṃskṛta*, Lamotte reads "inconditionné" rather than "inconfectionné."

the freedom and creativity of the Bodhisattvas. A supreme creativity, as it were, for the spiritual hero "from himself . . . makes spirit, though he is nothing but life."[16] This spiritual creativity pervades both the way and the goal of Buddhism. Ignoring its presence would be to imperil any attempt to understand the Buddhist nirvāṇa.[17] Acknowledging it, we are better able to interpret Paul Oltramare's profound and easily misunderstood comments:

> According to the principles laid at the base of the ontology, life—not nirvāṇa—annihilates life. The law of the momentariness of all things and that of Conditioned Production make life and not nirvāṇa a ceaseless destroyer. And it is in life and not in nirvāṇa that one is made conscious of the absence of a soul.[18]

The Buddhist nirvāṇa is admittedly an unsettling response to all those who, through the "sinne of feare," repeat John Donne's entreaty: "Sweare by thy selfe, that at my death thy Sunne/Shall shine as it shines now and heretofore. . . ." But we may not assume that it is annihilation, except insofar as it is indubitably the destruction of all that properly frightens us. Repeating the warning of Oltramare, I conclude with the reminder that the Buddhist nirvāṇa is a religious value only. It is accessible to the very few, and it is totally misunderstood when seen to be merely that sort of cessation which death supposedly assures everyone.[19]

[16] Paul Masson-Oursel, "Indian Techniques of Salvation," p. 212.

[17] In this element of creativity, the distinction between Buddhism and "Hinduism" is seen most unambiguously.

[18] Oltramare, p. 457.

[19] *Ibid.*, p. 460: "It is not enough to say that nirvāṇa is a religious value. It is only that. That is why properly it concerns only those beings, few in number, who have freed themselves through religion. It is apropos of a Tathāgata and his peers that one wonders: After death, does he or does he not exist? With regard to the others, the question does not arise. They remain the prey of saṃsāra. Buddhism's Western admirers completely denature the notion of nirvāṇa when they see in it whatever sort of peace it is that death would assure all men."

Selected Bibliography

Books

Barth, Auguste. *Quarante ans d'indianisme: Oeuvres de Auguste Barth.* 5 vols. Paris: Ernest Leroux, 1914–17.

Barthélemy Saint-Hilaire, Jules. *Le Bouddha et sa religion.* Nouv. éd. Paris: Didier, 1862.

Baudet, Henri. *Paradise on Earth: Some Thoughts on European Images of Non-European Man.* Translated by Elizabeth Wentholt. New Haven: Yale University Press, 1965.

Burnouf, Eugène. *L'Introduction à l'histoire du buddhisme indien.* Paris: Maisonneuve et Cie., 1876. (First published in 1844.)

———. *Le Lotus de la bonne loi.* 2 vols. Paris: Librairie orientale, 1925. (First published in 1852, Paris: Maisonneuve et Cie.)

Childers, Robert Caesar. *A Dictionary of the Pali Language.* London: Kegan Paul, Trench, Trübner & Co., 1872–75.

Colebrooke, Henry Thomas. *H. T. Colebrooke: Miscellaneous Essays*, ed. E. B. Cowell. 3 vols. London: Trübner & Co., 1873.

Conze, Edward. *Buddhism: Its Essence and Development.* Oxford: Bruno Cassirer, 1951.

———. *Buddhist Thought in India: Three Phases of Buddhist Philosophy.* London: George Allen and Unwin Ltd., 1962.

Csoma, Alexander (of Körös). *The Life and Teachings of Buddha.* Calcutta: Susil Gupta, 1957. (Two articles originally published in *Asiatick Researches*, Vol. XX, Part 1 [1836].)

D'Alwis, James. *Buddhist Nirvāṇa: A Review of Max Müller's Dhammapada.* Colombo (Ceylon): William Skeen, Government Printer, 1871.

De Lubac, Henri. *La Rencontre du bouddhisme et de l'occident.* Paris: Aubier, Editions montaigne, 1952.

Duka, Theodore. *Life and Works of Alexander Csoma de Koros.* London: Trübner & Co., 1885.

Dutt, Nalinaksha. *Aspects of Mahāyāna Buddhism and Its Relation to Hīnayāna.* Calcutta Oriental Series, 23. London: Luzac & Co., 1930.

Eliade, Mircea. *Yoga: Immortality and Freedom.* Translated from the French by Willard R. Trask. Bollingen Series, LVI. New York: Pantheon Books, 1958.

Foucaux, Philippe Edouard. *Doctrine des bouddhistes sur le nirvāṇa.* Paris: Benjamin Duprat, 1864.

Hanayama, Shinsho. *Bibliography on Buddhism*, ed. Commemoration Committee for Prof. Shinsho Hanayama's Sixty-first Birthday. Tokyo: The Hokuseido Press, 1961.

Hardy, Spence. *The Legends and Theories of the Buddhists Compared with History and Science.* London: Williams and Norgate, 1866.

Hodgson, Brian Houghton. *Essays on the Languages, Literature, and Religion of Nepal and Tibet.* London: Trübner & Co., 1874.

Hopkins, Edward Washburn. *The Religions of India.* Handbooks on the History of Religions, I. Boston and London: Ginn & Company, 1895.

Hunter, William Wilson (Sir). *Life of Brian Houghton Hodgson.* London: John Murray, 1896.

Jonas, Hans. *The Gnostic Religion.* Boston: Beacon Press, 1958.

Keith, Arthur Berriedale. *Buddhist Philosophy in India and Ceylon.* Oxford: The Clarendon Press, 1923.

Lamotte, Etienne. *L'Histoire du bouddhisme indien des origines à l'ère Śaka.* Bibliothèque du Muséon, 43. Louvain, 1958.

La Vallée Poussin, Louis de. *Bouddhisme et religions de l'Inde.* Paris: Gabriel Beauchesne et Cie., 1912.

———. *Bouddhisme: Etudes et matériaux.* London: Luzac & Co., 1898.

———. *Bouddhisme: Opinions sur l'histoire de la dogmatique.* Paris: Gabriel Beauchesne et Cie., 1908.

———. *La Morale bouddhique.* Paris: Nouvelle Librairie Nationale, 1927.

———. *Le Dogme et la philosophie du bouddhisme.* Paris: Gabriel Beauchesne, 1930.

———. *Nirvāṇa.* Paris: Gabriel Beauchesne, 1925.

———. *The Way to Nirvāṇa: Six Lectures on Ancient Buddhism as a Discipline of Salvation.* Cambridge: The University Press, 1917.

Monier-Williams, Monier (Sir). *A Sanskrit-English Dictionary.* New ed. Oxford: The University Press, 1899.

Müller, Friedrich Max. *Lectures on the Science of Religion.* New York: Scribner's Sons, 1893.

———. *Selected Essays on Language, Mythology, and Religion.* 2 vols. London: Longman's, Green, & Co., 1881.

———. *The Life and Letters of the Right Honorable Friedrich Max Müller*, ed. his wife. 2 vols. London: Longman's, Green, & Co., 1902.

Murti, T. R. V. *The Central Philosophy of Buddhism.* 2nd ed. London: George Allen and Unwin, 1960.

Obry, Jean Baptiste François. *Du Nirvāṇa bouddhique en réponse à M. Barthélemy Saint-Hilaire.* Paris: Auguste Durand, 1863.

Oldenberg, Hermann. *The Buddha: His Life, His Doctrine, His Order.* Translated by William Hoey. London: Williams & Norgate, 1882.

Olschki, Leonardo. *Marco Polo's Asia.* Translated by John A. Scott. Berkeley and Los Angeles: University of California Press, 1960.

Oltramare, Paul. *L'Histoire des idées théosophiques dans l'Inde: la théosophie bouddhique.* Paris: Librairie Orientaliste Paul Geuthner, 1923.

Pande, Govind Chandra. *Studies in the Origins of Buddhism.* Ancient History Research Series, I. Allahabad: Department of Ancient History, Culture and Archeology at The University of Allahabad, 1957.

Renou, Louis, and Filliozat, Jean. *L'Inde classique*, Vol. II. Paris: Imprimerie nationale, 1953.

Rhys Davids, Caroline Augusta Foley. *Wayfarer's Words.* 3 vols. London: Luzac & Co., 1941.

Rhys Davids, Thomas William. *Buddhism: Being a Sketch of the Life and Teachings of Gautama, the Buddha.* Non-Christian Religious Systems. 16th ed. London: The Society for Promoting Christian Knowledge, 1894.

———. *Buddhism: Its History and Literature.* American Lectures on the History of Religions, 1894–95. New York and London: G. P. Putnam's Sons, 1896.

———. *Early Buddhism.* Religions: Ancient and Modern. London: Constable and Company, 1914.

———. *Lectures on the Origin and Growth of Religion as Illustrated by Some Points in the History of Indian Buddhism.* Hibbert Lectures, 1881. 2d ed. London: Williams and Norgate, 1891.

———, and Stede, W. *The Pali Text Society's Pali-English Dictionary.* London: Luzac & Co., 1921–1925.

Schwab, Raymond. *La Renaissance orientale*. Paris: Payot, 1950.

Sebeok, Thomas A. (ed.) *Portraits of Linguists: A Biographical Source Book for the History of Western Linguistics, 1746–1963*. 2 vols. Bloomington: Indiana University Press, 1966.

Slater, Robert [H.] Lawson. *Paradox and Nirvāṇa*. Chicago: University of Chicago Press, 1951.

Stcherbatsky, Th. *Buddhist Logic*. 2 vols. Bibliotheca Buddhica, Vol. XXVI, Parts I and II. Leningrad: Academy of Sciences of the USSR, 1930–32.

———. *The Central Conception of Buddhism and the Meaning of the Word "Dharma."* London: The Royal Asiatic Society, 1923.

———. *The Conception of Buddhist Nirvāṇa*. Leningrad: Publishing Office of the Academy of Sciences of the USSR, 1927.

Thomas, E. J. *The History of Buddhist Thought*. 2d ed. London: Routledge & Kegan Paul, 1951.

———. *The Life of Buddha as Legend and History*. 3d ed. Routledge & Kegan Paul, 1948.

Trenckner, V. *et al. A Critical Pāli Dictionary*, Vol. I. Copenhagen: The Royal Danish Academy of Sciences and Letters, 1924–48.

Warren, Henry Clarke. *Buddhism in Translations*. Harvard Oriental Series, III. Cambridge, Mass.: Harvard University Press, 1896.

Weber, Albrecht. *Indische Skizzen*. Berlin: Dummlers, 1857.

Windisch, Ernst. *Geschichte der Sanskrit-Philologie und indische Altertumskunde. Grundriss der indo-arischen Philologie und Altertumskunde*, I, i. Strassburg: Karl J. Trübner, 1917.

Articles

Bareau, André. "Der indische Buddhismus," *Die Religionen Indiens III: Buddhismus—Jinismus—Primitivvölker*. Die Religionen der Menschheit, 13. Stuttgart: W. Kohlhammer, 1964. Pp. 3–215.

———. "L'Absolu dans le Bouddhisme," *Entretiens 1955*. Publications de l'Institut français d'indologie, N° 4. Pondichéry

(Madras State, India): Institut français d'indologie, 1956, pp. 37–43.

Childers, Robert Caesar. "Notes on Dhammapada, with special reference to the question of nirvāṇa," *Journal of the Royal Asiatic Society*. New Series, V (1871), 219–30.

Conze, Edward. "Buddhist Philosophy and Its European Parallels," *Philosophy East and West*, XIII (1963–64), 9–23.

———. "Spurious Parallels to Buddhist Philosophy," *Philosophy East and West*, XIII (1963–64), 105–15.

Das Gupta, R. K. "Schopenhauer and Indian Thought," *East and West*, New Series, Vol. XIII, No. 1 (March, 1962), pp. 32–40.

Foucaux, Philippe Edouard. "Un Mémoire espagnol sur le Nirvāṇa bouddhique," *Révue de l'Histoire des Religions*, XII (1885), 321–33.

Keith, Arthur Berriedale. "The Doctrine of the Buddha," *Bulletin of the School of Oriental Studies*, VI (1930–32), 393–404.

LaCôte, Felix. "L'Indianisme," *Société Asiatique: Livre du Centenaire*. Paris: The Society, 1922. Pp. 219–49.

Lamotte, Etienne. "La Critique d'authenticité dans le Bouddhisme," *India Antiqua*. Leiden: E. J. Brill, 1947. Pp. 213–22.

La Vallée Poussin, Louis de. "Buddhism," *The Legacy of India*, ed. G. T. Garratt. Oxford: The Clarendon Press, 1937. Pp. 162–84.

———. "Dogmatique bouddhique. La Négation de l'âme et la doctrine de l'acte," *Journal asiatique*, neuvième série, XX (September–October, 1902), 237–306.

———. "Dogmatique bouddhique II. Nouvelles recherches sur la doctrine de l'acte. Grand Véhicule. Système mâdhyamika. Les deux vérités. Prajna, karuna, bhakti," *Journal asiatique*, dixième série, II (November–December, 1903), 357–450.

———. "Nirvāṇa," *Encyclopedia of Religion and Ethics*, ed. James Hastings. Edinburgh: T. & T. Clark, 1908–1926. Vol. IX (1917), pp. 376a–79b.

Lovejoy, Arthur Oncken. "The Buddhistic Technical Terms *upādāna* and *upādisesa*," *Journal of the American Oriental Society*, XIX.2 (July, 1898), 126–36.

Masson-Oursel, Paul. "Indian Techniques of Salvation," *Spirit and Nature: Papers from the Eranos Yearbooks*, ed. Joseph Campbell. Bollingen Series, XXX,1. New York: Pantheon Books, 1954. Pp. 208–12.

May, Jacques. "Kant et le Mādhyamika," *Indo-Iranian Journal*, III (1959), 102–11.

Przyluski, Jean, and Lamotte, Etienne. "Bouddhisme et Upaniṣad," *Bulletin de l'Ecole Française d'Extrême Orient*, XXXII (1932), 141–69.

Rhys Davids, Thomas William. "On Nirvāṇa, and on the Buddhist Doctrines of the 'Groups,' the Sanskāras, Karma and the 'Paths,'" *The Contemporary Review*, XXIX (1877), 249–70.

Rocher, Ludo et Rosane. "Mokṣa: le Concept hindou de la délivrance," *Religions du Salut*. Bruxelles: Université libre de Bruxelles, Institut de sociologie, 1962. Pp. 169–202.

Schrader, F. Otto. "On the Problem of Nirvāṇa," *Journal of the Pali Text Society* (1904–5), pp. 157–70.

Senart, Emile. "Nirvāṇa," *Album-Kern: Opstellen Geschreven ter eere van Dr. H. Kern*. Leiden: E. J. Brill, 1903. Pp. 101–4.

Stcherbatsky, Th. "The Doctrine of the Buddha," *Bulletin of the School of Oriental Studies*, VI (1930–32), 867–96.

Thomas, E. J. "Nirvāṇa and Parinirvāṇa," *India Antiqua*. Leiden: E. J. Brill, 1947. Pp. 294–95.

INDEX

NOTE: Foreign terms are italicized and alphabetized according to standard English usage. Sanskrit, Pali, and Tibetan are abbreviated in parentheses as Skt., P., and T., respectively. Numbers in bold face refer to principal treatment of entry.

Abhidhamma (P.). See *Abhidharma*

Abhidhānappadīpikā (P.), descriptions of *nirvāṇa* in, 141, 141–43 *n*

Abhidharma (Skt.) texts: alleged nihilism of, 80, 123–24, 135–36, 136 *n*, 139–40; mentioned, 119, 150. *See also* Buddhist philosophy

Abhidharmakośa (Skt.), of Vasubandhu, 93, 292–93

Abhiññā (P.), defined, 244

Absorption, *nirvāṇa* as *vs.* annihilation, 94. See also *Nirvāṇa*

Aiśvarika (Skt.), Buddhist school, 38

Ākāśa (Skt.), *Sūnyatā* and, 39

Alexander Csoma Kőrősi. *See* Csoma, Alexander (of Kőrős)

Alexander the Great, 3

Alexander, Noël, on Buddhist atheism and *nirvāṇa*, 19

Alwis, James D'. *See* D'Alwis, James

Amṛta (Skt.; =P. *amata*), on Buddhist usage of, 124, 145 *n*. See also *Nirvāṇa*

Anātmaka (Skt.), defined, 95. See also *Anātman*

Anātman (Skt.; =P. *anatta*): E. Conze on Buddhist theory of, 95; C. A. F. Rhys Davids on, 242; T. W. Rhys Davids on, 228–29; F. O. Schrader on, 251–52. See also *Nairātmya; Nirvāṇa; Saṃsāra*

Anatta (P.). See *Anātman*

Andler, Charles, on Nietzsche, 187, 188

Anitya (Skt.; =P. *anicca*), defined, 264

Annihilation of the individual: Buddhist *nirvāṇa* as, 20–21, 29 *n*, 58, 60–61, 69, 74, 112, 113, 148, 196, 199–200, 275, 286; Buddhist *nirvāṇa* and Brahmanic *mokṣa* as, 64, 73; Buddhist *nirvāṇa* not, 21–22, 28–29, 30–31, 49–50,

199–200, 252, 276–77; *Śūnyatā* as, 39. See also *Nirvāṇa*
Anti-Semitism, Schopenhauer accused of, 166–67
Anupadhiśeṣa (Skt.), 210. See also *Nirvāṇa; Upādi*
Anupādisesa (P.), 210. See also *Nirvāṇa; Upādi*
Anupādisesanibbāna (P.), 152, 211, 213, 249. See also *Nirvāṇa*
Anupādisesanibbānadhātu (P.), 216. See also *Nirvāṇa*
Apathy, *nirvāṇa* as, 19–20, 28–29. See also *Nirvāṇa*
Apavagga (P.; =Skt. *apavarga*), epithet of *nirvāṇa*, 25, 143 *n*, 253. See *Mokṣa; Nirvāṇa*
Arahatta (P.; =Skt. *arhattva*): *nirvāṇa* as, 151–52, 228, 231, 232; Buddhist ideal of life, 198–99, 274, 275. See also *Nirvāṇa;* Sanctity; *Upādi*
Arhat (Skt.), defined, 209, 213. See also *Arahatta*
Arhattva (Skt.). See *Arahatta*
Arrian, 3
Āryasatya (Skt.), Buddhism's "Four Noble Truths," 302–3
Asceticism, spirit of: in Buddhism and Christianity, 168; virtue and, 163–64; Richard Wagner on importance of, 175–76. *See also* Denial; Renunciation
Atheism, alleged Buddhist, 18–19, 29, 63, 73, 74, 78, 83–84, 93, 123, 168. See also *Nāstika*
Atta (P.; =Skt. *ātman*), 249, 253. See also *Anātman*
Attha (P.; =Skt. *artha*), alleged original goal of Buddhism, 243–44, 245
Avadānaśatakam, cited, 61
Avyakta (Skt.), defined, 255 *n*
Ayuso, F. G., on Buddhist nihilism, 128–29, 129 *n*
Bāhyārthaśūnyatā, Stcherbatsky on, 288. See also *Śūnyatā*
Bareau, André: on Buddhism's "Four Noble Truths," 302–3; on *nirvāṇa*, 302–3 *n*
Barth, Auguste: cited, 221; as influence on Louis de La Vallée Poussin, 256, 258
Barthélemy Saint-Hilaire, Jules: 67–78; biographical details, 67–68; on Buddhist nihilism and nirvāṇa as annihilation, 68–78 *passim;* mentioned, 56, 103, 110, 126, 128, 129, 133, 148, 165, 187, 266, 267; views on Buddhism and *nirvāṇa* criticized, 79–100 *passim*
Basham, A. L., cited, 259 *n*
Basilides, Buddhism and, 8, 9
Baudet, Henri, cited on European images of non-Western man, 16–17, 20
Bayle, Pierre, cited on Buddhist quietism, 19 *n*
Belief, religious. *See* Faith
Bigandet, Bishop, 74, 109
Bodhisattva (Skt.), 97, 187, 191, 303–4. *See also* Buddhism
Bopp, Franz, 45, 45 *n*, 91
Bowring, John (Sir), mentioned, 79
Brahman-ātman (Skt.), 245
Brockhaus, Herrmann: as F. M. Müller's teacher, 103; F. Nietzsche and, 185–86
Buddha, the: estimates of character and accomplishments of, 62–63, 81, 82–83, 92, 139–40, 206; silence of, 264, 276; teaching of, 90, 116, 120, 121, 134–36, 226, 300. See also *Bodhisattva;* Buddhism; *Nirvāṇa; Tathāgata*
Buddhism: Christianity and, 4–20 *passim*, 225; discovery of,

D'Alwis, James: on *nirvāṇa*, 130–46; on Buddhist atheism, 133; on *Dhammapada*, 139; estimate of importance of, 145–46; mentioned, 100; critique of F. M. Müller, 131–44 *passim;* Pali Buddhist texts, 132, 135, 138; on nihilism, 134–35, 139–40; on religion, 133–34; on *upādi*, 144–45

Darśana (Skt.). *See* Buddhist philosophy; Metaphysics

Dasgupta, S. N., 283

Deliverance. See *Mokṣa; Nirvāṇa*

De Lubac, Henri: cited, 2, 8, 20; on F. M. Müller, 126–27; on J. B. F. Obry, 89

Denial of the will: Schopenhauer on, 168–71; Wagner on, 173–82 *passim*

Deussen, Paul, 184, 185

Dhammapada (P.), 119, 124–25, 139

Dharma (Skt.; =P. *dhamma*), 288–90

Dharmakāya (Skt.), 48

Dharmakīrti, 285

Dhyāna (Skt.), 75 and *n*, 144

Dīpavaṃsa, 57, 135

Discipline. *See Vinaya*

Dominicans, 12

Duḥkha (Skt.; =P. *dukkha*), vii, 290, 302–3. *See also* Suffering

Duḥkhanirodha (Skt.), defined, vii, 302–3. See also *Nirvāṇa*

Duka, Theodore, 42, 46

Dumoulin, Heinrich, on H. Oldenberg, 196

Dutt, Nalinaksha, 295 *n*, 299

Dvija (Skt.), 162

Eight-fold Path, 112 and *n*. See also *Ārysatya; Nirvāṇa; Vinaya*

Eliade, Mircea, 183, 295 *n*, 299

Emptiness. See *Śūnyatā*

Enlightenment, attitude of toward Buddhism, 20

Environmentalism, 153

Eternal Return, 187

Etymology of the word "*nirvāṇa*," 27–28, 59–61, 71, 80 *n*, 115, 233–34, 253

Extinction, *nirvāṇa* as. *See* Annihilation; *Nirvāṇa*

Faith, Buddhism and, 278

Fichte, Johann Gottlieb, Schopenhauer and, 157 and *n*

Flavianus Arrianus, 3

Formsgeschichte, 116. *See also* Text criticism

Forster, J., 159

Foucaux, Philippe Edouard: **89–100**; on *anātman*, 94–96; on F. G. Ayuso, 128–29, 129 *n;* on Buddhist atheism, 93–94; on Buddhism and Brahmanism, 92–93; mentioned, 72, 79, 269; on *nirvāṇa*, 89–100; on J. B. F. Obry, 89; his critique of J. Barthélemy Saint-Hilaire, 89–98; on *saṃsāra*, 93, 97–98; on *śūnya*, 96

Franck, A., on *nirvāṇa*, 77–78

Garnier, A., on *nirvāṇa*, 78–79

Goethe, Johann Wolfgang von, Schopenhauer and, 158, 159

Gogerly, (Rev.) Daniel John, 74

Goguel, M., 122

Goldstücker, Theodor, 103

Gnosticism, Buddhism and, 4–10

Grant, R. M., 7

Gymnosophist, 3, 5

Hardy, (Rev.) Spence: mentioned, 74; on *nirvāṇa*, 90, 117, 143, 151; on *upādi*, 145 *n*, 212. See also *Nirvāṇa; Upādi*

Harlez, Charles de, 256

Harnack, Adolf von, 7, 120

Herder, Johann Gottfried von, 159

Welbon, Guy Richard

The Buddhist Nirvana and its western interpreters

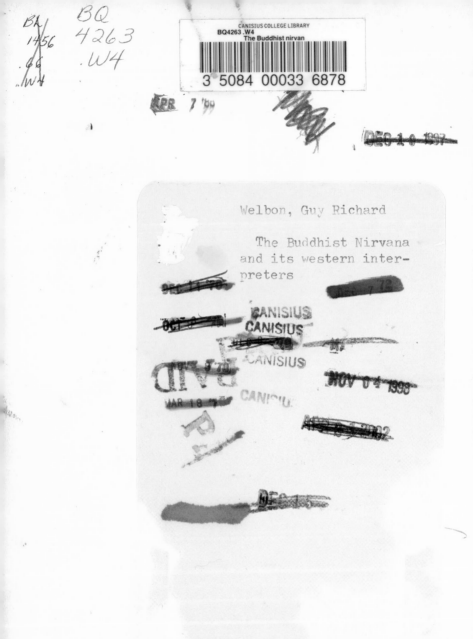